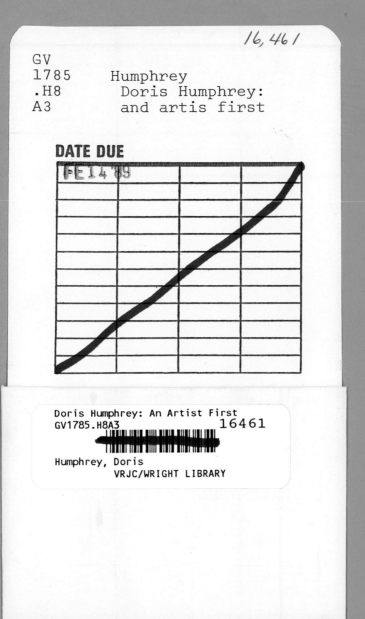

DORIS HUMPHREY: AN ARTIST FIRST

Doris Humphrey in costume for *Sarabande*, 1928. (Photo by Martha Swope from original by Edward Moeller; collection New York Public Library [NYPL].)

Doris Humphrey:
An Artist First

An Autobiography
edited and completed by
SELMA JEANNE COHEN

Introduction by JOHN MARTIN
Foreword by CHARLES HUMPHREY WOODFORD
Chronology by CHRISTENA L. SCHLUNDT

WESLEYAN UNIVERSITY PRESS
Middletown, Connecticut

Passages from reviews by Margaret Lloyd are quoted by permission from *The Christian Science Monitor;* copyright © 1936, 1937, 1946 by The Christian Science Publishing Company. All rights reserved.

Passages from reviews by John Martin are copyright © 1929, 1930, 1932, 1934, 1935, 1938, 1943, 1948, 1953 by The New York Times Company. Reprinted by permission.

"Interpreter or Creator?" by Doris Humphrey is reprinted by permission from *Dance Magazine.*

"Doris Humphrey Speaks . . ." is reprinted by permission from *Dance Observer.*

"Lament for Ignacio Sánchez Mejías," by Frederico Garcia Lorca, from *Selected Poems,* copyright © 1955 by New Directions Publishing Corporation. Reprinted by permission.

Library of Congress Cataloging in Publication Data

Humphrey, Doris, 1895–1958.
    Doris Humphrey: an artist first.

    Includes bibliographical references.
    I. Cohen, Selma Jeanne   ed. II. Title.
GV1785.H8A3   793.3'2 [B]   72-3695
ISBN 0-8195-4054-4

Manufactured in the United States of America
First edition

Contents

Illustrations

Introduction

Doris Humphrey spent the last months of her life writing—first that summation of her theory and practice of composition called *The Art of Making Dances*, published posthumously, which she had never had the time to write before; then the beginnings of what would have been a full autobiography if time (again) had allowed.

Having fought all her life for the creation, the development, the acceptance of the American modern dance, it was a foregone conclusion that she would continue the fight to the last minute of her power to do so. She was one of the half-dozen of women of great vision and total dedication who succeeded in giving entity to what was really a new art, if any art worthy of the name can ever be said to be new. Certainly it was the first completely and incontestably American manifestation in our artistic history.

Of this handful of pioneers none was of stronger mind or more indomitable purpose. When as a young dancer she became aware that she was being confined by the limitations of the dances she was called upon to do, she set about creating dances that would release her from remote and arbitrary traditions. From that point it was natural to proceed further to the discovery of the practicable processes of freely creative form.

When, because of a physical disability at the height of her powers, she was compelled to discontinue her rich and exquisite functionings as a performer, she turned at once with compensatory vigor to the exclusive matter of composition. Here she became the first artist in the field to find and harness the supreme creative objectivity demanded of a no-longer-participating choreographer, and to produce a repertory of truly great works of which she was not the pivotal figure.

When at last even this fruitful outlet was closed to her by further physical difficulties, she still refused to yield, and proceeded to record the principles of her artistic life as she had discovered and proved them, and ultimately the personal life that made these discoveries possible. That she was unable to carry this final section of her work to completion is a major misfortune, for her processes of written statement are as direct, clear-sighted, and unsentimental as her art itself. But there is a degree of satisfaction in the fact that she was able to bring the story up to the actual beginning of her independent career; from there on the public records continue the outline, at least, even though without the immeasurable value of her own insights and commentary on the revolutionary period to which she made such a large contribution. It is only one more evidence of her unconquerable spirit that she succeeded, as if by stubborn design, in carrying the record to this strategic point.

The medium in which she created is unhappily an evanescent one, and for all the intuitive mastery of form in which she had no rivals, the loveliness and the profundity of her work as both dancer and choreographer are lost. A few—alas, a very few—of her works have been scored in Labanotation, which she held in high regard. "Now," she said when her first short piece had been notated, "we belong to history." But if her works themselves cannot, in the nature of things, survive, the vital essence of her creativeness does survive in every notable bit of dancing and choreography that has come after her, and spreads its leavening influences, indeed, into all the forward-moving phases of our artistic lives and thinking.

With this brief but irreplaceable autobiographical sketch as a tangible point of departure, it was inevitable that sooner or later somebody would be moved to carry it further; to search through the reams of published material, to unearth the wealth of private and personal documents, and to build from them all the full story of one of the makers of our epoch. Selma Jeanne Cohen was clearly the one to do it, not simply because she had edited and published the autobiography, but most importantly because she was equipped with the background, the skill, and the sensitiveness to do it with taste and intuition. As a result, all of us who worked along with Miss Humphrey, fought with her (she was a good fighter), and knew at close range the greatness of her as both artist and woman have been made even more aware that we lived in a privileged time.

JOHN MARTIN

Foreword

In the fall of 1958 when my mother lay ill and unable to choreograph, she began to write—some short stories and her autobiography. Beginning with her earliest recollections she wrote of herself
as a child and as a young woman, probably taking pleasure in reliv-
ing those parts of her life when she was young and healthy. Death
cut short the autobiography, but boxes of letters, clippings, and programs remained, the raw material from which the story could be
continued.

Who would be the right person to make something of these
4540 diverse items? It would have to be a dance historian, a writer,
and a woman, I thought—a rare combination. Fortunately there was
someone who possessed these qualifications as well as having known
my mother and having seen many of her works—Selma Jeanne
Cohen.

She and I started to discuss the book without at first having a
clear idea of the shape it would take. Should the autobiography be
rewritten to include documentation? Would there be a jarring transi-
tion between the autobiographical and biographical portions? Would
it be impossible to describe dances, many faded from anyone's memory, in writing when the nature of dance is visual and ephemeral?

Selma Jeanne decided to leave the autobiography as it was, a
nostalgic remembrance of another age and of almost an entirely different person than the later Doris. The letters, with their feeling of
immediacy and their message of artistic and personal excitement,
introduce the era of the "new dance." An unforeseen effect of this
changed rhythm is to heighten the dramatic split with the past at

the end of the Denishawn period. Descriptions of dances, sometimes in Doris's own words and sometimes in those of critics, give extra depth to what otherwise would have been a purely personal account.

When the manuscript was nearing completion Selma Jeanne realized that there was a large body of important material, mostly Doris's own articles and statements, that could not easily be woven into the text. Her solution was to put several of them into a separate appendix, where they tell their own story of artistic achievement.

The first time I read the manuscript I was surprised that, in spite of an abundant supply of dates, it seemed unrelated to the larger history of the twentieth century. Was Doris as detached from her times as it appeared? Partly yes, for reality to her was in the theatre, the "magic box" as she called it, where choreographic invention could create its own relationships in time, space, and movement. Externalities were often merely to be put up with. Her credo was "no matter what happens, the artist survives."

On further thought, however, parallels can be drawn between aspects of her life and some of the major developments in twentieth-century America. She was a woman of accomplishment in an era of growing feminism. A comparison could be made between scientific and technological advances and her creation of a technique based upon observations of body movement. Her compulsive drive to work was both modern American and ancestral New England. Physically and spiritually descended from Congregational ministers from New Hampshire and Massachusetts, and a child of booming, turn-of-the-century Chicago, she brought to her art a combination of near-religious ideals, vitality, and missionary zeal. Indeed, she saw her dance as being of distinctly American origin. It came, she said, "from the people who had to subdue a continent, to make a thousand paths through the forest and plain, to conquer mountains, and eventually to raise up towers of steel and glass."

This biography is not a social history, then, but an attempt to chart the path of a creative talent through various experiences and accomplishments until a towering figure emerges.

CHARLES HUMPHREY WOODFORD

Somerset, New Jersey
April 1972

Acknowledgments

THE idea for this book began in 1965 when Charles Humphrey Woodford gave me permission to publish his mother's unfinished autobiography as an issue of *Dance Perspectives*. His further offer of access to his collection of letters to and from his mother made possible the completion of her life story. Without his collaboration the present study could not have been written.

To his father, Charles Francis Woodford, I am most grateful for permission to quote from his correspondence, as well as for the opportunity to hear his reminiscences of events that were known to him alone.

For permission to quote from other personal letters, I wish to thank Agnes de Mille, José Limón, Frederik Prausnitz, Helen Mary Robinson, and Ernestine Stodelle. For information on the existence of additional material, I am grateful to Clive Barnes and Selma Odom; for tracking down elusive facts, to Eleanor Frampton and Melisa Nicolaides Cassell.

Since I knew Doris Humphrey only during the last six years of her life, I had much to learn from those whose contacts with her were of much longer standing. I am indebted to her colleagues and friends who shared their memories with me; especially to William Bales, Ruth Currier, Olga Frye, Harriette Anne Gray, Martha Hill, Letitia Ide, Betty Jones, Pauline Koner, Ruth and Norman Lloyd, John Martin, Mrs. Robinson, and Charles Weidman. All gave generously of their time, their knowledge, and their insights.

I am deeply grateful to the Rockefeller Foundation for a research grant, which gave me the time to work on the extensive materials that had been placed at my disposal. And to the Mac-Dowell Colony, which gave me a glorious month of snow-bound isolation to make a start on the actual writing.

With the exception of a few letters that remain with the recipients, all of the documents cited here are in the Dance Collection of The New York Public Library where curator Genevieve Oswald and her staff guarded them for me. With the publication of this book, the materials become accessible to other researchers who, I hope, will make extensive use of them, for they contain much that was impossible to encompass within the scope of this work but that can yet contribute significantly to our understanding, not only of this remarkable American artist, but also of the great American art that she served all of her days.

SELMA JEANNE COHEN

New York, N. Y.
June 1972

PART I

THROUGH both of her parents Doris Humphrey was a tenth-generation American. Her mother's ancestors had come from England to Boston in the 1630's. Her father was a descendant of William Brewster, senior elder of the Plymouth Colony, who had arrived on the *Mayflower* in 1620. Congregational ministers were common in both families.

Julia Ellen Wells, daughter of Emily Taylor and the Reverend Moses Hemmenway Wells, was born February 3, 1866, in Hinsdale, New Hampshire. Her husband, Horace Buckingham Humphrey, was born February 25, 1857, in Newark, Ohio, to Susan Batcheller Hutchinson and the Reverend Simon James Humphrey. In 1869 the family moved to Oak Park, Illinois, where the father became pastor of the Congregational church. Humphrey Avenue there is named for him.

In the mid-nineties, when the younger Humphreys lived at 315 Grove Avenue in Oak Park, Horace was working on various Chicago newspapers, sometimes as a reporter, sometimes as a photoengraver. It was he who wrote the announcement when his daughter was born:

> a new woman
> Doris Batcheller Humphrey
> 7 pounds   Oct 17/95
>   Oak Park Ill.

The Palace Hotel

IN 1898 my father was working for the *Chicago Daily News*. Though he was not a practical man, it was apparent even to him that his job of compositor was not going to be good enough to support a wife and small daughter, so he began looking around. Somehow he heard about the Palace Hotel. They needed a manager, he was informed; so one lunch hour he went over there and got the job. Very likely the owner was impressed with his good blue eyes, that friendly manner, the general air of faithfulness and dependability.

There was great jubilation at our house: Horace had a new job, which paid twice as much as the old one; Julia, his Jewel, made eager plans to move and begin a new life in the Palace Hotel. When Horace told her that they could increase their income if she would also work as a housekeeper, she eagerly agreed to see about maids and linen and lace curtains.

Two more incongruous people could hardly have undertaken such tasks. Mother, a graduate of Mount Holyoke and the Boston Conservatory of Music, was really an artist, while Father had had a classical education at Beloit. Nevertheless, here was their little daughter, now three years old. Since it was all to be for her, they set about it with good will.

The Palace Hotel catered to a middle-class, theatrical clientele. It was always full of homey people, who happened to be on the stage—acrobats with several children, whole families with acts in vaudeville, and a few actresses somewhat on the loose. My father, with his kindly ways, would often carry these people on his books for weeks when they were out of work, somehow squaring these procedures with his boss.

Mother worked long hours in the linen room—giving out sheets and pillow cases, managing the maids, and inspecting the rooms for repairs. Near the sewing machine, which was lighted by an old gas lamp, there was always a pile of sheets and towels to be mended. Every six months all the lace curtains in every room came down, and then—as the years rolled on—I was pressed into service to help stretch the damp lace on huge frames set up in the cavernous halls. The sharp hooks on the edges were treacherous, but each one had to fasten a scallop of the lace even if fingers were finally bleeding from pricks.

Late at night—too late for a little girl—when the work was all done and the house put to rights, Mother would sit down at her piano to play music now no longer fashionable—MacDowell's "Witches' Dance," Sinding's "Rustle of Spring," and the "Carnival of Flowers." Sometimes her fingers, stiff with housework, would stumble. Then I would hear her close the lid with a bang and go stormily to bed. Father, in the meantime, was standing long hours at the desk in the lobby, often allowing the dead beats with their pathetic stories to move into a small room when the hotel was not crowded.

The Palace Hotel was anything but impressive or smart. It occupied one corner of two commercial cross-streets; the other three corners were blooming with prosperous saloons. Our corner clanged with trolley cars and drunks at all times of the day and night. Inside the hotel was roomy and comfortable, according to the standards of the day; but our family lived in an apartment full of big old-fashioned furniture, and it throbbed with furnace noises. There was no bedroom for Mother and Father. They slept in an enormous contraption in the living room, which looked like a wardrobe with a mirror by day, and which had to be turned laboriously into a bed that let down at night. One of the familiar noises of my childhood was the squeal of this cumbersome piece of furniture as my mother's tired shoulder was laid against it. But to me the Palace Hotel was a lovely place, with big sofas to slide on; marble-topped radiators, shiny and smooth; and cats—always cats.

By the time I was five, my formal education began. After long consultation, Mother and Father decided to send me to the Francis W. Parker School. Their little daughter should have the best; otherwise, what was all the drudgery for? Parker was the progressive school of its day, with advanced ideas for children and very advanced prices for tuition. No matter, nothing should interfere with the finest in education.

A new regime began at our house. Before breakfast Mother would see about the maids, then come flying back to brush up the curls and dress her child to go to the exclusive private school. Mother always had an eye for clothes, and all my outfits were in the most exquisite taste for the little girl of 1900. I had embroidered white collars, hats with velvet streamers, and satin hair ribbons. The children of the well-to-do often came in much simpler clothes, but—as Mother never saw them—she held pridefully to her own standards.

It was a lonely life for a child. School afternoons were spent playing with dolls, or cats, or sometimes learning cartwheels and other tricks from acrobats living in the hotel for free. Then there were always books, which became so absorbing that nothing else mattered.

There were plenty of friends at school, but all invitations to come and play at my house were politely refused. It took me quite a while to realize that this was because of the location of the Palace Hotel, with its three saloons and its questionable show-folk. Nice little girls were not allowed to visit me, although I was invited to their houses. This might be on a Sunday afternoon, on which occasions my mother would take particular pains to dress me up. At this time children were clothed for school in something known as Peter Thompsons, a dark blue sailor-suit style with a pleated skirt. For the party invitations, Mother had a special one made. This was white, with pale blue piping and a dicky, and it was very elegant. Off I would go, with curls tied in blue satin ribbons, to those Sunday parties which were full of roughhouse on the floor. The little girl from the hotel got very dirty indeed. Mother, with her elegant ideas, would not have approved of those parties at all.

After a year or two it became plain to Mother that something would have to be done about repaying all the party invitations. She knew very well that it would be useless to try to have an affair at our house; but, being resourceful, she came up with a solution. She would hire a bus, she explained, have it call for all the children in my class, and take them to a matinee that would be beyond reproach as entertainment. Then the bus would take them all home again, and the family honor would be saved.

Invitations were duly sent out. All the faces at school looked surprised and shiny-eyed with excitement—a theatre party! All the mothers answered for their children: Yes, they would be delighted. And the great day finally came.

The play was *Berkeley Square,** sentimental and charming, perhaps a little over their heads, but the novelty of a theatre was such a thrill that this alone insured the success of the afternoon. That queer little girl, who lived in a hotel, really gave them a good time. On the way home in the bus the girls strutted like the actresses, and the boys whooped with exuberance. Mother, in an elegant afternoon dress with a muff, presided over it all with the calm sense of a job well done and the social amenities being taken care of for at least another year.

The Palace Hotel was a ramshackle, old-fashioned building with great cavernous halls and a creaking elevator in a wooden shaft. Winding around this was a staircase, and at the back was another, dimly lit on its landings by a gas lamp. These were scarey enough in broad daylight, but in a series of fires we had they were positively terrifying.

At one time, every three of four nights there was a fire. A bell-boy would come to the door of our apartment, kick on it vigorously, and yell "fire" until my father got up, threw on some pants and a shirt, and answered him. There would be a hurried consultation with Mother. Then Father would disappear into the dark hotel, leaving her to cope as she saw fit. She dressed herself and me warmly in bathrobes, and as the proprietor's wife and daughter we went into the silent hotel to see about the guests. Father had given orders

---

* It could not have been *Berkeley Square,* which was first produced in 1928. However, since Miss Humphrey did not give the exact date of the event, I am reluctant to conjecture what it actually was—S.J.C.

that everyone should be awakened, so Mother led me to the top of the second-floor back stairs, where—she explained—I was to stand, directing the guests to go down to sit in the parlor. There she left me, with the awful smell of smoke and the flickering gas jet not il-luminating the corners very much, but merely emphasizing the great dark holes of the upstairs hall. Where had Father and Mother gone to; if the fire got worse, would they forget me?

Soon the guests began appearing, and I said timidly, "This way downstairs to the parlor." The first woman, in a flowered wrapper, carried a pug dog; then came another with a canary in a cage. They said, "Where is the fire?" But of course I didn't know, so I tried to be reassuring. "It's just a little one, go and sit in the parlor." Soon there were many: the women in curl papers, and the men in nightshirts with towels draped around their legs. Then came the acrobat family, all very dark and European; the children loaded with clothes and toys; the mother hysterical. She was crying and saying, "Oh, Anton, we'll never get out of here alive." The comedian came, wearing one of his fancy hats and a nightshirt, and carrying a cane. Then Mrs. Russell appeared, very elegant in a silk kimono, with all her dia-monds on, and her blond pompadour as neat as a pin-cushion. "What an awful bore," she said. All the while I was standing there shaking with fright, and wondering what would happen to me.

When the guests stopped coming, I didn't know what to do. There was really no reason for staying there any longer, so I went downstairs into the parlor, too. Here all was lightness and gaiety. Someone was thumping the piano, and everybody was singing "Nellie Gray"; then the comedian would crack some jokes, and the children were shrieking with laughter because the whole thing was such a chance to romp in the middle of the night. Even the acrobat's wife was smiling now, and nobody seemed alarmed over the strong smell of smoke coming from under the closed double doors. This went on for perhaps an hour, at which point my father came in and said: "Ladies and gentlemen, the fire, which was in the elevator shaft, is out. You may all go back to your beds."

The first time this happened we thought it was just an accident —perhaps a lighted match dropped carelessly in the elevator. But after three fires in ten weeks, my father Took Steps. He called in a detective. Then he sent his little daughter to stay with an aunt who lived in the suburb of Oak Park. To be sure that I did not return until the danger was all over, he arranged for me to visit several months.

This began, for me, a new and difficult regime. I was sent to the local public school, on the way to which I frequently got lost—sometimes on purpose. Here were strange new children and a teacher who expected me to know things I didn't know at all. I was lost and miserable. At the home of my Auntie Bess it was not much better. I had three small cousins there, who teased me and cried and were messy in their ways. The worst was the fact that my aunt was extremely religious, and obviously condemned the laxity of my upbringing in the Christian faith. So Sundays began with Sunday School; then came the regular service with a long sermon, much hymn singing, and prayers. She provided me with a nickel to put in the collection box so that all would be properly done. But this was not enough. She knew I had never been baptized or confirmed, and she began to get after me about this. "Next Sunday," she said, "several little girls will be confirmed, and you are to join them."

"No," I said, with surprising conviction for a nine-year-old.

"Oh, but you must come to Jesus," she said, and began to read to me from a pamphlet for children. Julia's child was being very stubborn. "No," she said, and "no" she stuck to. None of it seemed convincing to me, and I was determined to resist. How I longed for my easy-going life in the Palace Hotel!

Soon after this the welcome news came from home. The detective had uncovered a pyromaniac, one of the bellboys. Since he had been arrested, no fires had occurred. So Doris was to come home, now, and thank you very much. What a joyous return that was—to my mother with her music and her cats and no strict religious ideas; to my father with his kindly blue eyes, full of tenderness for me.

Since we lived in a big hotel, there was always plenty of room for guests. So a procession of relatives came to see us. There was Aunt Annie, who was a missionary to South Africa. Before she came I was full of anticipation about stories of wild savages, maybe headhunters, who danced and rattled all night, and threatened the lives of missionaries. When Aunt Annie turned up, she dashed all such ideas of adventure by being very prim and old-maidish—mousy even. On inquiry it seemed that she taught English and needlework in a church school in Cape Town, and had never set foot into the bush or seen a naked savage in her life. She wore her hair in a bun, had high collars on her dresses, and she hardly spoke at all in her timid voice. Mother was always restraining Father from telling some of his mildly ribald stories at the dinner table, for fear of shocking Aunt Annie.

Then there were Grandmother and Grandfather. They were big hearty people, with an enthusiasm for living. Grandfather was the head of foreign missions for the Congregational Church, and was a Reverend besides. Grandmother was sweet and jolly—she knew how to make a cat's cradle and could tell delightful stories. Grandmother was a second wife, and quite an ornament to the family because she was an Emerson, belonging to *the* Emersons, who included Ralph Waldo. So everything possible was done to make their visit pleasant. It so happened that they were very religious, which made quite a difference in the family routine.

Every morning after breakfast there were family prayers. This meant that everybody had to repair to the living room, and kneel on the floor facing a chair. Father might have urgent business in his office where new guests were arriving, or Mother might have visions of the maids standing around in the linen room just gossiping and wasting their time; but nothing could interfere with the first order of the day—the communion with God. The Reverend Simon James Humphrey would lead us in prayer, pleading earnestly for bounty and the virtuous life. After this Mother would rise from her knees and play a hymn on the piano for us all to sing to. Only then could I go to school, and Mother and Father escape as fast as was decorous to their respective jobs. At other times of the year religion was a very muted matter indeed; even church-going on Sunday was a casual, infrequent affair in our family.

The highlight of visits by relatives was undoubtedly that of my Uncle Will and his wife, my Aunt Marie. They were colorful, not only in their persons, but in the work they did. Uncle Will was a Reverend, too; but he had taken up with American Indians, belonging to the "Society for the Preservation of the Indian" or some such organization. He and his wife entertained for money to help their favorite charity. Uncle Will was handsome by the standards of the day; florid, with a fine flourishing mustache, and a tenor voice. Aunt Marie could accompany him, looking a beautiful figue of a woman as she sat on the piano stool. They were hearty, ate us out of house and home, and were always badgering my mother for the names of clubs or other organizations where they could perform.

Mother had a deep suspicion that the money thus secured never got to the Indians, or beyond the pockets of Uncle Will; but since they were relatives she tried to be cooperative. One of the ideas she came up with was for them to give a concert at the Francis W. Parker School. There the children were assembled every day for morning exercises, at which there were frequently guest artists—often musicians—so it was a most logical idea. She was in touch with the principal very soon, and it was all arranged: on a week from Thursday the Rev. William Brewster Humphrey would sing Indian songs, accompanied by Mrs. Humphrey. What an event for me! I told everyone at school that my Uncle Will was practically an Indian, and that he was coming to sing real Indian songs next week at morning exercises. This set me well apart as "somebody," and I sunned myself in their obvious admiration.

The great day came. The children all filed into the big assembly room, grade by grade. The principal, Miss Cooke, gave a little speech, outlining the plight of the Indians, their neglect by the government, and the efforts of the two good people who were on the program this morning to help alleviate their sufferings. Then Uncle Will and Aunt Marie made their entrance. They were handsome people, but their appearance that day plunged me into despair. They were wearing their concert attire: he, a frock coat and striped trousers, none too clean; she, a white lace dress, which I saw to my horror looked very dirty in the bright daylight. How could they, I thought, shrinking into my clothes. I hardly heard the songs, "From the Land of the Sky Blue Water" and "Indian Love Call,"* for the anguish pounding in my ears. It seemed forever until the last encore was sung and I could escape, avoiding as many eyes as possible on my way back to the classroom. I confessed the frightful aspects of

---

* Another lapse of memory. "Indian Love Call" was featured in Rudolf Friml's 1925 operetta *Rose Marie*. Quite possibly the additional offerings were also songs by the popular Charles Wakefield Cadman, who based them (or so he said) on authentic Indian airs.—S.J.C.

the concert in private to my mother, who was inclined to minimize the whole thing. "It probably wasn't so bad," she said, and went on keeping up appearances for all the relatives, whatever demands they chose to make.

By the time I was eight, my mother sat me down at the piano to explain the relationship between the keyboard and some simple exercises she had bought in a book. "This is middle C," she said, "and corresponds to this mark, and the rest of the scale consists of D, E, F, G, A, B. The bass clef is different, and the lines are. . . ." I got so I could remember the treble clef, but the bass was always a mystery. So perverse to have the two of them different! Sharps that went up and flats that went down made it all even more bewildering, and besides they weren't even marked—you had to remember them. It all seemed impossibly difficult, and piano sessions became stormy indeed. "No, no," she would say. "Don't you know that's an A flat?" When this mistake happened with maddening frequency, she would bang down the piano lid, crying, "To think I should have such a stupid child." Then there would be tears on my part, and a frowning, haughty mother, who was most remote and unsympathetic. I came to hate the ordeal of the piano lesson, and soon was not even trying.

But at about this time there came to the Parker School a dancing teacher, who held after-hours classes twice a week. This was an entirely different matter. She showed you how to move your feet, and you had only to make them go just like hers. It was all easy and a delight. There was music, too. The teacher had such great enthusiasm for her children and the dance that the afternoon classes were nothing but a pleasure. Mother said, "Maybe you can learn something, even if it's only dancing."

Classes with Mary Wood Hinman* went on for years, and on

---

* Mary Wood Hinman (c. 1880–1955) was one of the great dance educators of her time. A graduate of the Swedish College of Naas, she learned folk dances from her travels in Scandinavia, Britain, and Russia. In Chicago she taught, not only at Francis Parker, but also at the laboratory school of the University of Chicago, which was then directed by John Dewey. She also supervised dance programs in the Chicago settlements, including Hull House. In 1916 she published *Gymnastic and Folk Dancing*, which gave music and directions for performing dances and singing games.—S.J.C.

the infrequent occasions when my mother paid a visit, Miss Hinman would say, "Your little girl has talent." This was such sweet praise, such unexpected success, that I came to love my dancing classes, and I begged to be let off piano lessons entirely. My mother agreed, though reluctantly. It had been a foregone conclusion in her mind that I would be a pianist, and a better one than herself.

Soon a few opportunities came my way to dance in public. There was, for instance, the production of *A Midsummer Night's Dream* at school. Because I could dance, I was chosen—to my great delight—to be Titania. What elaborate preparations began at home! Every night after dinner the furniture was pushed away and, with an old broomstick for a wand, I would flit and turn to Mendelssohn's "Spring Song," which my mother played for me. New versions kept cropping up, and I would ask her, which looks the best: this way or that way? This was a subject for serious thought, and many a version of Titania's dance emerged in our parlor. Then there was the costume. Only the best would do for Julia's little daughter, so one glorious day we went to a professional costume house to pick out a ravishing, accordion-pleated shimmer of silk and spangles, with a crown and white kid slippers. As far as I was concerned, the performance at school was an unqualified success. I was delirious with happiness. After all, I could do something. I could dance.

Then Father, who had been taking note of all this quietly, came up with an idea. He was a most spontaneous and unself-conscious man, with a twinkling good humor emanating from him. "Why not," he said, "do a dance with me? I have an idea that will be fun." At first the notion of my untrained, thirty-five-ish-year-old father dancing seemed ludicrous. But when he explained I saw that it really would be fun. "We can do it at the next church social where there will be some entertainment," he said. Mother was quite skeptical, as it did not seem dignified to her, but she was cooperative about the music, and found something that would do for accompaniment.

It was to be a Dutch dance, Father said, so off I went again with my mother to find a Dutch costume and some wooden shoes at the costumers. This was not as beautiful as the outfit for Titania, but any costume was exciting enough.

Came the night at the church. My father was sitting in the

audience as I came on the stage alone, and began to do a few steps. Then I stopped. I came forward, saying, "I can't dance alone; I need a partner. Won't someone come up and dance with me? You, over there, come up on the stage." Great reluctance on the part of Father —he got up and sat down several times. Finally he made his way to the stage, pretending to be very bashful. Here, by coincidence, were a pair of wooden shoes and a smock, which he put on to join me in a rollicking, clumping series of steps that we had carefully worked out together. It was a great success. People laughed and clapped, and we took bow after bow. Then Father made his way back to his seat where his friends clapped him on the back and said, "What a cut-up you are, Horace."

As my lessons went on, Miss Hinman began telling my mother, "Send her to other teachers to study." Mother, by this time quite won over to a dancing career for me, sent me to a Viennese ballet mistress, a Madame Josephine Hatlanek. She was a plump, middle-aged, little lady who lived in a golden oak apartment very far from our house—a long trolley-car ride. Coming from a lesson with her I stood in a strictly turned-out first position all the way home. Lessons with Madame were faintly tinged with glamour, for she had danced with the corps de ballet in Vienna, and it was the nearest I had ever come to the real professional stage. She had a European strangeness and glitter about her that excited me, leading me to dreams of a wonderful future on the stage.

Madame had high button shoes, taught with a little stick to rap me on the ankles, and she had notions. One of these was that raw gooseberries were indispensable to the development of good dancers. Whenever they could be obtained, I was sat down to a dish of these before my lesson, enduring them only because of my great admiration for Madame. With these still setting my teeth on edge, we would go into her violently varnished, golden oak parlor, which had been stripped of furniture, and proceed to struggle with the five positions, *petits* and *grands battements,* and various *pas.*

Along toward spring Madame decided to give a recital. This was to be in the grand manner, with a rented theatre and a live orchestra in the downtown area of Chicago. Madame said I was to dance Paderewski's "Minuet," which she proceeded to teach me. Not on the *pointe,* though, she said, as I was a great disappointment to her in this respect. My feet would not stay firm in toe shoes—they had a tendency to buckle and collapse. Even so, Paderewski's "Minuet" was something to do even on the half-toe. Mother and I traipsed again to the costumers for something to wear. This turned out to be a pink-flowered panniered dress, complete with a white curled wig and a vanity mirror. Toward the end of rehearsals, Madame decided she wanted me to do another dance as well. This was to be comedy, and she instructed Mother to get me a Yama-Yama costume.

The day of this performance marked the first time I had ever been on a real stage, or had make-up on my face. The theatre was old and musty, with dressing rooms that smelled of cheap perfume and dust. What excitement to sit down at a real dressing table; to put pink on my cheeks and mouth like a real actress. Mother hovered around placing pins in the wig, tying on the slippers, and fluffing out the panniers.

I had never seen the rest of Madame's pupils dance, only passing them briefly on the way in or out of her house, so I was ready early to stand in the wings and watch the show. The one I remember particularly was Ada. She was obviously Madame's pride and joy, for Ada was very strong on the *pointe*, and Madame was featuring her that afternoon. My heart sank when I thought of my too flexible feet, and my "Minuet," which was only on the half-toe. Ada's performance began spectacularly. She came in with her black curls bouncing, her strong legs emerging from a tutu, and in her hands over her head she carried a chair. With this she made two complete circles of the stage on the *pointe*, which roused applause from the audience. Then she went into a series of *chassés, coupés, pas de bourrées, arabesques,* and *attitudes.* Ada is certainly the star of the afternoon, I thought. How will I ever become a dancer without feet like that?

However, when the time came for my dance, I forgot about Ada, and put my whole heart into doing it as well as I could. This must have had some charm, as it was followed by a round of applause and several bows. After this I hurried to the dressing room to change into the Yama-Yama costume. Madame's idea of comedy was to have me dance across the apron in a pseudo cake-walk style.

Then, after frowning at the conductor, I was to take from a concealed pocket a fake brick, which Madame had made with her own hands, and throw it at him. Immediately there was pandemonium. The conductor caught the brick with floods of German; the orchestra stopped playing; both Madame in the wings and I on the stage yelled at him, "*Schnell, schnell!*" We threw the brick back and forth several times till finally the dance came to an end at a furious pace with a wow finish. This didn't seem to be as funny to the audience as it had been to Madame.

Miss Hinman was there, waiting for me at the stage door. I met her with my discouraged heart in my shoes. But she put her arms around me. "I thought your 'Minuet' was the best," she said. This restored me completely, and I was happy with my first appearance on a real stage.

In her zeal for exposing me to as many teachers of dance as possible, my mother made engagements with several European dancers who passed through Chicago. Two of these were Pavley and Oukrainsky,* who were playing there with a ballet company. In the middle of their strenuous seven performances a week, one of them would get up early on a Saturday morning to teach a little local girl in the grand ballroom of the Congress Hotel where they were staying. Pavley was dark, with a mass of black curls and a faint look of mischief in his brown eyes, even at eleven in the morning. The Russian Oukrainsky was pale and gaunt, with an infinite air of sophisticated boredom, and a cigarette hanging out of his mouth. He was a phenomenon because he could dance on the tips of his bare toes, which he did in a sensational dance in an exotic Oriental costume. At this distance I can imagine what these two must have thought of

---

* Both men played extremely important roles in the development of ballet in America. Andreas Pavley (1892–1931) was born in Java. His principal teacher was Ivan Clustine, who was for some years ballet master to the company of Anna Pavlova. Serge Oukrainsky, born in Odessa c. 1888, studied in Paris. He was Pavlova's partner from 1913 through 1915, while Pavley was in her company. In 1916 both dancers began a long association with the Chicago Opera. They also directed their own company, the Pavley-Oukrainsky Ballet Intime, which made many tours of the country. Oukrainsky is currently living in Hollywood.—S.J.C.

an American woman who brought her daughter to them for a few private lessons. "Silly" was probably the kindest word that occurred to them. Both had been brought up in the grand manner in European ballet schools, and had begun their dancing careers as children, studying every day, and gradually arriving at their present eminence through the strict hierarchy of the school. A lesson or two was not only futile, but ridiculous. Still, Americans had money to throw away, and who were they to sneer at that?

To me, these lessons were the most exciting of occasions. The furniture of the huge ballroom was covered with ghostly sheets, and a place had been cleared of spindly gold chairs in the center of the room. Pavley and Oukrainsky didn't bother with music, but hummed some little tunes from Glinka, or made clicking noises on the beat when this seemed called for. I already had some idea of ballet from my lessons with Madame Hatlanek, and they found me a ready pupil. I could do all the preliminary exercises—the *pliés, petits battements* and the *ronds de jambe,* and such—so they undertook to teach me some steps from the czardas. I learned quickly, so soon I was flying around the ballroom, clicking my heels and turning in what I imagined was a very Russian manner.* It was more fun with Pavley than Oukrainsky. When the former danced with me, a little pink would begin to show in the pale face, and the black curls would bounce. Oukrainsky was full of Slavic melancholy, and would lean heavily on the piano while he said, "Do ziz one; now do zat one." At the end of an hour, they would bow from the waist, surreptitiously accept some money from my mother, and disappear into their mysterious lives.

Soon there was a chance to put these new skills to use. In my class at school was a boy named Albert Carroll, who could dance. One day he said, "My aunt is going to have a party, and she wants us to dance at it." The aunt, a Mrs. Morrison, had a very elaborate estate far out in River Forest, so my mother and I guessed that this would be an elegant affair indeed. Preparations began at once. Albert and I had rehearsals in the afternoons on the czardas, which

---

* Apparently the young student's imagination altered the nationality of the Hungarian czardas.—S.J.C.

I undertook to make up from the few meager remnants I had learned, adding what I thought was very Russian padding. We also had another dance full of bowings and pointings with the feet, faintly like a gavotte. Costumes were procured for these, as well as an evening dress for me to wear at the party later. This consisted of what my mother considered appropriate for a fourteen-year-old girl —white dimity, with rows of lace insertions, and bows here and there. I was also to carry a fan.

On the appointed day, quite early in the afternoon, a very elegant automobile with a chauffeur drew up to the Palace Hotel. I clambered in with my boxes of costumes and my fan to prepare for Mrs. Morrison's party. Such luxury, I thought, riding through the dingy streets of Chicago, which were more familiar to me from the inside of a trolley car. Being a dancer was going to be glamorous and fun. Above all, it would be exciting.

After an hour and a half of riding, we turned into some imposing gates, drawing up to a large, rambling white house with green awnings and ample porches, set in the midst of enormous lawns with a few huge trees. I was thoroughly enchanted and overawed. Albert was already there, a week-end guest of his aunt, who met me graciously at the door. "You two will want to do some rehearsing," she said, "so I'll leave you alone on this porch to go over your dances. Here is the gramophone and a pile of records. After that you can both dress for dinner."

There was some difficulty in finding music that would do. Nothing faintly resembling a czardas, with its snappy Slavic beat, was in the pile; but we chose a record with a strong waltz accent, and went to work making the dance fit to that. Albert wasn't much of a rehearser, soon wanting to sit down and cool off in the breeze. "They won't know the difference, anyway; let's take it easy," he said. So we sat, fanning our hot faces and enjoying the long shadows that were beginning to creep across the lawn.

Soon Mrs. Morrison came back, now very elegant in a dinner dress, to announce, "You two can have your dinner early on the upstairs veranda, and it will be ready in about fifteen minutes." I went to my room, put on my dimity dress, combed my hair, and tried to feel sophisticated meeting Albert for dinner; although it was difficult as he was just a boy I saw every day at school. "Your aunt is very nice," I said, trying to imagine other adult conversation that might go on at a dinner table.

After this there was a long wait, as it wasn't until nine-thirty that we were called on to perform. We had been in our costumes for hours, with time hanging very heavy indeed, but the moment we took our places to dance, everything turned to light and fire and thrills. The gavotte was first, full of arch glances and sentimental poses; then after a quick change, the czardas, which we imagined we did with true Russian vigor. There was a polite patter of applause from some thirty guests; then the resumption of laughter and the clinking of glasses.

I rushed upstairs to put on my evening dress, gather up my fan, and come down to join the party as I had been invited to do. I did not see Albert at all—he seemed to have disappeared somewhere— but several ladies spoke very kindly to me about my dancing. Then I was left alone on a sofa in the drawing room. Being very shy, I just sat there, not knowing what else to do. All the guests were out on the porches, enjoying what coolness there was in the hot night; but one lone, middle-aged man wandered through the drawing room. Seeing me, he drew up a chair close to where I sat. "You're really very charming, my dear," he said, "how long have you been dancing?"

"Oh, since I was eight," I replied.

"And you are now?"

"Fourteen," I said.

"Well, well," he said, "it would be very pleasant to have a little girl like you. How would you like to come and live at my house?"

Having no experience with light banter of this sort, and having a head full of romantic novels about lecherous old men, this sounded like a most immoral proposal to me. I stood up in the full dignity of my dimity dress, and retorted, "Certainly not; how dare you?" With this, to show my anger and contempt for him, I snapped my fan in two, threw it at his feet, and rushed from the room.

I went upstairs, got all my costumes together, changed my clothes, and crept quietly down to the ladies' cloakroom where I hid in a corner. I told the maid to let Mrs. Morrison know I was ready to go home whenever she could send the car.

At about two in the morning, a very sleepy little girl came back to the Palace Hotel, full of the sense of having been through one of life's experiences, and feeling older for having had an encounter with a man. My mother was waiting up for me, but to her question, "How did it go?" all I would say was, "It was lovely."

Not long after this my mother got wind of another visiting European. This one was a ballet master, who had come with a company of dancers that was attached to the circus. His name was Ottokar Bartik, and he was a real horror.* My mother, determined to see that nothing was left undone for her child, made an arrangement for a private lesson with him.

This man did not bother with a ballroom, but received us in his bedroom. He was short and frog-like, with a bald place on his head, not very successfully covered with a few thin streaks of greasy hair. He was polite, unctuous even, and appraised this woman and her thin daughter for what they were—fools who were eager to throw away their money on a dancing lesson in his bedroom. I changed my clothes in the bathroom, and stood before him, hanging onto the end of the brass bed which served as a barre. My mother sat inconspicuously in a far corner of the room as the *pliés* and the *petits battements* began.

He was very clever. When I turned so that my other hand held the brass rail and my back was to my mother, he would pretend to correct a shoulder, while tweaking me on the breast. Later corrections involved running his hand up the inside of my legs; always with a professional air. I was frozen with terror. Nothing in the books said anything about how to handle horrible old ballet masters with bulging brown eyes and wandering hands.

At the end of the lesson, my mother, who was about to make an appointment for another, was astonished to hear me say "no" in unmistakable tones. She prudently paid the man with no further engagement plan.

---

* Despite Miss Humphrey's unfortunate experience with him, Ottokar Bartik enjoyed a considerable reputation as a ballet master. Born in Prague, he came to the United States in 1908 to stage ballets at the Metropolitan Opera, where he remained until 1932. He frequently staged large pantomines and spectacles for Madison Square Garden and the Chicago Coliseum. At the time of Miss Humphrey's encounter with him, he was with Ringling Brothers Barnum and Bailey Circus. Bartik died in Prague in 1936.—S.J.C.

"What's the matter with you?" she asked on the way out. "You're a very ungrateful girl if you don't appreciate all the trouble I go to for you."

All I would say was, "He's a horrible man and I'm never going back. Never, never, never." Here was unaccountable recalcitrance in her usually tractable daughter.

Top left: Horace Buckingham Humphrey; right: Julia Wells Humphrey. Bottom: Kindergarten class at the Parker School; Doris Humphrey with curls and tam. (Collection Charles Humphrey Woodford [CHW].)

Top left: Father and daughter, ca. 1900 (photo by J. K. Stevens & Son Co.); right: Doris as Titania, ca. 1905. Bottom left: In *Minuet* costume, ca. 1907; right: as Pierrette to Effie's Pierrot, 1913. (Collection CHW.)

--◦-⊰{ **2** }⊱-◦--

Supporting the Family

I T was 1913, a fateful year full of endings and beginnings. First of
all, it was the year of graduation from the Francis W. Parker School.
I was good in some things, notably English, History, and Music;
but the despair of my teachers in others, like Mathematics, Latin,
and Science. Why they let me graduate I do not know. I remember
one awful day when the math teacher decided to make me understand fractions once and for all. He began with a simple equation
in the middle of the blackboard. I got that one right, and one or
two others. Then I was lost. He filled up that blackboard with other
examples, while the class watched with awe the fury of his persecu-
tion. Soon I was reduced to saying "I don't know" in a choked voice,
finally dissolving into tears. At this point he threw down the chalk,
and stalked out of the room. I never learned all the multiplication
table, nor conquered fractions, nor had any but a rudimentary idea
about geometry.

Latin was only slightly better, but this was because Mother
struggled with me over Caesar's legions on many a stormy night at
home. Science came to an abrupt end when I entered the laboratory
one day. Stretched out cold and dead on a table was a poor tiger
cat, which the teacher was preparing to skin and dissect for the
edification of the class. Having lived with and played with cats all
my life, especially with one lovable tiger, I vanished into the girls'
lavatory where I was sick, and vowed never to go back no matter
what they did to me.

I think they gave me a diploma because I was especially good in English (the teacher would say, "Did you write this yourself, with no help?") and because I could dance; but most of all because I was the first complete Parker product, the first student who had been there from kindergarten through high school. To fail me would really have been too disgraceful.

This laudable point of view was pushed to the very limit, however, when my mother proposed to take me out of school in my senior year for a short tour to the West Coast. So educational, she told them; it would take me through Indian Country, the Pioneer Trails, and clear out to Los Angeles. Parker was certainly liberal, considering the circumstances. They agreed without a murmur.

Mother knew a bass-baritone, who told her that the Santa Fe Railroad was sending out small companies to entertain their employees in the Railway Men's Clubs, which they had set up all along their lines. Mother and the bass got together a company consisting of themselves, an actress who could do dialect stories, and two dancers. My mother was accompanist for all. There was enough variety for everybody. The actress was alternately sentimental and funny. Charles Weeks, the bass, sang "Invictus" and "On the Road to Mandalay," and some folk songs; Effie and I did a Spanish dance, a Pierrot and Pierrette, and my Yama-Yama dance (now minus the brickbat). Effie had come into my life as one of my many teachers, but as she was young and attractive she was all eagerness to do some performing.

Nothing could have been less theatrical than the club houses provided by the Santa Fe Railroad. Their interiors were dark red or brown, full of pool tables, spittoons, large black leather armchairs, and plenty of counters for serving beer. A place was cleared of game tables for us, chairs were placed on three sides, and the show was on. The singer, my mother, and the actress always appeared in evening clothes for these events; while Effie and I changed our costumes behind an up-ended pool table somewhere. We performed in true professional style for the boys on the line, most of them far from home and lonesome.

There were incidents along the way. One dance called for Pierrot to go into a comedy spin, grow dizzy, and fall down until restored by his loving Pierrette. Since all the audience was right on the floor with us, this often happened at the feet of a chivalrous railroad man who couldn't stand to see a lady in distress. He would promptly rise, reeling a little, and say, "Ma'am, can I help you get up? Hey, Bill, get the lady a drink of water." Then he would lift Effie by the shoulders, dust her off, and say "Hope you're all right now, Ma'am," while the rest of the men would cry, "Atta boy, Charlie! You're a real ladies' man. Be nice to the little lady, Charlie." Effie, meantime, was thanking him and trying to shake him off. This would upset the sequence of the dance considerably. Mother would have to vamp till we were ready to go on, but everybody loved it, and we were a great success. The other two dances, most of which have faded from my mind, were undoubtedly horrors. I am glad that now no one can be expected to remember the little girl who did a fake Spanish dance to Moszkowski's music in a rented black and gold costume along the Santa Fe line in 1913.

Occasionally a town would have no club house, so the Santa Fe would rent the Sunday School room of the local church for our performance. However, Effie and I were never allowed to dance on these programs. It was impressed on me for the first time that there was a powerful prejudice in the church against my beloved dance. Since I had been brought up in a liberal family, and a liberal school, this was quite a shock—prejudice was something I knew nothing about. They considered our innocent performances immoral and sinful. How could they? I brooded over this considerably. Effie and I would wander around the drab little towns, not knowing what to do with ourselves, until it was time to meet the others respectfully at the outside door of the church. It was bitter to feel outcast and rejected. Soon, however, the performers were telling us the incidents of the evening, and good humor was restored. Among ourselves we were one family.

We entertained the boys all the way to Los Angeles, took a quick look at its sprawling wonders and tropical trees, then came all the way back across the country in the Santa Fe's best style—first-class Pullmans.

I got back in time to put some last desperate efforts into my worst subjects at school and prepared to graduate. The event had a great air of finality about it, but I sensed this only partially. I knew a period in my life was over, and that I had a career as a dancer stretching before me. But I did not realize that I would never see

my school or any of my classmates again. It all vanished as completely as though swallowed up in a fog. I entered an entirely new
life, in a new place, and with different people.

As a graduation treat, my mother allowed me to accept an
invitation from Uncle Herbert to visit him and his wife, Aunt Mira,
in their summer home on Cape Cod. This was another thrill—now
I would see the Eastern part of the country, too.

In the quiet surroundings of an old New England farm house
the summer was salty and refreshing. My uncle had a rowboat for
lazy fishing off the coast; and there were other delights, such as
digging for quahogs in the sand, bathing, and swimming. My aunt
had a younger sister who seemed very sophisticated to me. She
knew the popular songs of the day, so over the dishes she would
teach me numbers like "I Wonder Who's Kissing Her Now." To the
prim young girl from raucous Chicago this seemed very naughty and
daring. But I loved it. Also she told me all about her dates with boys
and a social world that was completely unknown to me. On hot Sunday mornings we would all go trudging to church through the sand,
drowsing through the sermon and the hymns. There were never any
embarrassing questions, however, about my own relationship to
religion. It was a happy, peaceful summer—the last I was to have
for many years.

At the end of it I prepared for one day in New York City
where Irene and Vernon Castle were teaching ballroom dancing in
a new way. They had started a craze that was sweeping the country. This would be an added fillip to a quite extensive dance education. I had already studied from Mary Wood Hinman clog, character, ballroom, and aesthetic; as well as character dancing, ballet,
and "interpretive" from several other teachers.

Out of a very slender store of money, I bought what I considered an extremely sophisticated new dress, and appeared in the
ballroom of a fashionable hotel along with dozens of other people,
all with twenty-five dollars in their hands. Irene and Vernon Castle
made an entrance, looking very sleek. The former had the new
hairdo, the short straight bob. To victrola music, the couple proceeded to show us the "one-step" and the new South American sensation, the "Maxixe." I had one turn around the room with Vernon

Castle, who was probably bored to death with this chore of instructing so many dancing teachers of assorted ages and sizes, and took little trouble to conceal it.

Somewhere during this session I was handed a telegram by a bellboy. It said: "HOTEL SOLD. MOVING OAK PARK. COME DIRECTLY TO STANDISHES."

No more Palace Hotel. It was hard to believe. I was well acquainted with the Standishes, a family of prosperous middle-class friends, who had a big roomy house in Oak Park; so there was no confusion in my mind as to where to go. But on the train that evening I had many dim, unanswerable questions about the future. What would my father be doing now; how would I continue to study and dance; how could this have happened so suddenly?

On a day in early September, after an hour's ride into the suburbs of Chicago, I arrived at the Standishes. There was my mother, looking exhausted and worried, but trying bravely to be cheerful. She led me to the two third-floor rooms that were to be ours, and that were already neatly arranged. We sat down on a bed, as she told me that the hotel had been sold suddenly, and the owner wanted new management. In this emergency the Standishes had very kindly taken us in; we were to be their guests until permanent plans could be made. Somehow she had made preparations for these already. She had samples of some nice wool material for a new dress for me, and that very afternoon we were to see some Oak Park people, who could organize some classes for children and some ballroom classes for adults. "You see," she said, "your father had been quite crushed by this misfortune. It is up to you and me to earn the living for the family now."

"What will he do?" I asked.

"He wants to set himself up as a photographer." (Photography had always been a hobby of his.) "But this will take time, and we must have some immediate income."

I looked around the bare, austere rooms, where the only familiar object was an old bureau belonging to the Humphrey ancestors, and I remembered seeing my mother's grand piano in the living room. There were no cats. "Your Auntie Standish doesn't like cats, so I gave them away," my mother explained.

I began to see the future: a dancing teacher in a respectable suburb, far away from the glamour of the stage; living with a kindly, but strictly religious, family.

We were immediately successful with my mother's class ideas. To begin with there were several grades of children on Saturday morning, and ballroom dancing two nights a week for their parents. On an evening in October one rather frightened eighteen-year-old became the teacher of twenty-five couples in the "latest thing from New York." Most of the men had been dragged there by their wives, and one of the first things I learned was to deploy the husbands to other women, who only smiled sweetly when they got stepped on. My mother had a huge supply of popular music, which made them all feel young again. At the end of a successful evening, when I actually got them to dance the one-step awkwardly together, I was no longer frightened. There was going to be a good living in this.

Classes grew. There were more children in the afternoons, and new ballroom classes in the evenings. Soon, outlying communities were asking for the new teacher. My mother took all comers. She was also business manager, and handled all the money, giving me a small allowance. Father, in the meantime, continued to be lost and hurt, and to make desultory plans about being a photographer. He, too, got a small allowance. One day I had a showdown with Mother about money. I asked for extra cash.

"Now what do you need money for?" she asked.

"I'm not going to tell you. I just want it," I said.

"You're just a little girl, who knows nothing about money," she retorted.

"I'm not a little girl any more. If I am old enough to earn half the living for this family, then I am old enough to have some of it to do with as I please."

In the end she grudgingly gave me a ten-dollar bill, but she kept a watchful eye out to see what foolish thing I was going to do with it.

What I did was to slip away to Chicago and buy tickets to see Anna Pavlova. I was beginning to feel stifled in Oak Park, with an exhausting round of classes to teach, and no end to them in sight. As a matter of fact, it took five years of constant teaching before I was finally rescued from being buried alive by a suggestion of Mary Wood Hinman's. My first teacher never lost interest in me, nor did she ever cease to try to plan for my needs. My mother, on the other hand, was well content with the success of herself and her talented daughter in earning a good living for the family.

In the meantime I had tickets to a paradise of glorious dancing. But one of these tickets chanced to be for a Sunday afternoon. The Standishes were a devoutly Christian family, who went to church twice on Sunday. Auntie Standish considered it a sin to pick up a needle on the Sabbath, or to read a book, or do any mundane thing. Moreover, these charitable people had taken us in under the direst circumstances of disaster, giving us shelter and food. Therefore, my proposal to go to a matinee on Sunday was a shocking breach of gratitude and good manners. When my mother got wind of it, she was all bristle and disapproval.

"Why are you putting on that dress?" she asked.

"Because, if you must know, I am going to see Anna Pavlova," I replied.

"You're not," she stated categorically.

Scolding and nagging, she followed me down the stairs and out the front door. I began running down the path that led to the front gate, with my mother after me, screaming like a banshee. I could run faster, though, and was out the gate, banging it shut before she could reach it.

It took the full hour's ride into Chicago to calm my nerves, re-clothe myself in my self-respect, and stop hearing my mother's voice screaming that I was a dreadful girl. The two hours in the theatre did the rest. I was transported to the wonderland of the Russian dancers, enchanted, bewitched, and blissfully happy. The only pang that remained was the seemingly impossible task of ever setting foot onto this glamorous world of the stage. Still, there was the vision to sustain me for a long time.

My mother faced her defeat calmly and bravely, as she did all crises. Never again did she try to make me obey her. Nothing so very dreadful happened in the Standish household either. If my Auntie Standish ever knew about it, she gave no sign, probably recognizing that there are transgressors of the Christian way, and meeting this fact with fortitude and prayer.

So 1913 came to an end: a year of beginnings and endings; full of the painful signs of growing up.

The first year of teaching in Oak Park finally ground to a halt in the spring. The season had been spectacularly successful from the point of view of numbers of classes; and we could confidently expect a continuance, or even an increase, in the fortunes of the family. But it was all most exhausting. Gloomy about being confined to teaching, I rebelled against the seemingly endless future of classes stretching ahead. I wanted to dance. My mother said that next fall we would take an apartment of our own, and be independent again. It must have seemed to her that all the long years of my preparation as a dancer were fully justified. She felt no lack in the status quo; only a relief and a satisfaction that we could be assured of a good living. She didn't feel stifled or frustrated; she merely took a great pride in the fact that her good planning had snatched success from a desperate situation.

In the spring I had an offer to teach dancing at the Outdoor Players Camp in Peterborough, New Hampshire. This was at least a change from the suburban respectability of Oak Park, and I welcomed it.

It was a brand-new experience. Up to now my social life had been practically non-existent. Never before had I lived, slept, and eaten with a whole colony of young people. We were housed in rough-built summer cottages, smelling of fresh pine and mountain air, and the rollicking atmosphere was something I thoroughly enjoyed. For the first time in my life I relaxed in the company of people my own age, all of them more or less intent on learning acting and dancing. My classes were held out-of-doors, which necessarily made them rather casual, as the niceties of dancing could hardly be taught on the grass.

Toward the early part of the season an invitaion came from the nearby MacDowell Colony. Mrs. MacDowell had engaged a young man, who was going to produce a play with dancing on her outdoor stage. Were there volunteers from our camp who would like to be in it? I was the first to offer, and there were two boys who wanted to go, too. Rehearsals were at night, so after supper the three of us would set off, in the beautiful New England evening, to walk the two miles to the MacDowell Colony. The play was titled *Youth Will Dance*, and called for English folk dancing, a form that was new and therefore stimulating to me. Besides, this was dancing on a stage, and taught by a personable young Englishman.

It was quite obvious from the start that I was the only dancer among an assortment of amateurs from other camps and the town of Peterborough, so it was no surprise—but nevertheless a pleasure —that I was chosen to be the partner of A. Claude Wright. What golden evenings those were! Dancing the age-old dances of England under the stars with a charming partner for hours on end on a real stage. Then there was the long walk home, often on pitch-black roads, all three of us singing to keep up our courage while going through the dense woods. It was not long before I was badly smitten with Claude Wright, who never gave any indication that he thought me anything more than a good partner. But the evenings began to take on the aura of a tryst for me—what could be more blissful than to be dancing and in love at the same time?

It all came to an end too soon; the play was costumed and performed, and that was that. But I had found out that Claude was going to teach a course in folk and sword dances at another spot in New England following the season at Peterborough. I wrote Mother that I was going to study for about three weeks before coming home, and prepared to follow Claude around to the last possible minute. Sword dances were hardly for girls but I brandished a blade along with the rest of them and enjoyed myself making rose patterns and jumping around with the boys.

Then I had another idea. I knew a small town in Vermont where an old aunt of mine lived,* and where I had seen American country longways and square dancing in the local grange hall. "Why not," I asked Claude, "see some American folk dancing while you are here?" To my delight he agreed with alacrity. But he said, "You know, I cannot stay long. England is mobilizing, and I must join."

Early in August we had heard the faint rumbling of war from a seething Europe. To us this seemed unreal, like distant thunder that never quite threatens to break into a storm.

---

* Miss Mary Miller, later Mrs. A. C. Walker, of Dummerston, Vermont, was not a blood relation but a close, long-standing friend of Julia Humphrey. Doris knew her as "Auntie May."—S.J.C.

In the meantime I announced to my astonished aunt in Vermont that I would arrive soon with a young man, and when would there be a dance? This way I could keep my charming Claude a little longer, although he never lost his rather impersonal manner with me. Fortunately, there was a dance soon in the grange hall, and it had all the true atmosphere, so impossible to find except in small towns. Everybody came, old and young. There was a pot-bellied stove; some paper streamers, naïve but gay; a fiddler and a pianist. What a wonderful night it was, trying to follow along in some of the really intricate dances with the glowing young man from England!

To catch his ship back home Claude had to leave the same night. This meant getting one of my cousins to hitch up an old-fashioned buggy to drive us the ten miles to Brattleboro where the nearest train line came through. On the surface it was a rollicking journey, full of laughter and songs, but underneath it all was for me the awful misery of the end. We were there in time for the early milk train. I waved goodbye gaily to Claude, whom I was never to see again, and who was swallowed up by the first World War.*

I climbed into the buggy alone, and cried all the way home.

In the fall of 1914 we moved to an apartment in Oak Park. This was a very modest affair indeed, set over some stores, with four rooms and a small back porch. Part of the latter was closed off as a dark room for my father, who by now had a couple of meager jobs as a photographer—one with an insurance company, and another with a real estate firm. Since these took only a small part of his time, he assumed the job of cook and bottle-washer for his two busy women.

By now I was a well-established dancing teacher, my mother having achieved her aim of seeing that every evening and every afternoon was filled up with classes. This often meant going far afield; some of the classes were twenty-five miles away in the north-side suburbs. Sometimes we had only an hour or so between the afternoon and evening sessions when my father would see that there was a hot meal on the table. Saturdays were particularly strenuous:

---

* She must have meant the second World War. On March 23, 1932, she wrote to her parents that she had had a letter from A. Claude Wright who was in Singapore with the British Air Force. He was married then and had five children.—S.J.C.

children's classes all morning and all afternoon; then a ballroom class far on the north side, followed at 10:30 with instruction for some enthusiasts who gathered in a private home. My mother and I would return from these exhausting sessions at about two in the morning, eat what Father had prepared for us, and fall half-dead into bed.

I was now in my early twenties. Rebellion was growing within me over being buried alive in Oak Park, Illinois; never having any fun, never doing what I wanted to do—dance.

Into the middle of this came a gleam of hope. I heard about the Marion Morgan Dancers,* who were playing in vaudeville in Chicago. On a Sunday I escaped to see them. They were beautiful, long-limbed California boys and girls, who danced barefoot some Bacchanalian sort of dances, full of leaps and runs. I loved and envied them. Why not, I thought, try to get into this company? I went backstage looking for Miss Morgan, who turned out to be brisk, and quickly agreed to see me dance one day between shows. I had, by this time, some quite advanced pupils, whom I told about my encounter. One of them, Carrie Bagley, was very enthusiastic indeed. "Oh, let me come too," she said. "I'd love to dance with them."

There were exciting preparations. Somehow I found an hour here and there when Carrie and I could practice some sequences, and I brushed up some of the more energetic ballet steps I knew. There were long conferences on what to wear, and the trying on of this and that, until the great day came. On a Sunday afternoon we found our way to the Majestic Theatre at the appointed time. It was a thrill just to be going in the stage door; to be, even briefly, in the rabbit warren of dressing rooms. Music was coming from the stage, performers were popping in and out of doors, call-boys were calling people. In short, it was the theatre world, where I longed to be.

Miss Morgan received us in the basement, which had a cement floor. "You'll have to dance here," she said. "We can't get on the

---

* Marion Morgan was on the Physical Education faculty of the University of California at Los Angeles, where she taught dancing in relation to science and history. Her group, which toured on the Keith Circuit, presented dances with such titles as *The Flight of the Sabine Women, The Overthrow of Napoleon, The Eruption of Vesuvius,* and *The Discovery of the Circulation of the Blood.* Their performance was described as having a "joyous abandon." They danced barefoot, and wore Greek-type tunics.—S.J.C.

stage." We both put on some short tunics, which we thought would be in the style she would approve of. Together Carrie and I did some movements, which I had taught her; then I did some ballet leaps and turns. Miss Morgan watched attentively, and made a quick decision. "I'll take you, Miss Bagley; but not Miss Humphrey." Turning to me, she said "You've had too much ballet training—you would not fit into my company."

I was absolutely stunned and crushed. Carrie was sympathetic, but, of course, thrilled to have an offer from Miss Morgan. That my pupil should be accepted and I rejected was really unbearable. We parted at the end of the long ride home; Carrie to tell her parents of the exciting news, and I to go home to an indifferent family, who were intent on keeping the status quo. Later I heard that Carrie's mother had vetoed the whole thing. "We could not allow Carrie to go on the stage," she said in her stuffy, suburban manner. So the whole episode came to nothing.

The weary years dragged on. The war in Europe had little effect on the dancing business in Oak Park. Parents were determined to have every possible advantage for their children, war or no war; married couples continued to want recreation with ballroom dancing in the evenings. I learned to knit wool socks for the boys in the trenches, and that was about all there was to it for me.

Mary Wood Hinman continued to keep an eye on me. She was sympathetic to my ambitions, and had faith in my ability. One day she came with an idea. "Ruth St. Denis and Ted Shawn are opening a school in Los Angeles this summer. Why don't you go out there? It will be different for you, at least. And something might happen."

The family being quite prosperous financially by this time, my mother readily agreed. I was elated. These people were on the stage; this was a chance to come within the glamorous aura of the theatre. So I set off one day for California in what Miss Ruth was later to describe as my prim suburban clothes and a preposterous pompadour.

Denishawn was another of those living-working arrangements, much like the Outdoor Players Camp, only this time in a solid building in the heart of Los Angeles. Oh, the joy of studying again, and of being with people my own age. There were classes every day in the outdoor pavilion, and fun at the beaches on week-ends.

Best of all, the course included one private lesson with Ruth St. Denis. I approached this with great excitement. What would she say? What advice would she offer? She watched me dance for about half an hour. At the end of it she said, "What do you do?"

"I teach," I said.

"You shouldn't be teaching, you should be dancing," she answered. I could hardly believe my ears. This is what I had been waiting to hear for five long years. She said, "We will talk about it."

Talk about it we did. As a result she invited me to join the company she was forming for vaudeville. Thus began an association that was to last ten years. I never went back to Oak Park again, except briefly for visits.

Vaudeville and Concert

I had an offer from the Denishawn Company that wild horses could not have prevented me from taking. At the same time I knew I could not abandon my family or the dancing school, which had been built up so laboriously. Fortunately a ready solution came to hand. In the Denishawn School was a girl who was at loose ends— she came from a nearby suburb of Chicago, and she liked to teach. Ethel Moulton was delighted with my proposal that she take over the classes with my mother. She considered it a break for her to be handed a going business, and I could happily write home that I would not be back, but that another girl would continue with my classes. Escape at last! This would cut down on my mother's income considerably. Still there would be plenty for the family to live on, and I could finally be dancing rather than teaching. This did not turn out to be quite accurate, however, as Denishawn, finding out that I could teach, made use of this talent in the many classes I taught for them in between dancing engagements.

Since it was still war time, Ted Shawn was in the Army, and the new company was to be headed by Ruth St. Denis alone. She devised an interpretation of Chopin's "Revolutionary Etude" with herself as the Spirit of Freedom and one of the girls as a Victim of War. There was a solo for me, and as I remember, an East Indian scene, with Miss Ruth doing a nautch dance. The time of happy preparation for these dances was by far the most exciting I had ever known.

After the summer school closed there were rehearsals, then

costume fittings, and a session or two in which Miss Ruth introduced us to the mysteries of make-up. This she did with incredible speed, slapping on the greasepaint, powder, and lipstick in less than five minutes. Beading her long eyelashes with melted mascara took another five minutes. We struggled to be as fast and as expert. We were also taught some of the Oriental mysteries of costume: how to fold and wear an East Indian sari, how to put on a kimono with its big obi. In between there was always talk of dancing, for Miss Ruth was anything but business-like, and she loved nothing better than an audience for listening to her reminiscences and dreams. These talks were perhaps the most stimulating of the many activities at Denishawn. She opened my eyes to the limitless possibilities of what dancing could be, always in terms of the stage and communication. I had been starving for such talk for years.

Finally, all preparations were made, and we started on a tour in vaudeville that was to carry us all the way across the country. I was on a professional stage at last; furthermore, vaudeville called for two performances a day—on some circuits, three. Each stage door was a thrill. The long hours never seemed tiresome to me, only more and more exciting. I wrote to Mary Wood Hinman, thanking her from the bottom of my heart for setting me on this path.

Early in my association with Denishawn two people came to the school who were to be my years-long colleagues. They were Pauline Lawrence and Charles Weidman. Pauline was a California girl, who came right out of high school to play for classes. She was plump and pretty, with cascades of black curls luxuriating on her head. She was fun to be with, and we soon became fast friends. Charles came out of the Middle West—Lincoln, Nebraska. He was tall, good-looking, and determined to be a dancer. He was fun, too. We became a closely knit trio.

By my second year at Denishawn I was no longer a student but a teacher. Ted Shawn had been mustered out of the Army, and plans were laid for another vaudeville tour, which would include him this time. New dances were rehearsed, but some of the old ones were retained, notably my solo—which was fairly brilliant— done in a gold leotard. We started again on the Keith and Pantages circuits. I never ceased thanking my lucky stars for this wonderful opportunity.

Along the way there was a bad shock for me. The stage manager said one day, "At the next show, and from then on, Betty [Horst] will substitute a solo of hers for the one you're doing." "But why?" I asked. He merely shrugged his shoulders. "Orders," he said.

I was stunned, not only by the cold way in which this was done, but by a dreadful fear of failing so much as a dancer that I might no longer be a member of the company. I did not fight the issue or demand explanations. I merely tried to hide my hurt and understand it. The solution dawned on me slowly. It was commercialism. Betty had rolling brown eyes, a plump figure, and could be very flirtatious. None of these virtues were mine, and the management had demanded a dance more appealing to the hoi polloi than the one I did. I swallowed my pride and tried to be grateful that I was dancing at all, with the horrible specter of Oak Park always lurking as the alternative.

By the end of the second tour in vaudeville, Miss Ruth had a new ambition—to form a concert company, while Mr. Shawn wanted to continue in vaudeville. So the forces were divided. I found myself a leading dancer in a program of music visualizations done to classical music, which I understood much better than vaudeville and in which I had an extensive background. Here I really began to come into my own, as Miss Ruth recognized my musicality and depended on it. She was sympathetic to an idea I had for five girls with a big scarf. With some help from her it was set to Schumann's "Aufschwung," which was called "Soaring" on the program.

One day we set off from Los Angeles to tour the West as the "Ruth St. Denis Concert Dancers."

Rehearsing and performing with the new company I was happy indeed. The program consisted of Miss Ruth's music visualizations, dances to scores that ranged from Bach through several Romantic composers. We had a company of nine girls and a concert pianist who could play beautifully. This was the kind of dancing I loved. I was thoroughly content to be the leading solo dancer in the group, especially because I had a quite brilliant dance with a long scarf ["Valse Caprice"], another one to Bach, and "Soaring," which had been included in the program. All the girls were costumed in basic,

Top: The young woman in her "preposterous pompadour." (Photo by Koehne; collection CHW.) Bottom: The pre-Denishawn dancer in performance. (Collection Walter Terry.)

The Denishawn dancer in her first professional creation — *Valse Caprice (Scarf Dance)*, 1920. (Photo by Arthur Kales; collection NYPL.)

short, transparent dresses of a dark cream color, which were worn throughout and were becoming to everybody.

We were well received, even though the style of the program was so different from the exotic Oriental dancing for which Miss St. Denis was famous. We played many obscure places in Wyoming, Idaho, North and South Dakota, and many other states where I am sure this sort of dancing was completely unknown. The audiences probably did not understand it, but the company of young girls was attractive and made a good impression.

We returned to Los Angeles to find that Miss Ruth and Mr. Shawn had bought a house and some property in the suburb of Eagle Rock, renting a nearby structure to house their company. Outside, under the romantic pepper trees, they had built a platform for dancing. It was a most idyllic setting. In the late afternoon, when the shadows were long and the heat had lessened, we would dance to the most beautiful music. It was a happy time—untroubled, full of beauty and contentment.

We were preparing another program to take on the road as the Ruth St. Denis Concert Dancers. After a preliminary concert or two in Los Angeles, we set off, this time with Pauline Lawrence as the pianist, on a tour that was to take us a little further east. In mid-January, 1921, we arrived in Little Rock, Arkansas, where a shocking surprise awaited us. There were no more dates, the manager said. Moreover there were no more plans for the company; we were to be disbanded and sent to our various homes. I never dreamed of such a thing; I thought I could count on years more of association with Denishawn and I felt completely abandoned. I knew they had other companies in vaudeville, but apparently there was no place for me in these. What to do? I certainly could not go back to Oak Park even if I wanted to, as Ethel Moulton was well established by now, and I couldn't oust her without committing an unpardonable breach of ethics.

After some quick deliberations I counted my money—I had a hundred dollars—and wired my family that I was coming home for a few weeks. My plan was to pick up some of my former advanced students there, form a company, and go into vaudeville myself. I also knew two attractive young girls in Minneapolis. They were good dancers, so I sent for them. I had nothing to start with—very little money, no costumes, no dances, no agent, no engagements. But I attacked all these problems energetically, and within three weeks things were well on the way. I found a theatrical agent, who set about booking us. I rehearsed the girls every day and supervised costumes, which were made at home with a sewing woman to help. I also sent for Pauline Lawrence, saying, "Come and be pianist-conductor for me." She agreed with alacrity. Although she had never conducted an orchestra in her life, she had plenty of nerve and was ready to try it. Out of the hundred dollars I also rented a black velvet cyclorama, decorated with some rather gaudy bouquets of flowers in a glittering substance. I bought five tickets to Detroit where we were to open.

That first rehearsal in Detroit was quite an experience. Rehearsals in vaudeville were usually brief indeed. Performers indicated the tempi they wanted, the orchestra played a few bars, and that was all there was to it. Pit musicians in vaudeville were probably the most hard-boiled characters anywhere. There were derisive remarks and laughter when my conductor began the rehearsal. But Pauline was pretty and charming; moreover, she had invested in a John Philip Sousa white suit and a baton for her new job. By playing the innocent female, she had those musicians eating out of her hand in no time at all. She was smart.

In the meantime, I was struggling with a reluctant stage manager who was in no mood to give me time for the lighting effects I wanted. In vaudeville lighting was simple: either a follow spot, or everything turned on full blast. But here came a company of dancers who had artistic ideas. There was to be all blue here, and a pink spot there, and he shook his head in annoyance over artistic females who wandered into his domain where all white light was the routine requirement. "Lady, you can't have all that in this theatre—there ain't time for it," he said. Nevertheless, he managed to give me most of what I wanted.

After the exhausting day of traveling and rehearsing, we finally arrived at the big test—the first performance. We were a success, and I breathed a sigh of relief. The manager came rushing back, exclaiming, "Say, your act is all right! I'm going to move you to fourth spot." This was a great compliment, as fourth was a very desirable spot indeed.

Our agent was pleased, too, and bookings began to roll in. As it turned out we played continuously all over the East, North, and Middle West for nearly two years, or until I was desperately tired of the whole thing. I thought longingly of the Denishawn days and wondered if they would ever come again.

By now it was 1922. I had heard occasionally what Denishawn was doing. They had been out in vaudeville, and had also done a brief tour in England. "Soaring" was still in their repertory, but was now done with either Charles Weidman or Ted Shawn in the lead. This I found very inappropriate for such a lyric dance, and so did the audiences in the industrial cities of Europe. I was doing the original version, which was one of the popular numbers in my vaudeville act. I also was doing my scarf dance to simple music, which the musicians in pit orchestras could cope with.

In September I received a letter from Denishawn, saying they had decided to form a big company to tour the country in concert engagements. Would Pauline and I join them again? The tour was to be preceded by a few concerts in New York City, and would I dance my scarf dance and some others in three weeks hence? All too eager to be rid of the boring business of week stands of vaudeville, I happily arranged to disband my company. Pauline and I travelled to New York and rejoined Denishawn with a sense of coming home.

There were many old friends still there, including Louis Horst,* who was musical director, and dancers whom I hadn't seen for years, but whom it was a pleasure to work with again. The concerts had a new formula. They began with a section of music visualizations, followed by several elaborate ballets on various subjects. In the next four years these gruelling tours took us all across the country. We were American Indians, Spanish dancers, East Indians, American square dancers, and Orientals of various kinds. There was something for everybody. It was theatrical; it was a good show.

---

* Louis Horst (1884–1964), pianist and composer, was with Denishawn from 1915 to 1925, later becoming musical director for Martha Graham. He was to be Doris's teaching colleague for many summer sessions at Bennington and Connecticut College, where he held classes in dance composition based on musical forms. As editor and critic for the magazine *Dance Observer*, which he founded in 1934, he was also to review many of her concerts.—S.J.C.

Now I met for the first time the sophisticated and enthusiastic New York audience. We had played many times in vaudeville in New York, but never to an audience like this. Not only was applause prolonged for almost everything, but I had the exhilarating experience of encoring my scarf dance, which obviously stopped the show. After the long dreary years of vaudeville this was exciting indeed. I could see a new admiration and respect in the attitude of the whole company, from the leaders down. Vistas of a new and more rewarding career opened before me.

Those tours were exhausting experiences, however. One-night stands with almost always early trains to catch, long hours of travelling, the unpacking, the show, packing up again, and very late to bed after having something to eat.

Denishawn programs were strenuous. The first part called for a pink and white make-up including a body make-up of glycerin and powder, as we danced barefoot and bare-legged. Then came the more exotic ballets. These were elaborately costumed; usually we wore wigs. In a Spanish ballet we were laden with petticoats, ruffled dresses, shawls, stockings, and satin shoes. There was also a dark-skinned make-up, which had to go over the pink and white. Often at the end there wasn't time to remove it all, so we would board Pullman trains in dirty feet and two layers of body make-up.

On the early morning moves a sleepy company would assemble on the platform for the take-off, preparing to wrap up in coats and sleep. Not so Miss Ruth. She had the energy of four people. Looking fresh and glowing, she would roam the aisles for dancers who were awake enough to listen to her crop of ideas and dreams, of which she had a fresh supply every morning.

These were very long tours, often extending from September to May, and they wore me out completely. I sometimes went for rest cures at the end of them, once to a sanitarium. In between, during the summers, there were classes offered, now in a New York studio where I taught. Though exhausting, the whole procedure was a fulfillment at last of my deep desire to be a dancer. I was performing every night, and meeting hundreds of audiences all over the country.

In the middle of one of these tours I had an idea for a new solo with a big hoop. I could see that it had great possibilities; it was original. But to have such a thing made in the course of a tour of one-night stands was difficult. As I remember, instead of having the nap that was to fortify me, I went looking in a Midwestern town for a carpenter shop. Yes, the old fellow in charge knew how to make a hoop out of the proper kind of wood; he would paint it gold and would ship it to me in about two weeks. I dreamed of my hoop, trying to imagine what it would do; but I said nothing to anybody about my idea until I had a chance to experiment with it.

Finally my hoop arrived, and I persuaded the stage manager to add it to the show baggage, unpacking it for me in the odd hour or two I could find to work on it. I found I could do quite wonderful things with it. I saw that it added a new dimension to the body; a new excitement to movement. I took Louis Horst into my confidence, and he came up with just the right piece of music. One day, after we arrived back in New York, I asked Miss Ruth and Mr. Shawn to look at my new dance. To my delight, they were very much impressed, had a few suggestions to make as to the choreography, and promised to put it on the program of the very next tour. This hoop dance of mine ["Scherzo Waltz"] was an immediate success, and was widely imitated, being featured in many Sunday papers and even appearing in sculpture. I danced it for years, until new ideas supplanted it, and it began to seem like a dated style of the 1920's.

The tours went on in every state of the Union until 1925, when something very dramatic happened to us. We were to go on a two-year tour to the Orient, leaving from Seattle, and beginning our engagements in Japan.

The plans for the trip to the Orient were laid far in advance; we were to go in the early fall of 1925. But first we had a long tour to finish, a performance in New York, and then a summer school. This tour, like the rest, was strenuous, and we arrived in New York for the climax in March with a very tired company. No effort was spared, however, for the important New York engagement. This was to be at Carnegie Hall where other performances were scheduled, so we couldn't get into the theatre for a lighting and dress rehearsal until after midnight. Miss Ruth was very particular about lighting, and there were long delays while the crew ran up and down ladders, changed gelatins, and angled spots.

Especially difficult was an elaborate ballet called *Ishtar of the*

Seven Gates. This was a re-telling of the story of Ishtar, who descended into Hell to rescue her lover Tammuz from the clutches of the Queen of the Underworld. This latter role had been given to me. Highly dramatic and dark, it was the sort of challenge I had never undertaken before. I sat on a throne swathed in black cheesecloth and a jet crown. There followed a stylized struggle between Ishtar and the Queen, in which Ishtar was successful in breaking the power of the Queen and escaping with Tammuz, who lay as though dead on a bier at one side. Heretofore, all the dancing I had done was lyric, so I was anxious to make a success of my dramatic part. An hour or so was spent on the lighting for this scene and the polishing up of the action. There were many other ballets, too. When we were finally released, the dawn was coming up; and we staggered to our hotel beds, more dead than alive.

The next night we came to the theatre early, prepared to give all for the dance in our most important engagement of the season. The long program began well, and was enthusiastically received. Then, toward the end, came *Ishtar.* The scene in Hell went better than it ever had, I thought, as I hurried to my dressing room to change to another costume for the rest of the ballet. In this there was an ensemble scene, which began with a ceremonial welcome to the upper world, and then Ishtar had a solo. The rest of us lay face down on the floor, while she moved sinuously to soft music in a celebration of the renewal of her life. This turned out to be my undoing, for when the rest of the dancers rose on cue to resume the dance, I stayed on the floor, sound asleep. I suppose this lasted only a few seconds because somebody soon came by and gave me a good push. Perhaps Miss Ruth never knew. But it was a most humiliating experience.

That was the end of the season. After a short vacation, Pauline and I took an apartment. I taught classes in the summer school, while she played piano for them. Preparations for the Orient went on at the same time. We were to be gone nearly two years, so clothes had to be assembled for all sorts of weather and occasions. Miss Ruth and Mr. Shawn gave us a very serious talking-to about our obligations as American dancers abroad. The girls were to have a chaperone; we were to behave at all times so that America and they could be proud of us. Also, we were advised that there would be many formal social occasions, and that we should be prepared for these. This meant buying evening dresses, and I remember investing in a couple of these and in an evening wrap. One of the dresses was a beaded yellow chiffon, very short to the knees in the style of the day, with slippers to match. The evening wrap was made to order of black velvet with a small chinchilla collar, but unfortunately this would not be finished until the very day we were to take the train for Seattle.

That last day was frantic. I went to say goodby to a girl who had been in my vaudeville company, and found her very ill indeed. Her young husband was standing around doing nothing, so I quickly arranged to have her see a doctor in the early afternoon. Several hours later I got the report: "Lenore is a very sick girl. She has tuberculosis and must go into a sanitarium immediately." I went into action: wired the sanitarium he recommended; notified her family; instructed the husband to take her away as soon as possible. By this time it was evening; the train left at eight, and I still had to call for my evening coat.

I hurried home for the rest of the packing, and rushed to the shop for my coat. The woman in charge had it ready. "But," she said, "it cost more than I thought; you'll have to pay another ten dollars." There was an agreed price, and I thought this outrageous. With nerves thoroughly frayed by this time I took a ten-dollar bill out of my purse, threw it on the floor, snatched the coat, and fled through the traffic to the station. I had only about five minutes to spare as I boarded the last car, and made my way to the company Pullman. We were on our way to the Orient.

The Orient

THERE was a great take-off from Seattle across the Pacific to Yokohama. Many press photographers, reporters, local representatives of the management, and well-wishers were in the staterooms and on the quay side. In the company the old trio was back together —Pauline Lawrence, Charles Weidman, and myself. I had invited Mother to come as my guest, since I was making enough money now to give her this share in my good fortune. Somehow she had managed to leave the school in working order, had provided sketchily for Father, and prepared, not only to go to the Orient, but around the world, which she intended to do when the company turned back toward the States.

Travelling on a big ship was a new experience. In spite of the continuous fog there was always something doing: a class every morning to keep us in shape; then games, food served every few hours, and dressing for dinner. Somewhere Charles had learned the newest ballroom sensation, the Charleston, and I had fun learning it from him. One night members of the Denishawn Company were asked to entertain at a party. Charles, in a tuxedo, and I, in my new yellow evening dress, put on an exhibition Charleston, much to the astonishment of the company, and possibly to the embarrassment of its leaders. This was hardly the high art we had come to bring to the Orient. But we were young. We enjoyed the captain's dinner with its firecrackers and funny hats. In general we had ourselves a thoroughly good time after the years of gruelling hard work.

Early one morning I looked out the porthole near Yokohama for my first sight of the exotic lands we were to visit. There were the most enchanting little sampans, with brown and blue sails, looking as though they had been painted on a Japanese print. I looked at the many people on the quay with great curiosity. They were all Japanese, but what a conglomeration of styles in dress. Some were in the traditional kimonos with tabis and getas on their feet; others, influenced by Western fashion, wore kimonos but sported straw hats and Oxford shoes; while still others were clothed in Western suits, shirts, and ties. I could see that many were already enamored of Occidental ways, which augured well for the reception of an American dance company. Miss Ruth and Mr. Shawn had carefully eliminated all Oriental dances from their programs; we had come with music visualizations and Americana.

Miss Ruth and Mr. Shawn were very publicity-conscious indeed, so between rehearsals at the Imperial Theatre, they arranged for the entire company, dressed in Japanese kimonos, to ride in rickshaws through the streets of Tokyo. This was to be photographed by the press at various points, providing advance notice of the opening of our company. Vast preparations went on for this expedition. Kimonos had to be made for all twenty-four of us, native maids engaged to dress us in them, and a long string of rickshaws hired for the occasion. With characteristic energy, Miss Ruth decided to select all the materials herself. Accompanied by an interpreter, she hied herself to one of the big department stores, which had a great variety of fabrics, and came back followed by a rickshaw laden with bolts of cloth. With incredible speed these were all sewed up and fitted to us in about a week's time. Then one morning, with obis tied by native women, and our Western hair done in an approximation of Japanese style, we all climbed into our rickshaws and were off for a tour of the city.

We certainly attracted attention. Hordes of children followed us for long distances, unable to control their giggles. Their elders were equally curious, but—like all Japanese—impeccably polite. They merely stared, not too obviously, at the procession of Americans. The tour went on for an hour or more, whereupon we returned to the hotel, were met by more photographers, and—still in our Japanese clothes—had lunch in the dining room.

Next morning the Tokyo newspapers carried large pictures of us at various stages of our tour, with enormous headlines proclaiming that the Denishawn Company had made a most unusual exhibition of themselves—they had toured the city in bath kimonos. Miss Ruth, in her enthusiasm for the beautiful fabrics and patterns she had seen, had selected all blue and white cotton cloth, which was used by the Japanese exclusively for going to and from their baths.

Even after this lapse in taste, we were a great success in the theatre. Houses were crowded. The Western dances were enthusiastically welcomed by a people who were enamored of Occidental ideas from the camera to popular music, which blared from shops everywhere. The theatre itself, though it had a good stage by our standards, was difficult to cope with in regard to its dressing rooms. Each of these was completely bare of any furnishings whatever, except for matting on the floor. The Japanese actor sits on the floor to make up, has a make-up box with a mirror, which he carries with him, and a chest to hold his folded kimonos. For the American dancers there was not a chair or a table or even a hook to hang up the big costumes. So we had to sit on the matting, too, throw the costumes on the floor, and prop up hand mirrors on whatever bit of support we could find around the stage.

The engagement in Tokyo was exciting and rewarding, however. Many distinguished actors of the Japanese stage came to meet us, and many were the parties consisting of very long successions of food ceremoniously served by exquisite girls in traditional dress. Then, too, lessons were arranged for the company with native dancing teachers. We struggled with the manipulation of fans and sleeves, and the subtle movements of head and feet.

There were many fascinating sights to see in each city: shrines, palaces, and just the look of a street of shops kept us enchanted. But after a few weeks of that, it was all over. One day we all embarked for the mainland and Shanghai.

China was next on our itinerary, but it always seemed like a vast blur to me. The streets and public places teemed with Oriental faces, but we never got to know any of them, for we lived strictly within an Occidental environment. The hotel was Western, and the food, and the theatre, and only the shopping expeditions revealed the riches of the country—the embroidered silks, the sumptuous coats, the tiny satin shoes. Audiences, too, were mostly American or British, with a few Chinese in the cheaper seats.

I remember being entertained a great deal at elaborate dinner parties, but these were given by Americans attached to Ford cars or Standard Oil. The parties, accompanied by much drinking, were preceded by highballs, after which I sat down for the first time in my life to a plate that was ringed with wine glasses. Even a few sips from each of these soon made me very dizzy indeed, so my concentration was fastened on staying in the room and listening to conversation, rather than flying off into space.

Next we headed for Singapore. Here we were in really hot country for the first time and all rooms, including bedrooms, were fitted with huge fans laden with wooden paddles to keep the air moving. Beds also were encased in netting to keep out the fierce mosquitoes.

At this point Miss Ruth and Mr. Shawn began to feel that they were out of touch with their company, as they saw us only briefly at the theatre during performances. At other times they were busy with high officials or with extensive shopping expeditions on which they collected, not only personal mementos, but fabrics and jewelry for possible ballets later on. But one day came an invitation. They would like us to gather in their rooms twice a week for talks and readings from the literature of the East. The book they chose turned out not to be Oriental after all, but a mystic and esoteric volume by the Russian Ouspensky, *Tertium Organum*. For most of us this was hard going indeed, but only I dared make any comment. At the end of one of these sessions I ventured to say that the mysticism of reincarnation somehow did not seem very convincing to me. Whereupon I was told that I could not understand, because I was such a young soul. I should listen and learn, if possible.

Personal matters began to be quite a factor in my affairs. There was, first of all, my mother, who began to show signs of being unhappy about the living arrangements. I had been working and living with Pauline so long that I never thought to change the pattern, so in each hotel I took a double room with her, engaging a single room for my mother. This she viewed as outrageous neglect on my part; she considered it her right to room with me—Pauline she saw as a newcomer and an interloper. So I roomed with Mother, but the trio of Charles, Pauline, and I was an old habit. Although we included my mother as often as we could in our activities, still there were many occasions—especially social ones—when she was left to her own devices. I would come back from a dinner party to find her in tears, miserably curled up in a chair, full of resentment and self-pity and accusations of neglect. I thought this unwarranted, and my relationship with her was filled with apprehension in the face of what became a raging jealousy. I hardly dared to go anywhere with my old friends, and was continuously fearful of her reactions which —in turn—bred resentment on my part, making us both miserable.

In addition to this a very attentive man appeared on the horizon. Wesley Chamberlain was an official in the National City Bank. He seemed to have plenty of time to take me shopping, give parties at his house, and have moonlit bathing sessions on the beach. He was unattached, attractive, and I enjoyed it all very much. I began to be really intrigued, wondering how it would be to live in Singapore, detached from the world of dance as I knew it. But I couldn't imagine giving up my career and devoting myself to a social whirl and beach parties. Long before it got to a point of decision, I knew that I was too committed to dance to be able to give it up and live happily with any man.

The company moved up-state to a smaller place in Malaya— Kuala Lumpur. Wesley engaged a car, driving me there through the most enchanting countryside—the road lined with bamboo forests and the many thatched huts of the natives. Arriving in Kuala Lumpur, I promptly came down with dengue fever, and had a new misery to contend with. This was a mosquito-borne disease, which had as its characteristic an intense itching of the palms of the hands and the soles of the feet, accompanied by a high fever. For several days, struggling to my feet, I went to the theatre for performances. But a doctor finally put a stop to this. I lay in my bed with hands and feet wrapped in cologne-soaked towels, which was the remedy at that time. My mother hovered around solicitously, and ardent letters of cheer arrived from Wesley, but to this day I cannot bear the smell of eau de cologne. Mr. Shawn had a very strict rule about illness in the company: if you could stand up, you could dance; if your legs wouldn't hold you, you could fall back on the bed. I fell back on the bed, and missed a week of performances, much to his inconvenience and annoyance.

When I had recovered, Wesley tried to persuade me to stay with him forever in the Orient. I was tempted. But my fate as a dancer, largely unrealized as yet, hung over me, and I could not consent. After that I saw Wesley less often, as the ardor had cooled off appreciably. I concentrated on trying to dance better performances to make up for lost time.

One steamy day in December, we arrived in Rangoon, the most exotic of the places we had yet visited, and we had a sense of being deep in the Orient. Most of the men were in sarongs, with small turbans; the women in wrapped skirts and transparent jackets fastened with jeweled pins. Most of them were barefoot, too, and the boys in the hotel moved noiselessly through the halls and in the dining room. According to the new pattern, my mother and I took a double room, which was fitted with the usual curtained beds, big overhead fan, and half-doors to catch any air there was.

On the very first night we heard of a fair on the outskirts of Rangoon. This was a chance to see something really Burmese, and we all got into rickshaws to go after dinner. The fair was a delight, although it was full of imported European gadgets like Ferris wheels, fireworks, and shooting galleries. Still, by following our ears, we came upon a native show, complete with an orchestra and two dancers—the latter being the most charming little creatures imaginable. Arriving before the show began, we were fascinated to see the dancers kneeling before little mirrored boxes, finishing their make-up, in full view on the stage. The make-up was not so elaborate, but the costumes were. These consisted of a tightly wrapped skirt striped in brilliant colors and reaching to the ankles. Over this went a white, transparent jacket with up-turned, quite exaggerated points on the hips, all edged with ball fringe. The front was fastened with three brilliantly jeweled pins. The arms were heavy with many bracelets; the neck hung with beads. The black hair was dressed in a most exotic way. It was cut short to just below the ears, with bangs; above this was a crown of hair wound smoothly over some solid base —quite high too, three or four inches. On this were jeweled pins and artificial flowers dangling on long skewers. To top it all, the dancers had lighted cheroots, which they puffed on from time to time. The dancers were very small—not more than five feet tall—

and as exquisite as flowers. We could hardly wait for the show to begin.

It opened with a couple of men who sang to the accompaniment of drums in the grating voices of the East. Then the dancers came on. They moved with bent knees and gliding steps, very close to the ground, and with incredible flexibility in the hands and arms. The fingers turned back almost to the wrist, a phenomenon we were to see many times later. The movements were quick and bird-like; without an interpreter to tell me I imagined that the whole dance and the costumes were derived from some magical feathered creature. Another dance used two brightly colored parasols, which the dancer whirled expertly while doing quite acrobatic feats, including a back bend to the floor. I couldn't know at the time that Miss Ruth would duplicate this dance for me exactly—with the cheroot, the parasol, and all. The little girl from Oak Park, Illinois, was to become extremely exotic in the Burmese manner.

I found someone in the crowd who could speak a little English and ventured backstage with him to see one of these bird-like creatures after the show. She was interested that a dancer from far across the sea had come to see her, and I offered her an invitation to have lunch with me at my hotel. She also spoke a little English, so I looked forward to this visit as a chance to find out more about the life of a dancer in Burma. Came the day, she showed up in bare feet and native dress, looking as strange as an orchid in a field of daisies in the all-European dining room. She sat cross-legged on the chair at the table, where the native waiters were not too deferential to this little cocotte of their own kind. They brought her Oriental food, which she ate with her tiny hands that were loaded with rings, and we had a halting conversation about ways of the dance in Burma. With her black eyes and hair, and her exotic, brilliantly colored dress, she made me feel very drab—like a big, faded Westerner. She had been dancing since she was three, she said. Soon she would marry, and stop dancing. She must have been all of fifteen.

We were nearing the end of December, and many thoughts were nostalgically wandering back home to the big turkey dinner, the cold crisp air of North America, and the families—so far away. But the Denishawns made a celebration for us in the Burmese manner with a few adaptations. On Christmas we were invited to a mid-day dinner in a private dining room, where long tables were laid, and in the middle of which was à brave attempt at a Christmas tree. Someone had found a small tree, stripped it of leaves, and hung it with bright objects that came to hand. There were tinsel balls, bits of tin, artificial flowers from the costume market, and tiny rings. This was a gay, if rather absurd, effort to put us in a holiday mood. At each place was a cheroot wrapped in a ten-rupee note, which was an imaginative gesture on the part of Miss Ruth and Mr. Shawn. There were toasts in rice wine, and much laughter and anecdotes. So we had a Christmas celebration after all, some ten thousand miles from home.

We said goodbye to Rangoon, and set sail for India, where we were to be five months, long enough to sample the many different climates and ways of this vast sub-continent. Calcutta and the south were very hot. But Darjeeling in the north was near the Himalayan mountains; cool in the daytime, even cold at night.

It was an adventure just to ride the train from one place to another. Some of these trips were very long, taking a day and a night. We were provided with bed rolls, as the second-class cars we rode in had only benches on either side of the car in two tiers; no chairs, or seats, or upholstery for comfort. We also carried food and a sterno stove. The train stopped for meals on the way, but these were so boiled away and unsatisfying, that we were always hungry. Food became quite a problem. To our surprise and delight, the station restaurants had big cupboards, well locked up, but full of American canned goods, which were for sale if you could find the manager to unlock them. American cans of baked beans and soups were a lifesaver on many an occasion.

The south of India was exotic indeed. Here were the elaborate temples, which the devout and European visitors were required to enter barefoot. This was quite an unpleasant experience, as the floor was covered with the dirt of many ages and the droppings of bats; but the eyes were fascinated with the elaborate carving of the vaulted interior as well as the ancient statues of the gods and goddesses covered with dripping ghee, the sacred butter, and more bat dung. This all seemed extremely pagan and remote. It was hard to realize that human beings really believed in these things, and we were amazed to see them prostrate themselves full length on the floor, mutter prayers, and finish backing away with many salaams.

Then there was the Taj Mahal. Very early one morning, Pauline, Charles, and I engaged a carriage to take us there. We were awed by the exquisite proportions of the place and the marble filigree with which it was decorated. We were only slightly disconcerted to find that Miss Ruth and Mr. Shawn were already there, posing for photographs in front of the elaborately carved doorway.

In India, our Russian manager, whose name was Asway Strok, persuaded Miss Ruth to put on one of her famous Oriental dances, a nautch. He argued that the art had fallen on such decadent times that few people in India had ever seen such a dance, and he proved to be right. It was easy to pick up in the bazaars the costume jewelry which was to adorn the nose, the ears, neck, arms, and ankles; and to buy thirty yards of material for a skirt. Miss Ruth was to appear in as authentic a costume as possible.

The balcony and gallery, full of East Indians, went wild with excitement. They had never seen a dancer of their country dressed in the sumptuous costume of a Rajah's court; a beautiful woman, too, with all the artistry acquired from twenty years of experience on the stage. We ourselves had seen what the ordinary citizen knew of dancing. Street dancers would appear occasionally, accompanied by a drummer or two. These were poor things, shabbily dressed, obviously poverty-stricken, dirty, dispirited. Truly the dance in India was in a bad way. There has since been a renaissance. Through the efforts of Uday Shankar and many cultural organizations, the dance has been rescued from its state of oblivion. But when we were there Miss Ruth was the darling of the people. She never did her nautch dance less than twice, and sometimes three times. Native audiences knew what was coming, and waited politely through the other items on the program. The rest of us might as well have gone home. The orchestra was filled with an American and European audience who didn't know what they were seeing. After the intermission they were half drunk anyway, as—according to English custom—a bar was provided in each theatre, and they regarded the whole thing as just another social occasion.

We were so long in India that there were several stretches of time off. In one of these Ted Shawn invited me to go with him to

Darjeeling, from which it was possible to see Mt. Everest, just inside Tibet. Everybody said the way to see Mt. Everest was at dawn, when the snow-clad peak would appear at its most magical. For this we had to travel some five miles on horseback, which made me apprehensive, as I had never been on a horse in my life. But the guide was reassuring. He said there would be a whole string of ponies in the party; they would all go at a walk and stay in line; there was nothing to worry about. Somewhere they found a pair of riding pants for me, and by four o'clock I was up getting into them along with a sweater and a scarf. These were by no means enough. The moment I stepped out of my room I was bitterly cold, and stayed that way until the whole thing was over. In the pitch dark they got me on my pony, showed me how to hold the reins, and backed me into line with the rest. Mr. Shawn was far up ahead somewhere, not available for counsel or encouragement. I kicked the sides of my pony with my heels as they told me, and soon we were moving over the mountainous trails. After an hour of this we came to a lodge that was provided for sightseers. Inside was a little warmth and a big pot of hot coffee, which I fell on with the most intense enthusiasm. The guide popped in and out of the building, saying each time, "Not yet, the sun hasn't hit her, we'll have to wait." After quite a while he came in looking morose. "She's covered with clouds this morning, you can't see her. But the next highest peak is lit up like a Christmas tree, come and see that." So we all dutifully filed out to look at the eerie snow cap of Mt. Kangchenjunga, the second highest peak in the world. It was beautiful, pink with the early light, and shimmering with snow. But in a short time one gets bored looking at a thing like that, and long before it was over I was yearning to get back and be warm again.

Back on the pony, then, for a ride through the beautiful dawn-lit countryside. At one point my horse lagged a little. Having a little more confidence now, I kicked him in the ribs to catch up. This had an alarming effect. He broke into a trot, and increased to a canter, passing all the horses ahead; eager, I suppose, to be home again and get on with his breakfast. I was terrified. I had no idea how to stop him. I could only hold on to the saddle with both hands and concentrate on not falling off. In a lather of fear and exhaustion, I got back to the hotel where I had to wait for someone to get me off the thing. Thoroughly upset, I collapsed in my room, piled all the blankets and a rug on my bed near the fire, and tried to recuperate. An hour later Ted Shawn came to the door in his urbane way to encourage me to get up for breakfast. After this I recovered enough to get on with the rest of the plans for the day. These included a trip to the market of the town, and a visit to a lamasery where a special entertainment was to be given for us.

The market had sheepskins and furs of several animals for sale, as well as big boots and fur hats to wear as protection against the fierce cold of the region. There were also prayer wheels, little boxes encrusted with semi-precious stones on a stick that revolved. Inside the box were Buddhist prayers, and the devout could rack up a formidable list of repetitions of them by whirling the thing. Each revolution counted as a saying of the prayers.

The lamasery was fascinating. A roster of Buddhist priests came into the courtyard, all in saffron robes, to perform a ceremony that consisted mostly of music. Some were playing on extremely long and slender brass horns, which were at least six feet in length; others were chanting and playing drums; while the remainder whirled prayer wheels—a colorful sight indeed. Suddenly the priests withdrew somewhat, and a troupe of dancers took over. There were men dressed in smock-like coats and baggy pants, with boots for all the world like something out of the Russian folk dance. The steps were Slavic, too, full of knee bending and wild jumps. Whether this was indigenous to the border of Tibet or had been an infiltration from the West we were never to know, but it was strange to see such familiar movements in this wild and otherwise most exotic country. At the end of the day we were again riding on a rattling old day coach, moving gradually from the discomfort of the very cold north to the equally uncomfortable and steamy south.

On our return I found that another publicity stunt was under way: the next day the Denishawn Company was to have a parade on the backs of elephants. This did not involve dressing in native saris, however; so we showed up at the appointed place in thin summer dresses, which were short to the knees in the style of the period. Miss Ruth never wore her clothes as extreme as this, so she was quite prepared to be modest on elephant-back. But she worried about the girls in the company. Gathering us all together in a dressing room, she proceeded to inspect what we had on. Pulling up one of the dresses she was shocked to find nothing underneath but a "teddy-bear," a garment of silk that hung from the shoulders and ended in loose panties. Remarking that this would never do, and that she always wore bloomers, she held up the whole proceedings while she sent to the hotel for a supply from her own wardrobe. Finally, duly fitted out in bloomers, we were allowed to get on the huge kneeling beasts, which lurched to a standing position, while the now modest Denishawn girls held on for dear life. Then there was a long ride, followed by press photographers, all to advertise an American dance company while the populace looked on with jaded, indifferent eyes. We all felt rather seasick from the constant pitching motion, and were only too glad to get off, go home, and return the bloomers.

From India we were to go farther southeast to Java. Here Mother decided she would leave the company, returning to the States across the Atlantic. There had been constant unhappiness between us, with accusations on her side and anger on mine. I put her on a ship, fearing that the close association had been a mistake, that she could never reconcile herself to the fact that I was leading a different life with new companions. Nevertheless, she said the experiences of the trip had been a highlight in her life. As I told her goodbye, I hoped the many impressions of the Orient would remain and that our personal differences—now that they would no longer be inescapable day by day—would fade. This, I think, came to be the case. She finally accepted the idea that I would never again be the little girl who went with her from class to class, with no other companion.

From India we stopped briefly in the principal city of Ceylon—Kandy, where we were fortunate in seeing a most colorful sight. This was a torchlight procession, all elaborately costumed and designed to show the people the Sacred Tooth of Buddha, which was embedded in an elaborate shrine mounted on the back of an elephant. We had a closer look at the Tooth in the temple at another time. This was mounted in gold and was some three or four inches long. One could only marvel at the credulity of a people who could believe in this, and at the brazenry of the priesthood for making it the focal point of ceremony and temple.

The procession was elaborate. Male dancers in white costumes and shining tin headdresses were at the head, followed by musicians and singers. Several men flanked them with lighted torches, which made the strange sight even weirder. Next came the priests; then the elephant with painted tusks and a highly colored, embroidered covering over most of the head and body. On top of the creature was a shrine of gold and crystal, which presumably housed the Tooth, although it was invisible. Following this were more priests, another troupe of dancers, torch bearers, and some stragglers from the general populace. We followed this procession through several streets where it was met by the most respectful behavior from the people. I think this was the strangest sight I saw anywhere in the Orient—primitive, superstitious—as far removed as possible from anything religious in the Western world.

Otherwise, Kandy was quite uneventful. We played to the usual European and American audiences, and in two weeks or so set sail for Java.

There we ensconced ourselves in the city of Soerabaja. One of our first excursions was to see the Bourabadour, a very ancient Buddhist temple, built differently from others we had seen. Unlike Hindu temples it was not closed in and mysterious. All in the open air, it consisted of tiers of curving corridors lined with hundreds of statues of Buddha set into niches. The building was so old that some of the Buddhas were broken, or missing entirely. The latter provided a fine opportunity for a publicity picture. We came on Ted Shawn, clad in the traditional draped robe, sitting cross-legged in a niche, with Charles Weidman standing below as a devotee with a begging bowl. They were being snapped at from all angles. Fortunately, the Javanese did not consider this sacrilegious, and the pictures were widely distributed in magazines and newspapers.

An exciting occasion in Java was an invitation for the company to see the ceremonial dancing at the palace in celebration of the circumcision of the seven sons of the Rajah. This took place in a pavilion with open sides, where chairs were set out for us. Seated on an elaborate throne, His Highness was served by native boys, who almost crawled on their bellies bringing him refreshments, cigars, a fan, and other luxuries. Exquisite girls danced in their elegant batik costumes and headdresses, all very different in style from other forms in the Orient. The men were vigorous. Their drapery was pulled up short around their hips and fastened between their legs to give them plenty of freedom in the knees. Through an interpreter we could follow the course of the story, which was an ancient legend concerned with love, intrigue, and fighting. The famous gamelan orchestra accompanied the dance with exotic music that we had heard about, but never heard. The picturesque musicians sitting back of their beautiful instruments were an aesthetic sight in themselves. It was sad to think that this was the private entertainment of the Rajah, for the fascinating sight was never seen by the people. Other dances were provided for them, but they were not so richly costumed, nor were the performers so skillful or beautiful.

In the internal affairs of the company an incident occurred that was to amuse us all. Late one night, Miss Ruth suddenly became very concerned about the whereabouts of her girls. About midnight, she began a tour of the rooms to see if all were properly in bed, or if any were still out on parties or dates—which was considered highly improper. The chaperone was there, all right, but one girl was missing. Where was Edith James? To check on this Miss Ruth had a list that she ticked off while striding along the veranda outside the rooms. Lights were still on in many cases, and these, falling on the half doors, threw disconcerting black shadows across the veranda floor. Peeking through the cracks we could see her not daring to trust the black spots, and lifting up her skirts to take great leaps across them. After a couple of tours around, she was thoroughly put out and sure that Edith was not there. The tone of her voice boded very ill indeed for the culprit.

We all expected something dramatic to happen in the morning, so everyone was down early for breakfast to be in on the scene. Nothing happened. Into the dining room came Miss Ruth, looking fresh and lovely. With the sweetest expression on her face she greeted everybody, including Edith James, with a cheery good-morning. Not a word was ever heard about it again, either. No doubt new dreams were cascading in her head, and her visions had quite banished the cares of the night.

The girls in the company were much sought after by American and European men, who scarcely saw young white women from one year's end to the next. These were the men who had come to seek a fortune in the East, or who had been tempted by huge corporations

and banks to run their businesses for them, at the price of exile from
a normal social life. Consequently, the girls had more invitations
than they knew what to do with, while our men were strictly ignored.
One of these isolated Europeans fell to my lot. He was a Dutch coffee planter, who seemed to have plenty of time to take me everywhere. There were not a great many tourist attractions in Soerabaja,
so these soon gave out as the focus of our afternoon rides, and my
Dutch planter took me on tours of the shops instead. He would stop
in front of one of the richly stocked stores, usually Chinese, inviting
me to come inside to choose something that I wanted. We would
roam the corridors looking at the endless bolts of Chinese silk, the
jade, the ivory and objets d'art, with me feeling very reluctant to
admire anything too much, because this meant that he would order
it wrapped up and placed in our carriage. I kept waiting for the
demands or liberties he might take, and was very wary indeed. But
when these were not forthcoming, I began to accept a few gifts and
got used to the unbelievable—that here was a rich, young man, who
just liked to give presents to girls. One day I asked to stop at a bank
—what did I want in the bank? Well, I had to send a payment on
my insurance back to the States. He wanted to buy even this for me.
A picture came to my mind of a permanent life like this—shopping,
and living on a remote coffee plantation in Java. But this offered no
temptation whatever—I thought it would be deadly boring and I
would be very unhappy. So the whole thing came to an amicable
but inconclusive ending. When our stay in Java was over, I thanked
my young man profusely for his company and his presents, and went
happily on my way with the Denishawn company.

We set sail on a French ship, belonging to the line Messageries
Maritimes, and were introduced to still another way of life. A bottle
of wine was on the table morning, noon, and night, as no French-
man considered it civilized to drink water. The food was not too
good, being a version of French cuisine prepared by native chefs.
An elaborate menu written in French turned out to be a bit of fish
with a sauce faintly reminiscent of the mother country, mutton with
a Javanese version of caper sauce, and a dessert of fruit and cheese.

Our destination was Saigon, Indo-China. Our only chance to see
Pnom-Penh, mysterious capital of Cambodia, where we were not

A *Burmese Yein Pwe*, 1925. (Photo by Martha Swope from unattributed original; collection NYPL.) Bottom: A Denishawn "Egyptian Ballet," ca. 1923; Ann Douglas, Theresa Sadowska, Doris Humphrey, Geordie Graham. (Photo by White Studios; collection Walter Terry.)

Soaring, 1920, posed at the Palace of Fine Arts, San Francisco. (Photo by Arthur Kales; collection NYPL.)

performing, was via a trip by car. Miss Ruth and Mr. Shawn asked Charles and me to come along and share expenses.

One hot early morning we started off in a chauffeur-driven car, with the four of us in back, and an enormous hat of Miss Ruth's in a box which seemed to be necessary, though it encroached on the space. In spite of the heat, we saw that several wool blankets were piled on the floor; we were soon to be grateful for them. The way was thickly littered with streams, whose only cross-over was a ferry. There was always a delay while several cars maneuvered for a place, and this meant stopping the car to wait. Immediately, swarms of gnats and mosquitoes descended on us like a plague. There were so many that it was impossible to fight them off, and so—in the sweltering heat—we wrapped up in blankets, with as little of the face exposed as possible. This went on till we reached the hotel in Pnom-Penh where guests wrapped very mundane blankets around their legs over dinner gowns, and nonchalantly removed the gnats that continually fell in the soup.

After our blanket-wrapped dinner, we started for the palace, which was marking a celebration. The first sight to greet us was a great display of fireworks, rockets, pinwheels, and all the appurtenances of a Fourth of July at home. This seemed odd in the middle of Cambodia, but we knew that Orientals were fond of the flashy display of fireworks. A guide met us at the gate to take us through some of the public rooms of the palace. One of these, an enormous throne room, had a floor entirely paved with silver. Finally arriving at an outdoor pavilion, we were courteously seated on chairs, wrapped in the absolutely essential blankets, and soon were enjoying an elaborate dance-drama with the richest and most elegant costumes.

The Cambodians wore the most elaborate costumes of the Far East. On the head was a high pointed headdress, made of intricately worked gilt with a great variety of design. Costumes were of brocaded silk, fastened with jeweled belts; and on the wrists and ankles were wing-like bracelets made of gold cloth. A whole floor full of these creatures was a dazzling sight indeed. The dance was based on one of the ancient legends full of drama, daring, and conflict in which the tiny enchanted princess was finally rescued from her abductors. Her little hands, like those of all the dancers, had been trained from childhood to be so flexible that the fingers turned all the way back to the wrist. Our stiff Western hands couldn't begin to do this, although Denishawn put on a Cambodian ballet on their return, which was authentic in most other respects.

Following the performance there was the long return to the ship through the tropical night. The mosquitoes were not quite so bad, but there was a new menace—birds, attracted by the lights, flew directly into the windshield, injuring and even killing themselves at horrifying intervals.

By now it was summer of the second year, and we were due to go back to Japan, and thence home. It was the last chance to buy souvenirs or presents, so we went day after day to the shops to purchase lacquer, kimonos, prints. I even went so far as to buy a large chest, which had to be crated and sent by freight. Although this was quite expensive, I never regretted it, and it is still doing good service in my house.

In the course of our wanderings, I came across a shop where postcards were for sale. Among the usual scenes was one that astonished me. It was a picture of a Japanese dancer doing my hoop dance, complete with ill-fitting underwear in place of the skin-tight leotard I wore, and a very wobbly looking hoop. This was the only dance of ours I saw, but I'm sure the Japanese made good use of all our other material, just as they quickly adopted other Western ways, like the phonograph, the jazz records, and dresses.

One day we took off on a Japanese ship, bound for San Francisco. We looked like a gypsy caravan. By this time everybody was loaded with booty. We all carried bundles, and quite a few had birds in cages. This was just before the law was passed forbidding the importation of parakeets, parrots, and cockatoos due to their tendency to carry psittacosis. Among others, Pauline had a white cockatoo that she intended bringing to a friend in the States.

In the winter of 1927 Ruth St. Denis and Ted Shawn began a tour with the Ziegfeld Follies, leaving Doris Humphrey and Charles Weidman in charge of the Denishawn School in New York. In addition to teaching, the two younger dancers occasionally presented their students in concerts.—S.J.C.

⊶⊰ 5 ⊱⊷

The Breaking Point

THE summer of 1928 Charles and I were teaching the classes at the Carnegie Hall studio, while Pauline played piano. The students were stimulated by our enthusiasm for some discoveries about movement, which had to do with ourselves as Americans—not Europeans or American Indians or East Indians, which most of the Denishawn work consisted of—but as young people of the twentieth century living in the United States. All this was quite nebulous as yet, but already vistas of a more genuine dance form could be glimpsed ahead. The bulk of the class work was, as always, Denishawn, however. This meant some modified ballet barre done in bare feet, a few adapted center exercises, and a dance or two from their repertory, such as "Bead Plastique" or "The Palace Dance." I was brought up sharply by Shawn, I remember, when he learned that I wasn't teaching straight Denishawn. This wouldn't do, he reminded me; their method was to be taught exclusively.

Toward the end of August an invitation came for me to attend a meeting to discuss the Greater Denishawn, which we had been hearing about for a long time. Miss Ruth had some property at Van Cortlandt Park on which had been built a large house, holding a huge studio and living quarters for the two stars, as well as provision for numerous students. No invitation came for Pauline or Charles, which was puzzling, since all three of us had been with Denishawn close to ten years. Not understanding this, I prepared to go alone on the appointed day when there was to be a meeting, beginning in the middle of the afternoon, finishing with a supper.

It was my first look at the new building and I was deeply impressed. A handsome pile, spacious and beautiful, a real home for the dance, I thought, as I was ushered into a large studio room where a long table was stretched out with several people already seated at it. I recognized Fred Beckman, the publicity representative; Hazel Kranz, the children's teacher; Margerie Lyon, who had a vague position, a cross between personal advisor and manager; and Olga Frye, the school secretary. I took my place, and shortly after, Miss Ruth and Mr. Shawn came in, graciously seating themselves at either end of the long table. I still saw no reason why Pauline and Charles had been excluded.

Miss Ruth opened the proceedings by explaining how the Greater Denishawn had come into being as an idea. They had been traveling so long, she said, and yearned for a permanent home where they could consolidate their efforts. Also they were tired of renting studios at high prices in New York City, and longed for a place of their own. The present house, though not complete, had been achieved by saving money from recent tours; particularly from the last engagement with a touring company of the Ziegfeld Follies, of which she and Shawn had been the stars. Now they were in a position, she told us, to plan the school and the future here. This is why we had been called today. She had two large charts in front of her: one a schedule of classes, the other a plan of the house in which, she said, there would be room for all of us to live if we wished.

Continuing about the classes: they had decided on some over-all policies, she said. The first one she mentioned was with respect to the Jewish students. It seemed best, she explained, to limit these to ten percent of the whole. This was the first time I had heard either director express a racial prejudice, and I was shocked. Also, I thought of the very talented young Jewish girls already in the school, and wondered what would become of them.

Then Shawn began to talk. There was another policy they intended to put into operation at Greater Denishawn, and this was with respect to the general moral tone. It had come to his attention, he said, that various affairs had been going on from time to time, and that these were questionable, if not downright immoral, as they did not result in marriage. A committee of faculty members would be established to hear the evidence in such cases. Permission to continue would be granted, or marriage would be advised. If the advice were flouted there would be an instant cessation of the affair, or the guilty parties would be dismissed at once. I thought this was the most extraordinary proposal, but said nothing.

Next there was the practical consideration of finding the money to finish the house, and make payments on the enormous mortgage. They had, he said, been carrying this heavy burden themselves, and had even accepted a gruelling season with the Follies for no other purpose than this. The house was not complete, and thousands of dollars more were needed to make the Greater Denishawn come true. He was going to call on Doris and Charles to do their share in earning money next year, by putting them into the Ziegfeld Follies. In the meantime, others would be found to do the teaching at the school. All eyes were turned on me for comment on this proposal, which so stunned me that I could not speak for a moment. I thought of the exciting new experiments in movement, and of my hopes for composing in a new style, all of which would vanish. Also I had a sharp remembrance of the current Follies. We had all traipsed over to Newark one night to see it.

"I do not think I could do that," I said. "I saw what you did in the Follies, and I was shocked. The dances had been altered, the tempi were much faster, and you, Miss Ruth, had your skirts pulled up four or five inches higher than they should have been."

This statement had a most surprising result—Miss Ruth burst into tears. Then she began to ramble almost incoherently about how she had always been respectable, while Isadora Duncan was running all over Europe having babies by different men, while she herself had always been a model of virtue. Also that the mysticism of the East had been her ideal and always would be, despite any deviations. Seeing her emotionally out of control, Shawn took up the defense and said to me:

"Do you mean to say that Jesus Christ was any the less great because he addressed the common people?"

"No," I answered, "but you're not Jesus Christ."

"But I am," he said. "I am the Jesus Christ of the dance."

This statement fell into a startled silence. There seemed to be no answer to it. Finally he began again on a long harangue about loyalty, obligation, devotion to ideals, and a great deal more to various nods from around the table. At the end he suggested that it was time for supper, and that the meeting would resume afterwards.

I don't remember much about the dinner. I think I sat very quietly trying to assimilate the various shocks of the afternoon. Also it dawned on me that I was surrounded by the opposition—alone, in fact, in my resistance to the Greater Denishawn, and that this explained the lack of invitations to Pauline and Charles, who would, of course, have backed me up. I thought to myself: these two people have no gifts for or interest in seeing into the hearts of others; they are intent on their own goals without considering that these might not coincide with those of their associates. I shuddered at the idea of a season with the Follies, and determined to resist.

When the meeting resumed, Shawn took over. Immediately he put the question to me: would I or would I not go into the Follies for a season to do my share for the Greater Denishawn? I said I would not, that some other way would have to be found. This roused a storm of protests from him and frowns from the others. Accusations were made of disloyalty, lack of responsibility, no ability for sacrifice, and so on, at quite some length. Seeing that this had no effect he called for an oral vote, asking each one at the table for a "yes" or "no" as to whether Doris should be considered a member in good standing.

Why I did not explain my attitude in more detail I do not know; surely some defense was in order. I can only think that my one accusation against Miss Ruth had had such a drastic effect that I did not dare bring up more unpleasant evidence. I could have said, "I do not think that compromises with artistic standards are worthy of Denishawn; moreover, I am most interested in some new experiments with movement, which I am not willing to abandon." This latter would merely have made them angry, as I had already been told: "Experimentation is unnecessary; Denishawn has thought of everything." Also, I could have added, "I don't approve of racial prejudice or moral coercion."

The vote was taken. Some just stated "no," while others added a sentence or two about disloyalty. I was voted out of Denishawn.

A depressing silence followed. The meeting broke up with angry glances from Miss Ruth and Shawn, answered by stony ones from me. I made no comment, but went home from this historical meeting with shock and resentment in my heart.

Charles and Pauline were waiting eagerly for the news. It was nearly midnight, but we sat up for hours talking it over. At the end we had a plan. Tomorrow we would look for a studio, hang out a shingle, and brave the dance world on our own. We knew an artist who would design a good-looking announcement. It was late summer, just the right time to make a break and begin again. We were a compact trio: Pauline to play the piano and manage the business; Charles and I to do the teaching and composing. The long years at Denishawn, fruitful ones and valuable, were over. We looked forward to a bright future with only ourselves to depend on.

PART II

Interim: Conflict

As she reached the end of her description of the Oriental tour, Doris Humphrey must have realized that her time was running out. Feeling urgently that the true story of her break with Denishawn must be told, she interrupted her narrative with the departure from Japan in November, 1926. Her last chapter begins with a time that she recalled as "the summer of 1928," though actually it was late spring, as her final break with the company came in June of that year. Despite her deliberate omission, the events of the intervening eighteen months were of the greatest significance, for within that period emerged the growing independence of thought and spirit that would lead her to new paths of creativity.

On May 30, 1928, Doris told her parents: "I've had a year to get a perspective on a great many things, and the results have been—to me—revolutionary."

The perspective had evolved slowly. Deep ties of loyalty and affection held her to Denishawn, yet her thoughts were seeking horizons beyond the vision of the leaders of the company. By nature, she was not impulsive, tending rather to repress her feelings, as she had during the miserable period of teaching social dance in Oak Park. She waited for circumstances to force her to act and then made a choice based on cautious reasoning. This was not simply lack of courage; a strong moral sense was involved. Earlier, there had been the feeling of responsibility to support her parents; now she was aware of a debt owed to the people who had given her the performing opportunities she had wanted so intensely for so long. Yet the time had to come for her to consider what she owed to herself—what she must do to fulfill herself as an artist.

Even before the company started back to the States, Doris was giving serious thought to her future as a choreographer:

> If I stay at home I want to be in New York and concentrate on producing dances. You see, as it is, I only do about one dance a year, and that's much too slow—life won't be long enough to get everything done at that rate. It's hardly any use planning how I'm going to get them put on, so I plan what they are to be like—and trust in the good luck that I have always had to see them really brought forth.

The Denishawn company gave the last performance of its Oriental tour in Toyohashi, Japan, on November 11. Almost immediately after their return, the dancers set off on a cross-country tour that began in Los Angeles on December 6 and finished in New York four months later. For impresario Arthur Judson, the tour was tremendously successful; for Doris, it was a grueling sequence of one-night stands. She was tired and restless. Her old dances were beginning to bore her. Ideas for new forms of choreography were stirring in her mind, but she could not find the time to work them through:

> I feel dissatisfied with all my dances. The polka—is the polka, you know. Never could do it. The Spring misses—people don't understand it, and the movement isn't interesting enough if you don't. The Burmese is Oriental apple-sauce. So I think next year is the thing to hold to.

A month later, she wrote home that she was "experimenting with something different for The Spring." There was so little time. She wanted to visit Oak Park, but when? She suggested the two weeks after the tour finished in April, or perhaps later, but not much later, for she would have to start teaching by the first of August and must be settled in a New York apartment by that time.

Her relationship with Miss Ruth and Shawn was becoming increasingly strained, though there is no evidence that she allowed this to become apparent to the company directors. She was, however, nursing a few plans:

> I'm going to try desperately to make an arrangement by which I can stay in New York next year, and still keep their good will

—because another tour is just an almost unthinkable horror. The money I have in the bank I'm determined not to touch—it's dedicated to production which I firmly believe I will get sometime. My idea would be to do a few dances or a ballet next year with appropriate settings and music.

At this point, she seemed to feel that she could remain with Denishawn and still develop as an artist in her own right. Yet the situation began to look more and more threatening. She told her parents that she was concerned about the fall:

[Miss Ruth and Shawn] promise us an increase in salary [on tour] in proportion to their increase. That, of course, would knock out our school & creative work for another year, and by that time, they probably won't resist some other offer, Europe, for instance, then they'll have to do America again so the concert field won't get away from them—so I can't see where we are going to stop. I really don't know what to do—what do you think?

Doris had to investigate the facts, then weigh the evidence, pro and con. What motivated her now was not anger (though it must have been smoldering) but rather a mounting conviction that she had something of importance to accomplish on her own. Could she accomplish it within the frame of what was now being talked of as the "Greater Denishawn"?

The plans were ambitious. There was to be Denishawn House, the private home and studio of the directors, as well as a theatre and a school. While the company was on tour, Shawn took advantage of a break in the schedule to rush to New York where he purchased the corner lots that adjoined Miss Ruth's property near Van Cortlandt Park and selected an architect to start work on the building. The problem the directors faced was money. And this created a problem for the young choreograher:

It would be the biggest thing in the dancing world undoubtedly and I'm sure it would be better to be with it than outside. My fear is that such a tremendous organization would either swamp me, or I will be required to work for the good of the institution to a greater extent than I want to. I'm sure it will take at least two years, and probably more to get the money and the buildings, and another fear I have is that they would expect everybody to spend their entire time for the next two years campaigning for the money. For instance, they talk of accepting a tour next year in order to give speeches and spread propaganda for the big project. That would mean four years, including those in the Orient, just wasted as far as my own work goes—and [it] seems to me two more years would be too great sacrifice. I'd rather leave now and take a chance on being invited as a guest artist to use their theatre after they have it built. But of course they would think it thoroughly disloyal . . .

The first week in May, however, Doris went off to Westport, Connecticut, for a vacation, and was quite willing to let the problems of the future rest in abeyance for a while. She enjoyed staying with Nell Alexander, whose home was surrounded by small cabins that she let to guests. Here Doris could relax—and eat. Everyone agreed that Nell's cooking was marvelous.

But news of Denishawn trickled persistently into Westport as various members dropped by for week ends. Shawn came one week, and Miss Ruth the next. The word was that he had decided to let his wife have her own way about the better part of the planning for Greater Denishawn, and that she was absolutely thriving in her new role of authority. "He will stay out, he says, until they need him, which is the most unselfish thing he's ever done I think."

The next visitors were Martha Graham and Louis Horst. Doris had seen little of either of them for some time. Louis had left Denishawn before the Oriental tour, going to Vienna to study music. He had returned to New York in 1926, becoming Graham's musical director. She, having left Denishawn in 1923, had already given her first independent New York concert.

Since thoughts of a similar defection were now stirring in Doris's mind, the consequences of Graham's move were bound to concern her. The two had never been on especially friendly terms. Actually, however, they had spent few of their Denishawn days together; one touring most often with Shawn, the other with Miss Ruth. (Consequently, the complete absence of any mention of Graham in the *Autobiography* is not so strange as it might first appear.) Now, though, with her own growing feelings of independent ambition, Doris felt drawn to the earlier deserter as to an ally:

The Shawns, I'm ashamed to say, are jealous of Martha. It's disgraceful, and as Louis knows the bitter things Ted has said about her, he hasn't been near them. So there's a breach wide & deep that may never be spanned. They think Martha should mention Denishawn on her programs, and in her interviews— and that is the fly in the jam. She considers that she has broken away from everything they do, and is individual. (Mr. Shawn having emphatically pointed out to her before she went away that she had no right to any Denishawn works.) So there it stands. I'm much more in sympathy with Martha & Louis and have looked forward to seeing them for ages. It was rather difficult at first, because they thought all of their old friends in the company shared Ted's viewpoint, and it took aggressiveness on our part to assure them of our friendship.

The feelings of friendship were only enhanced by further contact:

Martha could stay only one day—although she needs a vacation badly. She has worked so hard to keep her studio going. I like her a lot—seeing her after such a long absence I get a fresh impression as of a new person. Of course she's extremely artificial—not silly, I mean, but like a hot-house flower that grows best in a hot, moist climate, intensely feminine, not a flaming obvious flower—but a night-blooming thing with a faint exotic perfume. Whereas Louis is the same old bundle of contradictions. He believes in equality & freedom of the sexes, but dies of jealousy, and says no man can love a woman who is unfaithful to him. He believes there is no happiness in love, and that art is the only fun that lasts, and in the next breath says that half an hour with the one you love is the greatest ecstasy! He's a hopeless romanticist and sentimentalist—full of Neitsche [sic] in his brain and romance in his heart . . .

At this point, Doris herself was making an effort to resist romanticism. The same letter reveals her attraction to a ballet Louis had written and titled *Viennese Serenade*. It is the nineteenth century— night, a lamplighter, lovers meet, they dance, dawn breaks, they embrace and part. Tempting, yes. "But I'm tired of darling little dances and I long for a good thick juicy beef-dance-steak that I can chew on hard."

She thought of starting with an idea for which music would then be written: " . . . the whole thing would be absolutely my own." She was concerned that she had always depended on someone else

—like a composer—for inspiration. Now: "I want it to be a symbolic or ritualistic thing—with some direct connection with our own human emotions and desires."

By the following week she had an idea—not just a theme, but the entire design of a dance clearly worked out in her mind. *Color Harmony* was to be one of her first major breakthroughs:

> Following my theory that any abstract idea can be danced, I chose "Harmony," although in working it out I find that closely crowded by the "Art versus Nature" idea. Briefly it is this— there are three groups personifying the primary colors, and each has a short dance, a slow waltz for the blues, vivacious rythm [sic] for the yellows, and a sturdy brilliant dance for the reds. The warmer yellows and reds are attracted to each other— the cool blues are aloof. Inevitably one red after another becomes entangled with a yellow, and immediately a flame of orange scarf goes up between them, afterward to encircle them both as they madly whirl & dance. Then the blues are drawn in and all the couples swoop and clash in the utmost confusion —(all the combinations possible between the three colors are made). In the middle of all this a streak of white light appears, and down this path a silver creature runs which you can call intelligence or thought or the power of art form, whatever you like. This creature separates the couples, drives them into a design. They all grow more calm as it weaves in and out between them making form out of confusion.

While the creative ideas were brewing, life at Nell's went on pleasantly enough until Shawn came by with a new Packard, chauffeur, and dog:

> He is most interested in building the institution of Denishawn, which he wants to do by everybody's cooperation with himself as dictator. And he's right, I think, if your aim is a smooth-running organization . . . which would be all well and good for me if it were merely a business, but it happens to be that and more. More important to me than any organization is the dance, and more important than loyalty is sincerity. . . . By his insistence on obedience to his will we would be drawn into art-expressions that we do not believe in—and that would be a lie and is false. . . . it's in the blood to cling to an ideal.

However, the air seemed to be cleared when Doris learned that Shawn and Miss Ruth had accepted a contract for a forty-week tour with the Ziegfeld Follies. Knowing that she did not want to travel, they had refrained from inviting her to join them, asking instead that she remain with the school in New York. Their decision immediately erased her need to consider leaving Denishawn. With the directors away, she would be free to work on her own choreography. And wasn't that enough?

In early July Doris visited her parents in Oak Park, returning to New York later in the month to get settled in the apartment she was to share with Pauline. By August, the dance studios were open. Martha announced a student recital "and went through the usual Graham emotional pyrotechnics, being afraid to invite us, and fighting with Louis about it, telling us we couldn't come—and changing her mind, ending by calling at the studio twice and telephoning three times to be sure we were coming." Within the Denishawn fold, Doris found sufficient independence: "I feel more free to do as I please now that the year has really started, and I let my imagination run—instead of teaching the old routine things."

She was not laying claim to unique innovations. Many of the new German and American dancers were using the same general principle:

> . . . which is that of moving from the inside out; so I don't feel that I'm stealing anybody's stuff. . . . It's the dominant expression of our generation, if not of the age, and ballet is as out of style as bustles and leg o'mutton sleeves. Miss Ruth and Isadora were the first of course—but Miss Ruth allowed Ted to dominate the training in the school with his bar and technique . . .

By September, Doris was back at the serious business of choreography. Three dances were in progress: a Debussy waltz, Ravel's *Fairy Garden,* and Scriabin's *Pathetic Study*—the last a duet for Charles and herself:

> None of these three involve a hoop, scarf or other prop, are not startling, and I hope will be safe from democracy. I'm just at that in-between stage when the first glow of enthusiasm has cooled, and I'm struggling with phrases and continuity—and that annoying way the music has of going on, leaving you far behind.

When she noted that the dances were not startling, she failed to mention that *The Fairy Garden* was to be danced in a costume consisting only of a shift of very thin chiffon—as close to nudity as she dared go.

The schedule was busy now. There were classes from ten in the morning till eight at night, and there were more students than expected. Doris inaugurated two weekly "creative nights" for all the pupils to come and "give birth to their ideas." Another evening she set aside for a select few to help her with her own work. The remaining nights she reserved for work on solos and duets. A strenuous life, but one that she loved.

After living out of a suitcase for more than two years, she was glad to be settled. Home-cooked food seemed a real luxury. The apartment near Carnegie Hall had a kitchenette "that two people can get into." The studio, its walls hung with dull blue theatrical gauze, was kept quite bare, since it was meant for work. The Chinese chairs were lovely, but "so very straight and small that we had to buy an armchair for people Louis's size." The former tenants had left behind a black kitten who, for the tan sprinkled in its fur, was known as Dusty.

The choreography was progressing, though Doris was finding it hard to work on solos: "I like groups of people so much better— but the people are not so good, so there we are." The new group piece was Bach's *Air for the G String*, and she was pleased with the costumes for the five girls, who had long trains hung from their shoulders, reflecting the drawn-out, sustained effect of the music. She was pleased too with the score for *Color Harmony* that she had commissioned from Clifford Vaughan, who had been musical director at Denishawn for the past two seasons: "Of course, it doesn't always go well—I have bleak days when nothing seems any good— but some of it is right, I am sure."

Hearing that Shawn and Miss Ruth would be back in the city at Christmas time, she was anxious to get some of the dances in shape in case they might like a showing. And she wanted to give a recital before the year was out. Apparently she was not at all apprehensive with regard to what the directors would think of this idea.

However, she was a little fearful that her combined freedom and security in the Denishawn school might not last. It was one thing for Miss Ruth and Shawn to look at her dances and then leave to rejoin the Follies. But the tour would have to come to an end. And what then?

> We haven't heard a word as to what Ted's plans are—but I bet he has at least one. I'm going to have one too as in defense, in case his includes me in a way I don't care for. What would be difficult would be for him to take over the school and want us to stay and of course eventually that would involve giving concerts with him—and to get out of that is going to take some very high class manipulation. Nobody thinks much of him as an artist—not even the members of his own company and his school—which makes it difficult to work for him—and try to avoid upholding him as an example to his pupils. He's about ten years behind in his theories of movement.

But there was no mention of Denishawn in Doris's next letter to her family, for her mind was too absorbed with the concert she had just given at Studio 61 in Carnegie Hall. The place was already historically significant to dance, for music-educator Alys Bentley had previously let it to Isadora Duncan. It was an auspicious spot for a beginning:

> The recital used me up completely, and the classes went right on, of course, and it was a fight to keep up. The thing went pretty well, although it was not the pleasure I thought it would be, because lots of the most critical people were there—and that made it difficult. I enclose a program. I had taught the girls the Sonata [*Pathétique*] in class, and like the old thing anyway, and wanted to do something of Miss Ruth's as a tribute to her. The girls did it quite well—they're all Jewish you know and quite emotional. I thought I would be awfully tired of it, but it came to life unexpectedly, and bloomed beautifully. Most of my numbers were soft—as I've had such a reaction against the brilliant things—and they all came out pretty well, only need more work, as a new style always does. The Papillon is more like my old things—in a short yellow accordion pleated slip, with large long pleated sleeves—very fast and frothy. Only the first three numbers of the Color Ballet were done, but they can stand alone, so I had the girls do them. I think they are original and modern. Clifford's music is stunning—even Louis [Horst] liked it, so you can imagine!

The press agreed, one critic placing *Color Harmony* "among dance masterpieces."

Doris wrote the Shawns about the concert, telling them that her new dances were delicate and romantic rather than brilliant: "Of course it takes time to develop new facets of one's expression—so these are still 'imperfect.'" Feeling secure, she was bold enough to criticize their plans for the coming winter. Agreeing that it was a good idea to have a plan, she nevertheless felt that they were trying to move too fast. For the company to put on two programs a week was asking far too much if they were to maintain a standard of excellence; two a year would be as much as she would care to venture. Besides: "How do you know any of them could organize a program —see that it balanced—had quality and finish?"

Meanwhile, she concentrated on building her own repertory. She was considering a solo about Penelope at her loom. And there was to be a dance using labor rhythms. So many ideas! Soon another work was under way. Having met Henry Cowell, whom she liked immensely, she began a new piece to his music. It concerned the wailing creature that bore departing Irish souls to their new homes in another world: "The 'Banshee' will be fun to do. . . . I'm going to be covered in a moldy green, head and all, and try to move like a lost soul." The concept succeeded, for she impressed a viewer as "a spooky spirit and most realistic spectre that made me turn up my coat collar and look to see if all the doors were shut."

How peacefully and fruitfully it might have gone. But Doris's critical appraisal of the plans for Greater Denishawn had not pleased her superiors. On March 7, Shawn phoned her from Altoona, Pennsylvania, asking that she meet him wherever the tour happened to be as soon as possible to discuss business. Her next concert was scheduled for March 24 and she was in the midst of the (as usual) frantic preparations. So she sent Olga Fry in her place. Shawn considered Doris's "demands" to be "impossible," and quickly sat down with Miss Ruth to draft a statement of the aims and purposes of the organization. Then he rushed up to New York on a Sunday to confront his recalcitrant protegée:

> I had an awful time with Ted over the summer school and that involved absolutely everything before we got through, from our personal faults to what is art. He was difficult as usual—but it wasn't all his fault as I hadn't told him what was going on. . . .
> We finally got it settled but God knows it was a frightful ex-

Top: Doris Humphrey with Students of the Denishawn School in *Concerto in A Minor,* 1928. (Photo by Martha Swope from original by Vandamm Studio; collection NYPL.) Bottom: *The Shakers* (1931) in a 1941 revival; Nona Schurman, Beatrice Seckler, Marie Maginnis, Katherine Litz, Doris Humphrey, Lee Sherman, Charles Weidman, Peter Hamilton. (Photo by Martha Swope from original by Barbara Morgan; collection NYPL.)

Top: *Color Harmony*, 1928. (Photo by Vandamm Studio; collection Walter Terry.) Bottom: Doris Humphrey as the Old Queen in *Life of the Bee*, 1929. (Photo by Marcus Blechman; collection Walter Terry.)

perience. Lots of it I sympathized about, but could scarcely see that it was my fault. For instance, he said he had been on the road all year, was stale—had no new material—would go right from the road to the summer camp [the studio and school he had built at Nell Alexander's] with no time to prepare any. And here I was with a lot of fresh ideas etc.

For the time being, then, matters were settled, though probably Doris was willing to compromise on at least some issues simply to cut short the wearing discussions and get back to work on her concert. A "Dance Program presented by Doris Humphrey and Charles Weidman and Students of the Denishawn School" was given at the Brooklyn Little Theatre on March 24:

> It was so much better than the little one at Miss Bentley's studio —everything more finished and I was sure of what I was doing—without a quiver of stage-fright. I even enjoyed doing some of it—so if I can make the inevitable a pleasure—what more could I ask? Everybody—almost—was crazy about the [Grieg] Concerto, and I think myself that it is the best & most sincere thing I have ever done—very serious and vital. I felt that it was real—which is a great satisfaction after all the whipped cream and apple sauce of other days. The Color Harmony was the least finished—it is such a big thing I had to stand off & look at it to get the proper perspective—and I know at least what is wrong now, even if the remedy isn't clear yet. The Air for G. String is lovely, if I do say so—although Louis says "That's a scream, a medieval Christian dance done by five Jewesses." However, I think they move like angels, and that's the important thing. . . . I had a set of screens made to use instead of a cyclorama—[a] set of platforms & steps—which were most effective for the big ballets.

There was little time for rest, since the next concert was set for April 15 at the John Golden Theatre. It was preceded by a series of crises. One was provoked by the New York law forbidding entertainments of any kind to be given on Sundays, the only day that the dancers had access to the theatres. Their established practice was to obtain permission to present a "sacred concert." This time, late on Friday and without warning, the license was revoked. After a sleepless night, the performers checked with the authorities, only to find that someone had made a mistake on the application and asked for a license for a "dance concert." A simple change in the wording legalized the whole thing.

Then, on Saturday night, Clifford Vaughan came to the rehearsal, heard the tempos, said he couldn't sacrifice his art, and walked out—with the score for *Color Harmony*. This too was resolved, for he came back Sunday morning. By evening, all was well though some frazzled nerves remained:

> From the response of the audience, the box office receipts, and the general enthusiasm afterwards I should say it was a great success—but from my own it could have been a lot better. The two big events were the Color Harmony & the Concerto, the second of which was almost perfect. The color thing is done by sixteen of the girls and Robert [Gorham] you know—and to present sixteen amateurs to a New York audience takes some nerve and training. . . . There may have been other abstract ballets done in America, but I've never seen one—and I'm quite proud of it. The girls had so many handicaps—Clifford is a rotten director—the tempos were very uncertain, the lights went wrong—but they kept on marvelously. People were simply stunned—they said [they had] never seen anything like it. . . . The Concerto I can always throw myself into—it's such superb music—and the orchestral tone intensified the emotional quality —until both we & the audience at the end were at such a pitch of excitement everybody wanted to yell & did. Imagine the thrill of having a whole house crying "bravo"!—not once but every time the curtain went up. As the critic said in the Times— after the two ballets the solo numbers with piano seemed pale —and with the exception of [Charles's] Minstrels and the Banshee which is blood-curdling, nothing else went so very well. I told you Mr. Cowell was going to play for me—somebody said he drew it from a tortured piano! I had a small green screen— fixed like a chimney—around which I oozed and wailed. It made quite an impression—but I wasn't satisfied with it. It takes me longer than two weeks to learn a dance—and a thing like that becomes merely sensational unless it is done very well. The expenses of the thing were staggering—over $1200—but I think we took in $1400—or so—which is an untold relief.
>
> I haven't even thought of what comes next. I'm too tired— didn't get up at all yesterday until dinner. Well this is what I wanted to do all along—and as I said before—I have at last a sense of living instead of getting ready to live—or a sense of flatness after having lived. And now that I've smelled blood— God help anybody who stands between me and my meat!

The next month, relaxing in the course of a two-week vacation in Westport and with the triumph of the concert fresh in her mind, Doris could see the true extent of what she had accomplished in a single season. Though she could not so commend herself in writing to her family, she was obviously aware of how far she had outdistanced her mentors of the past ten years. To place herself again under their artistic dominion was inconceivable. Miss Ruth was planning a summer concert at Lewisohn Stadium, with a program consisting of old numbers. The prospect was distasteful: ". . . our ideas of values are totally different and will lead to serious difficulties I foresee that."

Yet she persisted in hoping that independence might be possible within the old framework. She had found a new studio for the Denishawn school—the fifth floor of an old building at 9 East 59th Street. Obviously, she expected to continue teaching there.

Then the blow came . . .

The Start of the Struggle

A<small>T</small> the close of her Autobiography Doris recalled her optimism at the end of her years with Denishawn: "We looked forward to a bright future with only ourselves to depend on."

There they were, the group Pauline had christened "the unholy three," ready to face the world on their own. What a crew they were to be setting out on the adventure of life together!

There was Doris, her slender body and delicate features belying the steel-strong will. Cool, detached, intellectual, always in control. Artistic sensitivity tinged with bits of the New England Puritan and the Middle Western schoolteacher. A perfectionist, so unstinting in her demands on herself the artist that she had little time or energy to spare for the person. Hers was a single-minded purpose; for that and that alone, she was ready to sacrifice.

Pauline: the aider and abettor. The person behind the artist. Pianist, costume designer, lighting expert, manager—generally indispensable. Remarkably competent, efficient, and versatile, she could come to the rescue in almost any situation. Always ready to minister to Doris's needs. Not that Doris voiced them often, but Pauline was rather clairvoyant. Always knowing better than anyone else what was required, what was right. Capable of organizing everybody's lives—and needing to do so. Yet it was all for her colleagues. To them she was utterly devoted.

Then Charles: gay and outgoing, full of fun. He improvised brilliantly, onstage—and off. When disciplined, he tended to sulk, but invariably came through in performance. He stuttered a bit, but chattered incessantly. Quick and impulsive, he easily reminded one of the chipmunk he later portrayed in his staging of Thurber's *Fables for Our Time*. Childishly delightful. And childishly irresponsible. He borrowed money from everyone. So—the unholy three. On their own.

Doris was happy and confident. Yet she was much too clear-headed, too realistic, to envision anything like easy, immediate success. She may not have anticipated the extent of the hardships that lay ahead, but certainly they came as no surprise to her, and she was prepared to cope with them. She knew that independence could be hers only for a price.

The first cost was a purely practical one. Heretofore there had been an organization, a school, and a company behind her. Now all the chores of administration were in the hands of the unholy three. They agreed to take over the 59th Street studio when the Denishawn lease expired in the fall, a daring step because the space was expensive and a good number of students would have to be attracted. This could present a problem, for the trio had cut themselves off from the aura surrounding the parent company. While Doris Humphrey and Charles Weidman were known to the dance world of New York, their names alone did not carry the prestige that the general public had so long associated with Denishawn. The new group had to establish itself.

Another problem was the title of their art. "We have no name," lamented Doris of the new style she had embarked on creating. It was called by some "modern," but no one really knew precisely what that meant, especially since each of its exponents seemed to interpret it in a different way. Martha Graham moved in one manner, Tamiris in another, Humphrey-Weidman in still another. This was independence with a vengeance. But it was deeply motivated.

The new idiom was based, as Doris had told her parents, on working "from the inside out." Modern? In principle, it was as old as man himself, for it came from the primitive instinct to let the body mirror the impulses seething within it. But to the American theatre audience of the late 1920's it was practically unknown. Their chief source of exposure to the idea had been Isadora Duncan, and she, largely rejected in her own country, had danced far more in

Europe than at home. For three centuries American social convention had censored such intimate revelation, had hidden the original
impetus of dance movement under a patina of cultivated elegance,
erecting over it a superstructure of beautiful but artificial forms. For
such audiences, the visible manifestation of inner feelings, unmasked
by either balletic prettiness or Denishawn exoticism, was shocking.
The breakthrough was violent, and it was largely misunderstood.
Yet personal integrity demanded that it be what it was. With her
few colleagues, Doris could not subscribe to accepted concepts of
movement simply because they were accepted. If the audience was
bewildered by the unfamiliarity of the concept—well, one just had
to persist.

Looking back from the 1970's, Charles could say: "We were
young and strong. It wasn't so hard." And at the time, his partner
kept reiterating that she was doing exactly what she had always
wanted to do and she loved it. But—there was always a "but." Her
letters home became less and less frequent, more taken up with
apologies for not writing and with descriptions of the work that left
so little time for personal relationships. There was never enough
time; there was never enough money.

Before launching the struggle for survival there was—fortunately—a summer of comparative quiet, with only classes to be concerned about, for Doris honored her commitment to teach at Denishawn until September. There was even a little time for social life, a
most unusual situation and one that was not to recur for some time.
Wesley Chamberlain, whom Doris had met in Singapore, turned up
in New York in August, to her admitted delight. As usual, however,
nothing came of it. With considerable acuity, she analyzed her reaction for "Mama-San" (the title acquired on the Oriental tour) and
"Pop":

> Quite a man—and I'm very fond of him—a complete contrast
> to most of the men I know and in that lies his fascination. Lots
> of power, with a look like a lion tamer, which appeals to the
> feminine part of me, but which paradoxically would make me
> snap like a turtle if he tried to use it on me.

One consequence of the episode, however, was the gift of a yellow,
part-Persian kitten. There was a difficult period of adjustment for

Dusty, but in time the two pets became good friends. In Oak Park, for some reason their daughter could not understand, the Humphreys went on living without a cat.

Faced with planning her own school, Doris used part of the summer to give some thought to her ideas of teaching. She told her parents that she had completed an article for *The Dance Magazine,* "On Learning to Dance," but ". . . I'm sure they won't use it—it's too high-brow for them—and I'm inexperienced at that sort of thing and I packed in too much, and got mixed up in my psychology which I don't know anything about." Contrary to her expectations, the magazine did use it. Retitled "Interpreter or Creator?" it was published in the January, 1929, issue. There is no evidence that the article had any startling effect. Undoubtedly it was admired by the author's friends and ignored by nearly everyone else. The modern dance was like that. It was to take a long time . . .

Although the Humphrey-Weidman studio did not start its full schedule of classes until October, a single session was offered daily through September. The arrangements were informal: at the end of each class, the students paid Pauline and the trio divided the receipts. The plan was to have as few classes as possible—just enough to bring in some money—so there would be time to prepare an October concert. Some numbers from the spring program would be repeated, along with *Water Study,* which had just been done at a dance teachers' convention. Doris was also composing a new group dance based on Maeterlinck's *Life of the Bee,* and a new solo to a sarabande by Rameau.

Consciously experimenting, she analyzed her intentions for *Water Study* in a program note:

> Probably the thing that distinguishes musical rhythm from other rhythm is the measured time beat, so this has been eliminated from the Water Study and the rhythm flows in natural phrases instead of cerebral measures. There is no count to hold the dancers together in the very slow opening rhythm, only the feel of the wave length that curves the backs of the group.

The rhythm built gradually as the waves gathered momentum; first only bending the torsos of the kneeling dancers, then raising them to crouching positions, then sweeping them to their feet, hurtling them headlong across the stage until the crest was reached and finally subsided. Mary Watkins found in the dance "the authentic feeling of the sea casting itself relentlessly, in torpid or in stormy mood, against the wall of some New England shore. Real genius has gone into the creating of this."

The *Bee* was also based on natural phenomena, in this case the struggle of the young queen to wrest her position from the aging ruler. The movement material was firmly rooted in insect behavior: bodies huddled together defensively, wings quivered in fear, groups ran as if flying in frenzied trajectories. John Martin, America's first full-time dance critic, wrote with enthusiasm:

> . . . in the literal sense of the word, thrilling. . . . Never was music missed less. The humming of an off-stage chorus in varying rhythmic phrases, punctuated at rare intervals by a point of open vocal tone, provides a sinister aural background for a sinister picture. A fight to the death between the two principal figures, with the chorus massed on the floor at the side and back in frenetic expectation, contains as much excitement as almost any three melodramas I can mention.

Only two of the sixteen girls who had danced with Doris in the spring had failed her. One left to get married, but the second defection was troubling, for this one went to her "enemies":

> Yes—I have them—for the first time in my life—and the sensation is strange. The Shawns are very bitter—and listen to all sorts of lies and slander—and have convinced a number of people that I am most unethical in every way—I have wheedled and inveighed the pupils into leaving Denishawn with me, not only at the studio, but under their very noses in their own house. I am dishonest, I am grasping and greedy and selfish, ungrateful, and no loyal Denishawner is allowed to take lessons of me on pain of dismissal.

Under the circumstances, she was especially grateful when Miss Ruth, along with several members of the school staff and some of the students, came to the concert at the Civic Repertory Theatre on October 24. Miss Ruth did not come backstage after the performance, but she sent Olga Fry to tell Doris that *Color Harmony* was "stupendous." "It is the great part of Miss Ruth who could do it," Doris told her family. The concert had been a great success: a sold-out house and standing room besides—eleven hundred people had come.

Still, the work of the school had to go steadily on. Exhausted, she wrote home that "it is simply impossible for me to keep up, both as a person and an artist." But when her parents pleaded with her to come home for Christmas, it was not only the burden of work that made her say no: "You see I'm in debt. And can't see my way to taking vacations on other people's money. And so you are paying the penalty of being born to honest parents and having an honest daughter." The school was doing well. There were sixty students who came at least twice a week, but the expenses of maintenance were high. Still, Doris expected the debt to be paid off by spring, and a summer vacation would be a necessity; last year she had taught without a break, and she knew she could not manage that again.

Despite financial worries, the trio had a merry Christmas. Mrs. Picard, a rich private student of Charles, came with a tree, gifts, and a goose that Pauline cooked for dinner. Doris's students gave her a movie camera, for they knew she felt this was the coming way to record dances.

By February, rehearsals were under way for the spring programs scheduled for March 31 and April 7 at the Guild Theatre. She sent her parents a program, writing plaintively on the back of it: "I do wish you could even see one of these concerts." Of course they could not, for they had their own school to manage and no more money than she had.

There was no question but that the emphasis of the Humphrey choreography for the new concerts would be on compositions for the group. This was one of her unique contributions to the modern dance of the period when Martha Graham and Tamiris and Charles Weidman were all concentrating on the solo dancer. The programs went well, though this time they lost money. The first night was Easter; the second was very hot. Doris was overworked to the point of almost unsupportable fatigue:

> But every time I felt myself sinking, I remembered Ruth St. Denis telling me I couldn't do it without a rich boy friend or an entertainment standard—that is, a compromise in life or art— and I pulled myself together again. Of course I haven't done

anything very positive or concrete to point a finger at yet—but I'm still going, without being much in debt or giving the vaudeville public what it wants.

On May 10, there was a successful concert at the Philadelphia Academy of Music, and in July a strenuous two-week teachers' course, the latter a device to pay the summer's rent. Before her anticipated August vacation, Doris was trying to finish two new dances. The first was to Ravel's *La Valse:*

> The other is my first attempt at a work which is really what the dance should be I think. I call it "Motion Concerto" [this became *Drama of Motion*], without music or theme, in three parts —that is the first part is based on design, the second on rhythm, third on contrasting quality in motion. Sounds awfully stiff, but I'm [doing] it. Anyway we need something a little stiff to offset all this self expression and personality boosting. All this is having a logical result on my work. I take so little interest in solos that it isn't funny—and am at a point where I must decide whether to give up dancing entirely or dance much more—becauses this half effort is hopeless.

She justified her concern with group dances in a program note titled "The Ensemble":

> Through the new conception of significance in the ensemble which has developed during the last ten years, the dance promises to come to its full stature, just as music flowered through the symphony. A group of bodies is as varied and colorful a medium as the orchestra, and gives the composer equally rich material to fulfill the range of his vision. The new ensemble also has the architectural and impersonal attributes of the orchestra as distinguished from the personal and expressionistic, unique qualities sadly needed in the dance to place it more seriously among the arts.

Never content with mere theorizing, Doris implemented her ideas with careful, deliberate, practical measures. This year she devised a letter to be sent to all prospective members of the group. After outlining the aims and structure of the company, emphasizing the seriousness of its artistic aspirations, she laid down the laws:

> Rehearsals are twice a week at night usually, but that increases to three or more before concerts, and in addition there are cos-

tume fittings during the day. I expect everyone to come to rehearsals faithfully and to arrange vacations and family events so it is possible to do so.

After a concert at the Lake Placid Club on August 2 and a brief vacation in Maine, Doris returned to New York where the school opened in mid-September. The merry-go-round started again:

You see it seems to be necessary to live in a four ring circus to be the kind of a dancer I've picked out for myself. First there is the studio and classes. There is piles of competition in New York—schools are listed by the dozen. . . . Then I'm trying to develop individuality in people—and since nobody ever did that for me I am groping for the right way, and I'm not always successful. I think back over the teachers I have had from dear Miss Hinman through to Ruth St. Denis & T. Shawn and I can't remember a single lesson in which any of them ever suggested that I make a move of my own. What I had was instruction, not education—and the fact that I did do something for myself occasionally was just the grand old family independence coming out—and added to that circumstances and necessity—which was all in spite of training & not because of it. But when it comes to applying this drawing out theory of education to actual pupils, the path is very thorny. In the first place there is no cooperation from them. The majority of people and especially of girls are docile lambs who love to be mastered—and since there are plenty of strong and vivid personalities in the field who dote on mastering them—it is hard to keep them. The most difficult are those who have already been through years of academic training—academic in the sense that they have been told exactly what to do every minute. But with raw beginners I have considerable success with the more spontaneous method. The general idea is—you tell me—or show me what you want to do and I'll tell you if you're doing it and how to go at it if you're not. Well all that is just one of the problems—which should take all of one's time and attention. Then there is the group. With one hand I try to encourage them to be individuals—to move and think regardless of me or anyone else—and in rehearsals it is necessary to contradict all that and make them acutely aware of each other, so that they may move in a common rhythm. I'm probably crazy to try to do exactly opposite things with the same people. Of course my main interest is in the group—from an objective art standpoint I am convinced that it will carry the dance to the highest point in art—that the group can express more subtleties, more power—more variety than one single dancer ever could, no matter how intelligent or talented he might be. Just the composition for the group, and the training of them as an entity would be another job to take all one's time. Then there is me—and I'm probably the greatest problem of all —because if I cannot adjust the various parts of myself so that they harmonize and work smoothly together—none of the other things can be done at all.

The main undertaking for this winter was the first season of the Dance Repertory Theatre, a project that was to combine the forces of Humphrey-Weidman, Graham, and Tamiris. The idea had been initiated by Helen Becker, a renegade from the Metropolitan Opera Ballet, who had taken the exotic name of Tamiris to set out on a career of artistic rebellion abetted by a timely concern for social and political causes. Her Dance Repertory Theatre was not intended to be, nor to become, a single company. Rather it was a device to offset some of the practically unsurmountable problems attendant on the staging of single, independent concerts. The participants hoped that, by using the services of a manager (which no one of them could afford alone), each would be saved the tedious tasks of coping with theatre staffs, advertising, and the rest. Sunday evenings had also become a problem, with several choreographers often competing for the eager but still small audience. By taking a theatre for an entire week, the cooperating groups could hope to pull in larger houses than any one of them could manage alone. Hopefully, the broader range of programing would also help to attract the general public who had not yet shown much interest in the modern dance.

From the beginning, Doris was apprehensive about the enterprise, though she recognized its potential value:

> It has seemed necessary for us to incorporate, and of course I hate that idea because organization has come to be such a hateful thing. They simply organized the life out of Denishawn. And besides I haven't much faith in Martha Graham. She is a snake if there ever was one. In spite of all misgivings, it is the best thing to do—the thing is to be ready for double crossing.

Even if all did not go smoothly, the project did go on. Six performances were given at the Maxine Elliott Theatre, each company offering two programs. The Humphrey-Weidman group had the evenings of January 6 and 9. When it was over, Doris had to admit that the strain had been worth while. Major articles in the newspapers had drawn attention to the venture, to its individual participants, and to the existence of the modern dance itself as a vital, contemporary force. Some of the houses were very good and so were some of the reviews, *Drama of Motion* receiving special praise from John Martin, who called it "quite the most extraordinary creation that has come from the mind of this highly gifted composer . . . a dance composition that has plunged into the hitherto almost untouched wilderness of plastic potentialities, and has retained at the same time its contact with humanity and genuineness." But the young choreographer was not swayed too much by the opinions of the critics. "After all," she told her family, "you can only keep your mind on the jump over the fence and not on the cheers or the hisses." Just as well, for a few months later a Boston critic found the same work "considered prose rather than glowing poetry."

Knowing that *Drama of Motion* was an extended foray into previously unexplored territory, Doris had presented it with an explanatory program note:

> The three parts of this dance constitute Miss Humphrey's first attempt to establish the dance as an independent art. This experiment has no program, no music, almost no costumes. In positive terms, it has three contrasting qualities expressed both in movement and design. The first is slow and sustained, moving with a warm strength in its curving flow. The intricate patterns weave in and out only for the purpose of pleasing the eye with an ever-changing series of lines and spaces. The second part is introduced by a brief dance which modulates from the slow movement of the first part to the sprightly jigging of the second. This part is all sharp, surprising accents and odd quirks and jerks, with the solo keeping a remnant of the first movement through it all. The third movement opens with a thundering rush of power through the bodies of the entire group. This powerful accent is reiterated in different ways until a contrasting delicate quality emerges. Rudely the first theme returns and sweeps up the softer group, bursting beyond the limits of the stage in its crude gusto. The last spurt of power spends itself in a fall circling the stage.

But even the much less esoteric works, Doris often felt, required some preliminary analysis. The modern dance was so new and, to a

large portion of the public, still so very strange. Its uneven, broken
rhythms and lines could be disconcerting if the audience was not
provided with a clue like the one she devised for this program note
on her solo *Descent into a Dangerous Place:*

> This fantastic creature has the utmost difficulty in finding its
> way home. Through crevices and broken rock it slips and slides
> —a most perilous descent even for a supernatural being. The
> music is written in dissonant harmony by the contemporary
> composer, Adolph Weiss, which forms a fitting accompaniment
> for the creature's angularities.

Doris delighted in such theorizing, but there was never enough
time for it; and after this season she found herself, however un-
willingly, even more deeply involved in organizations. This was
clearly the only way for the dancers to protect themselves. In February there was a fight with the Sabbath League, which was determined to preserve the 1879 law forbidding Sunday entertainments.
The situation became urgent when the theatres began to refuse to
rent to dancers for fear of losing their licenses. Realizing they would
have to put pressure on Albany, the performers organized the Concert Dancers League to work toward getting the old law amended.
So, in addition to all the usual work pressures, Doris now found
herself attending numerous meetings.

There were personal problems as well. In February, Mama-San
fell ill. Doris assured the family that she could send them $25 a
week and kept in close touch with Ethel Moulton for continuing
bulletins on her mother's condition. By March 7 the nurse was allowed to leave, but soon afterward her father suffered a stroke, and
the worries persisted.

At the end of March, rehearsals started for the Norman Bel
Geddes production of the lusty Greek comedy *Lysistrata,* with Doris
and Charles as choreographers. She suspected that this would be
an exasperating job, but the musical was scheduled to open in New
York on June 25 for an indefinite run, and she hoped to make a
contract for $50 a week to last as long as the show did. With a cast
including Fay Bainter, Ernest Truex, and Miriam Hopkins, *Lysistrata* seemed bound to be a hit. However:

Another time I won't be drawn into such a production because it just can't be right. I'm not in control sufficiently to make it so. And one of the things that is wrong is the inexperience of the dancers. Half of them are studio-bred entirely—which is all right as far as it goes. But they don't know how to simulate abandon without being abandoned night after night. Result— they hurt themselves—especially the greenest ones.

Though she did not mention it at this time, one of the greenest of the dancers in the company was José Limón. Just twenty-two years old, the Mexican-born Californian had been at the Humphrey-Weidman school since 1928 when, completely untrained in dance, he had turned from his ambition to paint and decided to pursue a career in the theatre. He had been judiciously placed in the back line of the chorus of *Lysistrata*, where he abandoned himself nightly in the bacchanale.

At the same time, Doris was rehearsing the Schönberg opera *Die Glückliche Hand,* scheduled to open in Philadelphia on April 11, prior to its presentation at the Metropolitan Opera House in New York. It was an important production, sponsored by the prestigious League of Composers and enhanced by the presence of Leopold Stokowski conducting the Philadelphia Orchestra. Doris's role was that of The Woman, symbol of the protagonist's dreams and desires. It was a mime part, as was that of Charles who played The Stranger, representing material power. But the leading role was taken by a singer who used the good, old-fashioned, conventional gestures, and Doris found it impossible to make the two styles fuse or even seem remotely related. When the premiere was over, she told her family that Philadelphia had taken it pretty well. "I don't yet understand it myself."

Lysistrata gave Doris considerable trouble: "I'm going to rehearse the daylights of it," she declared on May 18 and kept declaring well after the success of the New York opening. Meanwhile, she took on still another job—the dance entries in Webster's *Dictionary*. By June 1, she was having difficulties tracing the origin of "antique Greek dance," but had successfully completed "arabesque" and "assemblé."

In the midst of all this activity, an interlude for Rostand's *Les*

Romanesques, to be presented at a garden party in Newport, was a pleasant diversion:

> All except Hymen make a very stilted entrance—and then the dances follow each other—the Graces do a very amourous one, much entwining with pink roses, I do a tambourine dance as Terpsichore, Hymen does a solo, and greets Terpsichore fondly. The Amazons entertain them, and every time there is a pause Hebe pours a drink for whoever will take it. It is grand fun to do as a satire—but I doubt if anybody at the party will get it. You know society people after a few cocktails.

Les Fêtes de L'Hymen et Terpsichore delighted the audience at "The Glen" on June 18 and was kept for a while in the Humphrey-Weidman repertory.

Then there was the summer teachers' course, which the young choreographer enjoyed as much as usual. A ballet dancer had turned up in the classes:

> You can't change an old war horse like that in a few weeks. She'll go to her grave in fifth position. It all just continually bores me to death—sometimes I can't finish a class without going out and slumping for a few minutes.

Since the summer had been so busy, Doris tried to arrange a less tiring schedule for the fall. *Lysistrata* had proved to be a real hit, and she had been asked to rehearse it again, this time for the road. Hopefully this, along with a single class at the Dalton School, would carry her through financially and still leave some time for choreography. By September several new ideas were stirring:

> I'm interested in doing a dance based on religious cults—the general theme being Shakerism. They did a dance, you know, with definite formations and gestures and music. The subject is fascinating to read about—but is chiefly important as a starting point for the composition. The subject never is the point— you know—I agree with Roger Fry who insists that Cézanne's apples are as important as Raphael's madonnas.
>   Then there is Scriabin's "Poème de L'Extase" [sic] which is a tremendous work which I will labor over long and lovingly. I also have in mind a ballet about women which will have to be written [i.e., the music.] There are others but three will be enough for now. I made the mistake last year of trying to do too much.

For some time, the trio had realized that they would have to find a less expensive studio, and in October they moved to their new quarters at 151 West 18th Street. It was a dreadful location, Doris had to admit, with a machine shop on the first floor of the building, a shoe factory on the second, and Humphrey-Weidman on the third. The interested people would come anyway, she insisted. As for the rest—good riddance. The studio was 32 by 38 feet, with seven windows, four skylights, and three old wooden rafters. "The whole place looks exactly like a barn, with whitewash and everything but the cows—and I daresay we'll even have those—we usually do during the season." Each of the trio now had an apartment of his own at 248 West 17th. This too was a bad street, but they were in a new building with open fireplaces and electric refrigerators.

The last week in October, Doris had a chance for a brief visit with her family while she was in Chicago with *Lysistrata*. As usual, though, she saw little of them, since she had to rush back to New York to rehearse for a concert at Hunter College on November 12. She wrote home that she had christened *The Shakers* then "with considerable success."

The success was fated to grow, for *The Shakers* became one of Doris's most popular works. Despite her insistence that the subject was not the point, she remained intrigued with it, for she was reading books on the Shakers years later and one of her most prized possessions was a Shaker bench.

Later she told her students that the Shakers attracted her because they believed in dancing; their religious ritual was, in fact, a dance and its original steps and formations served as the basis for her choreography. But beyond this, the disposition of the sect was bound to appeal to her temperament, which was drawn always to the art of disciplined simplicity. Directness, meticulous structure, immaculate line devoid of superfluous ornament—these were qualities she admired. The Shakers admired them and gauged their conduct by them—in the uncluttered rooms of their functional dwellings, in their fastidious dress, in the austerity and practicality of their lives. Yet within these calmly balanced lives dwelt also the passion of religious exaltation and the tension of sexual frustration. And there Doris had a dance.

The basic themes were few: hopping, swaying, falling forward

and pulling back, shaking. The dancers moved in straight, symmetrical lines, often in unison but with individual "shaking" movements.
Against the formal processions of the ritual, she pitted ecstatic falls;
inspired speech; man and woman trembling as they approached one
another, knowing they must not touch. The Eldress turned and
turned, rooted to a still center, as her congregation jumped high off
the ground, falling to their knees at the final "amen" in a climax of
sublimation. Though Doris was unable to share the religious faith
of the Shakers, she could appreciate the drama of their ceremony,
so essentially simple yet equally, theatrically exciting.

Christmas was uneventful this year. Doris gave a party for the
company and let it go at that. With the second season of the Dance
Repertory Theatre scheduled for the first week in February, followed immediately by Humphrey-Weidman concerts in Philadelphia
and Washington, she had no time for frivolities.

Most on her mind in January was a lecture-demonstration to
be given at the New School for Social Research, which had just
opened. This was one of a series, the first of its kind, that had
originally been suggested to Doris and Martha Graham by Henry
Cowell, who was on the New School faculty. The women, in turn,
had asked John Martin to organize and preside over it. The programs were so successful that they were continued for some eight
years, introducing a large public to the principles of the modern
dance and helping to build its concert audience. This time Doris's
subject was movement, composition, and appreciation of the dance.
She was worried about it:

> I am continually discovering gaps in the theory that I am work-
> ing on. After some twenty years of working and thinking, I'm
> still not sure of much of anything—and especially within the
> last two years has everything changed. You know I have com-
> pletely reconstructed all my ideas of the dance in the years
> since I left Denishawn. It's been a difficult process, partly be-
> cause I've been groping for a new approach and partly because
> in the few extra hours that I have I want to concentrate on
> composition—and the demands of theory have often been
> neglected. You know I teach only one class this year—and even
> that is irksome mostly because I have never made up my mind
> how to do it.

A month later, she had settled on several principles: all movement patterns fall into three divisions—opposition, succession, unison; all movement qualities fall into three divisions—sharp accent, sustained flow, rest. No dance, she declared, is well balanced unless it uses at least two elements from each division; the hardy perennials have them all. (Doris took time to reach conclusions, but once they were established, she stuck to them. The principles she described to her family at this time are the same that she reiterated— though with far more sophistication—in *The Art of Making Dances,* which she wrote in 1958).

Despite its christening at Hunter College, *The Shakers* was undergoing considerable revision and taking up a good deal of her time. She was also working on *Dances of Women,* so the schedule was strenuous, and it may have been fatigue—at least in part—that caused Doris to sprain her knee during a performance of *Shakers* at the Craig Theatre.

But she was unhappy about that whole season of the Dance Repertory Theatre—the manager had been atrocious, she had been cut out of stage rehearsals, the stagehands had made mistakes. Now she could not dance for two weeks and she was furious.

There was some solace, however, in making plans for the summer. In May she would finish the dictionary job; in June she would see the Indians in Arizona as the guest of Mary Wood Hinman; in July there was the teachers' course; in August, rehearsals for concerts at Robin Hood Dell in Philadelphia. She hoped to visit Oak Park on her way both to and from the West. It was all beautifully plotted; the scheme was as intelligent and neatly organized as her choreography. But none of her choreography ever went so far awry as her well-laid plans for this summer of 1931.

The first signal came on April 22 when she wrote home that Miss Hinman had decided to go to Russia. Doris, however, would go West anyway. On May 7 she suddenly wired her parents to please send her birth certificate, which she needed to get a passport, for she was going on a vacation cruise to the West Indies. Eleven days later, Cleo Atheneos—writing as the school secretary—informed the Humphreys of a change in their daughter's plans. She was still bound for the Caribbean, but—instead of the ship she had originally

named—she had sailed on the S.S. *Dominica* of the Furness Line.
Friends who had accompanied her to the pier had been horrified at
the appearance of the vessel she had chosen and had booked passage
for her on another that was sailing the same day. A minor matter,
really, since her destination was the same.

Only it wasn't.

And Afterwards a Woman

THE carefree atmosphere of the cruise did not rub off on Doris immediately. Unaccustomed to relaxation, she was also unpracticed in casual sociability. Her life revolved around the studio and the group; she was surrounded by dancers who all thought and worked and talked dance. What point of contact could she have with these people sailing for pleasure to the West Indies?

The first letters home bore her usual marks of thoughtful reflection. From Trinidad on June 1 she wrote that she was observing island architecture—"very gingerbread." She preferred the Japanese approach to houses. Ten days later: "I have been feeding on Havelock Ellis and Nietzsche, the two most inspiring people I know of." Only when the trip was over did her comments about it take on a more personal tone:

> I found out that I can still be foolish, that people are fun to play with and that they are kind and generous to strangers. In short, I've found a big slice of just the life I need exactly. . . . I've had so much more fun on board this ship than I did on the Oriental trip. The whole point is in getting to know people. As I remember I never spoke to a soul outside of the company. Very dumb.

While she provided no details about the people she was meeting, she did make a confession:

> One of the lesser events—but one that will surprise you is that your erstwhile chaste pure daughter has now succumbed to the tobacco habit. You see it was this way—You only have so

much resistance and I was slipping fast under the constant barrage of cigarettes and bridge and men that something would break soon. I chose cigarettes as the lesser vice.

Back in New York, Doris started teaching again on July 6 and began a rather long letter to her family by telling them all about it. There were three hours of lessons every day and a recital each week. She had been pleased with the first program of original dances by some half-dozen members of her group who had "bloomed at last." Then—three weeks after her vacation had ended—she finally gave her parents some idea of what had happened:

> I feel better, look better, generated some new ideas and last but not least acquired an Englishman who is one of the better specimens of the human race. By acquired I mean that he will probably be a permanent addition to my scheme of things in one capacity or another. Name—Leo Woodford, second officer on the S.S. Dominica. If this is a surprise to you, it was nothing less than a sunstroke to me as I was not on the warpath, I assure you when I went there. . . . This man is 28 and a seaman from the time he was fourteen—a good mind, especially for mathematics—good taste in literature and talent for drawing and painting—well built, although short, he's a good boxer and swimmer. Not particularly handsome but a great smile. A tender and imaginative lover. I see a few faults too, but there will be plenty of time for those later. He comes to port every three weeks, but will take a whole trip off pretty soon. This strikes Pauline as hasty, Charles as aggravating. What's your reaction?

Then, after a few comments about other matters which filled the last of her pages, she jotted in the margin: "I'm not thinking of marrying him—don't believe in it."

Years later, her husband viewed the episode from another perspective:

> I think of you as saying to yourself—'and now is the time to do the next thing—and now is the time to get me a husband.'—and getting up, drinking three cups of coffee, and with apparent casualness and hurry but actually with precise surety— doing the 'next thing' without too much fuss and bother.

Was she aware of such motives now? Maybe. Maybe not.

The August, 1931, issue of *The Dance Magazine* quoted Doris as saying: "I believe that the more impersonal and abstract art is, the greater it will be. The farther from the individual, the farther from personality, the closer to perfection." And there is the statement of *Color Harmony* where "intelligence or thought or the power of art form" is needed to pull the clashing emotional factions into ordered design. In art, Doris wanted perfection, and to achieve it she had to hold with the reins of intellect the confusing mass of human emotions—including her own.

Yet she knew that art was the product of a whole person, that it was not only mental but emotional. If the person was not completely fulfilled, the art would suffer. For a woman, fulfillment meant marriage and motherhood. Therefore she should have them. Such reasoning would have been characteristic of Doris, though it would have been equally uncharacteristic of her to allow her feelings to show.

A year later and a month after their marriage, Leo recalled their meeting on the *Dominica*. He had found her sunbathing in aloofness; she did not answer his friendly words. Since most unattached women on the Furness Line cruise ships were overly eager, he considered this lady a challenge. He proceeded to make his approaches. In time, she responded politely, but "looked preoccupied. . . . You only appeared to be friendly, but you had unbent. . . . Your demeanor was a cloak for your warmth and responsiveness. . . . I felt you would give love to your man, but for a short while only. . . . I was skeptical and feared." They swam and danced together before he knew who or what she was. By the time he found out, it didn't matter.

Charles Francis Woodford had been seeking the one woman. Born in Hull, he came from a family of seamen. Raised in circumstances of poverty, he had gone to work during World War I, educating himself with voracious reading during the long watches he served on shipboard. While the other men played cards, he absorbed volumes of literature and philosophy. Though he was casually interested in the theatre, he knew little of it, for he was seldom on shore long enough to sample the New York offerings. He had seen some dancing at the Roxy.

Possessed of a naturally keen, analytical mind, his thoughts turned to history, politics, and sociology, but they also functioned well on the arts. After the light banter on the ship's sun deck (which could have sustained neither of them for very long), he and Doris let their conversations turn to philosophizing. He had a mind that she could respect and enjoy.

For his lionlike quiet strength, she called him Leo. He had always been "Charlie," but she was close to another Charles and she wanted to keep them distinct. He never particularly liked being Leo, feeling the name did not suit him, but he went along with it to please her. Claude Wright, Wesley Chamberlain, Charles Weidman, Charles Woodford. . . . Strange, she thought, how many men in her life had the initials C.W. . . .

After Doris returned to New York, Leo took advantage of a leave to rent a small cottage on Fire Island. He bought a 16–foot boat in Barbados, arranged to have it brought up free on the deck of the ship, and then had a friend get it to the house on a truck. He taught Doris to sail. While the teachers' course was in session, she went out to the house for week ends. With uncharacteristic feeling, she told him what he meant to her then:

> Every day I know again that my love for you is the impalpable white center from whence I draw new strength for work, new love for people, increased sensitivity to all things in my world. All the materials for completeness are within my grasp. I feel at last that life *is*, not might be or should be. What more can I tell you of this? Expression deals with hopes and fears, unbalance, effort to achieve, remorse over past deeds. But what can I say when the spiral curve varies only a hair's breadth from the heart of things? You remember I foretold this. I can tell you of things that happen far out on the rim, the less important things. . . . The little house at the beach was fragrant with our love when I was there again. I look forward to our reunion with everything in my soul and body.

Realistically, he wrote her from St. Thomas:

> It's hard for a sailor to love and be loved, but harder still for her who loves him. For my own part I have always known this and accepted it, but you, how can you bow down to a thing so sudden that there's no time for adjustment? How can we learn to know and understand when each time after a day or two together we are flung a thousand miles apart? This is but an aggravated form of slavery. Still, however, beneath this hor-

ror, there is a note of happiness for having you which runs in a melodious whisper and keeps me mentally stable.

She missed him. But there were so many distractions:

This absence is too cruel, I think, especially now at first. Yet the days are crowded with necessary things. They prevent me from holding you in rapt remembrances and from writing in visions. You see New York in these short sentences, the breaking off of movements and ideas that should go into phrases. Temperamentally I lean toward the flowing things. . . . My days are full of rehearsals and classes and weekends at the beach—almost nothing else. I am on somewhat better terms with Charles, and my Pauline is always a joy—well almost always, except for a malicious streak she has.

In the years to come, Leo would often hear these themes reiterated—the pressures of work and the tensions that erupted among the members of the closely knit trio. Much as Doris loved her colleagues and they loved her, the unholy three had many problems to cope with in their working relationship. This summer, Charles was concerned that he and Doris did so little dancing together. Pauline, the sharp-tongued taskmaster, whose pessimism was to earn her the name of Cassandra Legree, was chiding Doris for an inadequate performance of *Dances of Women*—they should have spent more time together with the composer, the costumes were wrong, they had gone on half-baked.

Tenaciously protective, Pauline was especially aggressive at this time, since she did not approve of the love affair with Leo. For one thing, it took Doris's mind off her work—not very much, actually, but any distraction was something to begrudge. Then, too, if Doris must have a steady lover, Pauline felt he should be someone of superior stature—physically, intellectually, socially. Leo she considered as failing to meet a number of her demanding specifications. He lacked the distinguished aura that would enhance the claims of America's greatest dancer; therefore he was simply unsuited to the job. Since Doris found him attractive and intelligent if not always socially adept, and since she had no intention of breaking off the relationship, her friend's attitude became a nagging annoyance.

Artistic problems were also persistent, like the constant struggle to enlighten and convert the public. Doris taught two sessions for the American Society of Teachers of Dancing, which was holding its fifty-third convention at the Hotel Astor from August 24 through 30. Her theme was rhythm, which her notes stipulated "must be sensed in muscular effort, not as a mathematical beat imposed from without." She began with exercises in natural body rhythms without music, then with contrasting music or drum beats. She then illustrated natural rhythms combined in dance form for ensemble, followed by studies of natural body designs to show oppositions, successions, and symmetricals. Her class was followed by "Dainty Miss Milkmaid," a "toe routine" taught by Sonia Serova. One of the students had a question: "What do you call your work, Miss Humphrey, dancing?"

September was a bad month for classes, so resources were low and Doris needed money to pay a deposit on a new apartment, as she and Pauline, for reasons of economy, had decided to live together again. At 171 West 12th Street, they had three closets, a nice fireplace, and a view of the Empire State Building. They now kept the cats at the studio.

Unfortunately, the Humphreys were desperately in need of money too, for the school was not doing well, Julia was ill, and Horace depressed by his own helplessness. Ethel helped as much as she could, and Doris managed a brief trip home before starting rehearsals for a concert in Cleveland. In October, Leo was in England where she cabled him frantically for help. He sent her $10, "more than half of what I possess." From Newcastle-on-Tyne he wrote her:

> I am sorry to know of your parents' attitude towards us, not that I care myself, but I suspect you may feel a little disheartened. I told my dad about us and he agreed that it was good unless of course there was offspring, and ventured to caution me regarding such.

By the time he returned, however, they were beginning to discuss the pros and cons of marriage. Stubbornly, Doris persisted in her assertion that she didn't believe in it. Leo agreed that they were removed from the traditions and conventions of "the common herd." Yet, he pondered, "marriage would give us certain rights and privileges. We might use convention and not be used by it."

From Oak Park Mama-San wrote plaintively that they had been thinking about Doris's concerts. "Would I be able to follow and understand the new idiom?" she wondered. Her heart trouble now required treatment and rest, and the recovery would be slow. No, she could not come to New York for a visit because she had to care for Horace and because, as usual, there was no money for travel since the school business was so slow, even worse than last year. She did not feel sorry for herself; only useless and humiliated at letting everyone down.

What could the daughter say? After some words of sympathy and "chin up" encouragement, she told her family more about her work. A concert in Rochester had been especially successful, the manager suggesting that the group come back to perform with the orchestra, which was a good one, as was Cleveland's. Doris was optimistic about future programs with fine musical accompaniment, though she already knew from experience that her tastes could create trouble:

> Cleveland is afraid to death that we'll come with modern ballets—and since they won't have the Grieg Concerto the problem is difficult. They had the Lewisohn things last year and were over-awed by stuff that seemed sweet enough to us. On the other hand these conductors, as ever, balk at the use of absolute music for dancing. And there we are. Hard to find music written for dancing, scored for orchestra, not too modern (no dissonances) and not too stiff.

She was teaching at the studio, at the Dalton School, and at the New School for Social Research. At the same time, rehearsals were intensified in preparation of concerts in Pittsfield, Massachusetts, on November 19 and New York five days later. "So you can see that the next two weeks will be a battlefield."

Nevertheless, there was time for a pleasant Thanksgiving dinner. Pauline cooked (as usual), and their guest was José Limón. Since his debut in the back line of *Lysistrata*, the young man had shown steady improvement. He had now been initiated into the concert group, though his first performance was notably inconspicuous. Crouched invisibly behind a large box, he had held it at appropriate levels for *Dances of Women*. With the strength and stature of his Yaqui Indian ancestors and the elegance of his Spanish progenitors, José made a striking figure on the stage. Charming in person also. The two women found him a delightful holiday companion.

Doris's parents remained a source of constant worry. Julia was getting better, but for Horace it was only a question of time—another stroke was sure to come. With the school enrollment constantly dwindling, the Humphreys lived on the meagre funds their daughter managed to provide, and these constituted .a considerable burden for her. To help ease the financial situation, she decided this year to hold an intensive teachers' course right after Christmas. Classes were offered daily from ten to one in creative dance composition for solo and group; the fee was $50.

After the teachers' course came a concert at the Guild Theatre on January 17, to be followed by another on March 13. For the latter, Doris was choreographing two new group dances, *Pleasures of Counterpoint* and *Dionysiaques*: "Getting them composed and costumed is a man-sized job. . . . I don't much care for dancing myself, getting fed up," she told her parents. (Though John Martin had just described her movement as "steel and velvet; strong, resilient and accurate.") Apparently she had also written something of the sort to Leo, for he noted: "Once you told me that you were an artist first and afterwards a woman. I wonder if that letter means a change?" And a little later: "The decision of continuing work or not rests entirely with you." Noting that his income alone would then have to suffice for them, he added that he rather liked the idea of her being more dependent on him. At one point he suggested a move to Bermuda: "We could get married there. I would like to give you a child."

At the Guild the two new dances were both successful, though Mr. Martin was most excited about *Dionysiaques*:

> Here Miss Humphrey has touched new heights as a composer. It is strong, simple, pagan in feeling, and its mood is matched in design of sheer magnificence. It is by way of being a contemporary restatement of the 'Sacre du Printemps' with all the force and passion which must underlie such a subject, yet with no tinge of emotionalism in its projection and no taint of self-consciousness in its hieratic suggestion. Though Miss Humphrey is one of the great choreographers of the day, she has here outdone herself.

Top: *Lysistrata,* 1930. (Photo by Martha Swope from original by White Studios; collection NYPL.) Bottom: "The Dream of Sganarelle" from *The Schools for Husbands,* 1933. (Photo by Martha Swope from original by Vandamm Studio; collection NYPL.)

Top: *Dionysiaques*, 1932; Doris Humphrey in central role. Bottom: A Humphrey-Weidman lecture-demonstration of the 1930's. (Photos by Martha Swope from originals by Edward Moeller; collection NYPL.)

Though an artistic success, the Guild concert was a financial disaster:

> I enclose criticism which was more enthusiastic than usual. . . . [*Pleasures of Counterpoint is*] very simple and not as Mr. Martin has so pedagogically explained a dance done to the strong and light beats of music. However his general idea is correct, that there was a theme done by three girls, accompanied on the syncopated beats by a group of girls behind them. The joke is that the dance was all done long before the music was composed and we had a devil of a time getting them together.
>
> As far as I am concerned, the concert was more than I was equal to. Seven strenuous dances with costume changes was too much for my strength, consequently they were not done as well as I would have liked. Also we lost money as usual. The two new dances I thought would be good, and were. But this is the last concert I am going to give without a guarantee against loss—and how long do you have to wait for that?

Despite the financial disappointments and her assertions of "getting fed up," Doris made no changes in the proposed course of her professional life—except to expand it. She planned to start teaching an additional class at the Henry Street Settlement in March, though this was only to earn money to put into concerts, since of course she was not serious about waiting for that guarantee against loss. She was in a kind of bondage:

> Every moment now is consumed in making every move in my dances as finished as possible—or in thinking about them. Early in the morning I begin seeing a figure, myself, dancing on a stage, and I, the onlooker, am always above and at a distance from it. Quite often, as it is going through the sequence of a dance, it will do a new gesture, and if this pleases the onlooker, the figure will do it over and over quite obligingly, in fact with considerable satisfaction. But this is a tiring process, my bones ache and I want the dancer to let me rest. But she won't. She fades into a mist temporarily, and then begins again on some other dance, quite amazingly bright and strong. And this goes on all day—day after day, on subways, on buses, anywhere, an absolute slavery.

Lest the slavery isolate Doris from her lover, she determined to involve him too. Together they would write a theory of the dance.

He understood her absorption and was pleased by the idea of col-
laborating with her, but he was becoming resentful of what he
considered her attempts to make an artist out of him:

> I'm troubled by your assertion that to grow together we must
> make something. . . . I think you are dissatisfied at making a
> match with one diametrically opposed to you in disposition. . . .
> You are a creator, one of the elite. Not me. I'm a hedonist, a
> loafer. You despise this so you invent attributes I don't have.

They did have a common interest, however. Through the mail
they enjoyed parrying philosophical questions, such as: Can an artist
compromise and still get on as an artist? Doris replied:

> I have no theories to bring to bear on the question because for
> so many years the non-compromising atitude has been so much
> a part of me that it has never been attacked and analyzed. I
> am as non-plussed for an answer to you as I am when people
> say, "You love to dance, don't you, Miss Humphrey?" The point
> is, of course, that life is unimaginable without it, and there is
> no question of liking it or not. It seems to me, looking back,
> that I was from the beginning fertile ground for causes of any
> kind to grow in. I like both the fortitude and drama of the
> uncompromising attitude. The Christian martyrs, the ascetic
> Shakers, the starving artists all seem brothers to me. They all
> had a bulwark of faith in something which they adhered to and
> defied the world for. There must be a kernel of that in every-
> body—no sane man is without a belief in something, but to me
> it is more desirable to have a disinterested belief in a religion, a
> pattern of life, or an art-thesis, and to make the man conform
> to that than to make of the man the pattern to which every-
> thing else must conform. . . . Leonardo da Vinci noted that the
> artist should not have even one friend to influence or distract
> him from the pure contemplation of his art.

Did Leo distract her? Not when they corresponded like this.
But when he was on shore leave and they had to deal not with
abstract principles, but with the practical realities of their personal
relationship, the results were often less than serene. The difference
in their ages, backgrounds, and temperaments was considerable.
Soon there was what Leo called a "near quarrel." Knowing and loving the woman, he wanted to know her dancing and had come to

the studio to see her at work. Probably it was a minor incident, and he told her that fundamentally he felt he had been wrong, but:

> . . . my sense of male superiority was outraged that you dared to presume to rebuke me. I felt the impulse to walk away from you forever. You implied openly that I was not too among the stars. I am miserably aware of this, but it was a most unkind cut. That you say I am bored at the studio places me on the artistic and mental level of an ape. I had thought you didn't want me there.

Soon, however, Doris turned to him for help on an article she was writing. From his new ship, the *Monarch of Bermuda,* Leo wrote that he found it "quite good"; the ideas were fine but the organization was somewhat faulty. Also some sentences ended with weak words. In dance, he commented, "I feel sure you would not complete a phrase with a feeble gesture." When "What Shall We Dance About?" appeared in the summer issue of *Trend: A Quarterly of the Seven Arts,* the sentences ended with good, strong words.

Much as Doris may have wanted to think only of aesthetic problems, she had to concern herself with earning money. In May J. J. Shubert auditioned the Humphrey-Weidman company to see if some of their dances could fit into his forthcoming review *Americana.* This meant work for all fourteen of the girls in the group as well as for Charles and two of the men. The contract was signed before the end of the month. Talks were also underway with Sol Hurok, who seemed interested in trying to raise money for American dancers. At one point in the negotiations, Hurok even offered to manage the company, but it was under contract to William Gassner's Concert Guild and, despite prolonged maneuvering, the Hurok deal eventually fell through.

While Doris found that she could manage both a multifaceted career and a lover, Leo was pressing the idea of marriage:

> Up to a certain point one can live without it. In a great city like New York, it is possible to go on indefinitely, but just try and give your theories a practical reality in some one horse town in any part of the world, and then you'll have the avenging hordes of society snapping at your heels. You would likely find your man denied any employment which also presupposes

some sort of social status, and you would find your child possibly unable to have playmates, whilst you yourself would have to endure the contumely of the virtuous females and the lascivious leers of the equally virtuous males. Under such conditions I maintain that the sacrifice of self to ideals would not be justified.

As for the attitude of your studio associates, I am perfectly aware of that, but I am not quite clear of the superstition that marriage lends validity to a relationship even amongst the most rebellious. However the correct solution of that is that being unable to give myself identity there because of the essential exclusion of myself from certain esoteric relationships, I would attempt to break through by definitely stating my relationship to you. You might deny it if you will, but even amongst artists the loose relationships of their friends are not openly acknowledged, whilst marriage is a relationship which definitely places them in juxtaposition. And if you still assert that all your girls who can and do ignore my existence now, would do so were we man and wife, well, I say you are mistaken. Not that I really care about that. Probably any undue recognition of my presence would embarrass me very much. I rather prefer to remain as I am at present, just a quiet man hunched up in a corner.

Of his arguments probably the most persuasive for Doris was the one about the child. She did want one, and she was in no position to change society to accommodate her beliefs; she had crusading enough to do on the dance front. No, she could not wait for the perfect society, nor could she wait for the perfect man. She admitted to her parents that she was about to capitulate:

I have changed my mind about the blessedness of the single state and am thinking seriously of marrying Charles Francis Woodford. This is a highly desirable young man, I think, and if he hasn't all the virtues he has *practically* all of them. I hope this meets with your approval.

When the Humphreys saw their daughter's summer schedule, they may well have wondered how she would find the time to get married. From June 18 to 22, she would be with them in Oak Park; June 23 to 30, working with the opera in Cleveland; July 3 to 23, teaching at the Perry-Mansfield School of Theatre and Dance in Steamboat Springs, Colorado; July 25 to August 8, rehearsing in New

York for *Americana*; August 3 to 30, directing the teachers' course at the studio.

On June 12 she wrote them about furbishing up her wardrobe for six weeks of travel and of Charles's preparations for the Cleveland season. Then she added a P.S.: "I forgot to mention that Doris Humphrey married Charles Francis Woodford on June 10th, 1932, in Morrisville, Pennsylvania. This information to be used as you see fit."

Casual. But it had taken a considerable amount of planning, for the couple wanted privacy and Doris had volunteered to find a place where they could be married without attracting the attention of the New York papers. She told no one—not even Pauline. In fact, Leo had hardly any warning. Docking at nine in the morning of June 10, he found a letter: "Meet me at ten at Pennsylvania Station and we'll get married today." Much as he wanted her to say it, his first reaction was one of near-panic. He had one hour and only $2 in his pocket. Frantically, he appealed to one of his shipmates, who loaned him $10. Then he rushed to the station where Doris directed him to buy two round-trip tickets to Trenton.

When they got off the train, the bride had a sudden thought: "Leo, don't we need a ring?" There went another $5. They walked over the bridge to Morrisville.

There, the justice of the peace informed them that he would have to go to Doylestown, the county seat, to get the license. It would cost $12. They should either give him a deposit or drive with him. "Sometimes," he explained, "I go there and buy the license and when I come back the people have gone—changed their minds, I guess. I don't want to get stuck."

Leo turned to Doris. "Have you any money?" he asked. She had $6. So they drove to Doylestown, where the justice bought the license and they got married. After indulging in the luxury of dinner at a Trenton hotel, they had just ten cents left between them. In 1932, that was enough for two people to get from Penn Station to West 12th Street on the subway.

Hopes and Fears

Iɴ contrast to Doris's perfunctory announcement of the marriage to her family, Leo wrote them with ingratiating frankness:

> Dear New-Parents:
> I have an apology to offer you for thrusting myself into your family without your sanction. I hope sincerely that you will accept it and excuse the unceremonious manner in which we of the post-war generation conduct our affairs. But our ideals are high enough, as high indeed as those of any other time, the difference lies in the manner of our approach.
>
> So we two embraced respectability after a short but ecstatic revolt in which we learned the lessons which all revolutionaries learn and by which we hope to profit.
>
> Thus we set out with high hopes for our future, and I ask you to give us your formal blessing.

There was hope also in his first letter to his wife:

> It seems scarcely possible to me that—with the weight of tradition behind us—that Friday will not mark the beginning of a new phase of our life together. . . . I think if we escape from the idea of possessing each other we shall be unique. But then we are so, are we not?

Yet his confidence was tinged with wariness:

> Your words of encouragement to me are ever cause for much pleasure. Of course I've never had anyone whose opinions I valued to care before, and it is a unique experience for me. Coming from the woman I love makes it very precious indeed.

But I ask you not let your affection for me blind you to my very grave shortcomings so much that you learn to expect too much from my limited faculties. Else you will be greatly disappointed and it interferes with the divinely ecstatic physical union we enjoy.

At times, her criticisms made him concerned, not only for the immediate hurt he felt, but for their ultimate consequences:

It is not that I mind having the actual thing pointed out, but that you, in doing so, show your superiority to me in being aware of the small matters of life, and bring to my mind the fact of your undoubted supremacy. . . . Something must be done about this or you will come to despise me.

But the tensions were seldom long-lasting, since, if nothing else intervened, physical separation served to resolve them. For, though the relationship was now "respectable," marriage did not give the couple any more time together. Leo had to sail regularly on the *Monarch;* Doris had her professional commitments irrevocably worked out. As would happen again many times in the future, he would be in port in New York while she was off dancing somewhere else. Their married life, in the conventional sense, could be maintained only intermittently. Of course both of them had known this from the beginning. While there were to be discussions at various times about Leo's taking another kind of job or of Doris's relinquishing her career to devote more time to her family, neither could, or really cared to, change the basic nature of his life that much. They had chosen their mates wisely.

For the husband, the separations were cause for almost constant anguish, which he expressed fully and directly in his letters. For the wife, unhappiness was usually the subject of brief, almost dutiful, comment. Unlike Leo, who worked only to provide for his family, she pursued her career with passionate dedication. Her letters to him are filled with accounts of her activities—teaching, performing, choreographing; they are almost completely devoid of comments on their relationship. Yet they should not be taken at purely face value. By nature, Doris was reticent, seldom capable of exposing her feelings. In this respect Leo was her opposite. He could tell her that he was lonely or angry or hurt, and he could analyze in detail the reasons for his feelings. She could rarely respond in kind, though sometimes she tried.

Now, at the age of thirty-six, Doris's defenses were deeply entrenched, so much so that there were times when Leo found her almost unapproachable. If he had hoped that the marriage would destroy the last of the reserves, he was mistaken and he soon recognized this:

> This parting is going to be harder than the one before. Or is it because this time it is I who remain in the nest, as it were, whilst you, who are afield having new experiences, may find it less hard. . . . In those days, the days of our first long separation, we were but lovers, now we are two whose lives have intertwined about each other like two trees whose trunks stand separate but whose topmost branches interlock till the leaves kiss each other in the wind. Yet there is a strangeness between us like a broad road upon which we stand together each upon his own side. Often I catch you looking at me as if I were a perfect stranger and I do the same also, indeed for disturbing moments you are an unknown person —a fleet second and the sensation is gone and you are you again, nose, eyes, and red lights in the hair, crushed mouth, and the proud poise of your head upon delicate shoulders—the you I know and love. See how I begin to paint little pictures of you which fail miserably in serving for your presence. I see you sitting in my bunk, munching an apple. The light from the window falls strongly upon your dear face and shews up all its dramatic qualities—yet you were munching an apple—dearest of dears, you would terrify if you didn't do such things. There is an enormous figure of you in the orgiastic throes of Dionisques (?spelling) which also makes me feel somehow gigantic and fills me with a desire to fly at you and be primitive. What drives me almost frantic though is that air of abstraction from your surroundings —to wit myself—when you are doing little things like powdering the nose or arranging the hair. I have no weapons to penetrate this, and your elusiveness almost drives me to desperation.

Though Doris's reply to this letter has not been preserved, it may well have been much like the one she wrote to her family that week: Cleveland's *Carmen* and *Aida* were going very well; Eleanor Frampton, a former student and now a friend, who was teaching dance at the Institute of Music on Doris's recommendation, was a charming hostess; Charles and José were living upstairs; it was all great fun.

On July 7, the Cleveland *Plain Dealer* carried the story of the suicide of Nikolais Semenoff. The ballet master, who had escaped from Moscow during the Russian Revolution, had been teaching in Cleveland for the past eight years. When Doris had done a lecture-demonstration there the previous year, Semenoff told friends that she had slandered the ballet and he threatened to leap to his death from Niagara Falls, asserting that "maybe my jump will set back the self-inflated modernists." Actually, he did not jump but waded into the river where the current carried him over the Horseshoe Falls. The reporter noted that acquaintances believed Semenoff had been disappointed at not being chosen to direct the dances for the summer operas. That Doris Humphrey had been selected in his place was the crowning insult. Doris was horrified, though no one other than Semenoff himself thought to put any of the blame on her.

The news reached her in Steamboat Springs, where her stay was otherwise restful and uneventful. She taught only one morning class and hoped to gain some weight before facing August in New York. Relaxed for the time being, she felt interested only "in ideas, mine and some other people's, in living richly and extensively, and in loving and enjoying a few friends and my Englishman. Doesn't sound like the credo of an artist, does it?"

Of course the mood did not last, for she was soon back in the throes of the teachers' course. The enrollment was good, but since the proceeds had to be split three ways (equal shares going to Doris, Charles, and Pauline), she still had no more money to spare for her parents. While apologizing to them, she felt helpless to remedy the situation.

At the end of August Leo was home for all of two weeks, but Doris was busy teaching. Still they saw each other every day at breakfast and dinner:

> I really think a once-a-month husband is better, because, although I loved having him home, I inevitably found out little faults in him during that close contact which I wasn't aware of much before.

Back on the *Monarch*, Leo admitted that the visit had not accomplished as much as he had hoped:

> I thought that we would straighten out many things, instead there was very little talk at all. Or is it my naive mind which thinks that nothing is accomplished without talk? . . . Much was added to our intimacy during the two weeks. Particularly I have come to appreciate more the difficulties of your work and the enormous tax upon your strength. It tore me to see you come home day after day and collapse. I had always thought you to be physically strong, foolish because I know where the strength and endurance of athletes lie—the palm goes to big bodies— and you are small. I see you now dancing with that big heart of yours and it pains me.

The work had gone into *Americana,* which opened in Philadelphia on September 17, with Doris's *Shakers* and *Water Study,* some numbers by Charles and a *Waltz Finale—Blue Danube* that she had staged. *Water Study* was performed in a cellophane set which delighted her because it made the dance look "very blue and watery." But there had been trouble with *Shakers.* Unaccustomed to dealing with modern-dance artists, Shubert had asked for some changes. It needed livening up, he asserted, and demanded that the dull gray costumes be redone immediately in bright purple and white. Citing the clause in her contract that forbade any changes without her approval, Doris was adamant. She won.

The drama critics were impressed. "A stunning historical passage," one wrote of *Shakers.* It "strikes deep and strangely at the very core of ecstacy and art." Brooks Atkinson asserted that the work of the Humphrey-Weidman company "gives the dance a new prestige in the theatre."

At this time the Humphreys decided to move to Auntie May's in Dummerston. Though they would be paying guests of Julia's girlhood friend, Vermont would be a less expensive place to live and the country air would be good for Horace. Ethel could care for the school without them. Still Doris knew that their financial problems were far from solved:

> I know how you feel about paying debts, keeping up credit, and all the rest of it. I have these same problems, and a perfect mountain of bills and notes to pay & so I know too well how

pressing obligations become. Also, I remember how improvident it is to be without any savings, so that you have to borrow when the income is low. So of course it is difficult to know what to do with money as it comes in. Here is one of the things that complicates it for instance. I have a twenty year endowment policy which will lapse unless I send a hundred and fifty before November twenty-fourth. Also, for instance the Shuberts have cut everybody ten percent. . . . Leo makes very little money you know, and I never see it anyway because he is saving it for the hypothetical offspring. He puts it a Bermuda bank where more value can eventually be purchased for pounds than dollars. All this is by way of explaining that financing the family has to be done carefully, which is why I asked for a budget, and also how little will your creditors be satisfied with a week? Now I *can* send twenty-five dollars a week just now, but I have not forgotten how we nearly starved last year, and you know I haven't a penny in savings. Almost anything can be done if it is planned carefully enough—so let's do it.

Unfortunately, *Americana* closed in December.

It would be some time yet before the anticipated offspring would put a stop to dancing, for the baby was expected in late June. Probably Doris telephoned her parents about it, since there is no announcement in her letters (not even in a P.S.) and, in fact, very little mention of the coming event at all till near the end of her pregnancy, though she did note in January that she planned to write "the theory book" in the spring when she would not be dancing.

The book would incorporate the ideas she had been developing since she left Denishawn. While the theory had been put to the practical test in the dances she had choreographed over the past five years, it had also been intellectually formulated for the various lecture-demonstrations she was presenting with the group. This season she had offered them at the New School, George Washington University, Hood College, and the Rye Country Day School. While these brought her no money, she found them worth while under the heading of "missionary work." She also used them to try out her theory.

The talks were most carefully planned, and numerous versions of them exist among her papers, usually in outline or summary form and written on any kind of scrap paper she could lay her hands on—stationery from various hotels and old studios, announcements for courses at the school, concert flyers. The changes she made in the lectures most frequently involve wording or choice of examples and sometimes the ordering of ideas, for—from this time on—the ideas themselves remain quite consistent. She had hit on a theory that worked for her and, while she refined its details and extended its applications, she never altered its basic principles.

Usually, she began her lectures by describing the motivation of the modern dance:

> It is a theatre art of our time. Pioneers in the field were all dancers who searched in their own souls and bodies for new means of communication to audiences. . . . If one word were selected to characterize the whole trend that word would be subjective. Dancers found that they were people first with new attitudes and feelings about life in a world of vast sociological, psychological and historical change. Wrapped in emotion and suffused with a vision, they spoke to us not only of themselves, but in a different language of movement which had to be discovered to convey their meaning. The old forms would not do, the resources of the human body had to be enlarged (renewed), revitalized, to contain the new dance.

Depending on the nature of the audience—whether dance students, teachers, or laymen—she went on to discuss the training of the artist, technique, forms of composition, subject matter, and the relation of dance to music and décor or its place in American life.

In each case, every facet was carefully thought through and the whole scheme neatly structured, for Doris never relied on improvisation. If the lectures lacked the charm of spontaneity, they contained the forcefulness of conviction. Later, in *The Art of Making Dances*, she would inveigh against the public speaker "who runs on in a monotone of logical thought . . . we prefer some passion . . . and, if possible, some wit." She had these too, but they were calculated.

The theory itself was developed with logical precision. Though its movement ideas dated back to the *Water Study*, the conscious formulation began on that fateful trip to the West Indies when Doris told her parents that she had been reading Nietzsche's *Birth of Tragedy* (probably before she met Leo, but possibly afterward as well) and that it had profoundly influenced her thinking about dance. From the German philosopher she took the contrasted concepts of the Apollonian and the Dionysian, the dual drives in the human being that impel him, on the one hand toward rest, order, balance, and security; on the other, toward activity, exuberance, excitement, and risk. Surely the concepts would not have struck her so deeply as the motivating forces of dance had she not recognized in them the principles underlying her own experiments with movement. As the mind desired stability, the body sought equilibrium; as the spirit yearned for adventure, the body longed to explore the "dangerous place."

Standing before a mirror, she tested the theory. Stillness, security, was comfortable—but theatrically uninteresting. As she let her body reach out, challenging the threat of gravity, her muscles tensed, sparking dramatic conflict. Movement—life—excitement. Dance, then, lay in the arc between two deaths, the lassitude of the body erect and of the body prone. When the standing body began to sway from its security or when the lying body began to fight its way upward—there was dance. Its essence was the polarity of fall and recovery, the self-imposed challenge and the conquest. Fall and recovery, climaxed by that moment of suspension when the person asserted his freedom from the powers of nature. The dancer and space. Man and his environment.

For the theatre, the concepts could not be left at this elemental stage. As she fought gravity, Doris saw the body making shapes in space—design; and in time—rhythm. These varied with the degree of energy applied—dynamics. The result—drama. So there it was: the theory, complete and whole. Waiting only to be used for the myriad dance ideas she had stored in her mind. And to be set down in the book that Leo would help her write.

It was not, however, to be written that spring, because there were just too many other things to do. Classes went on. The 18th Street studio was freezing cold in winter even with the gas radiators turned on full force. However, it was better than 59th Street, where they had had no heat whatsoever. While she still could, she performed: "I'm between hot and cold about dancing. Leo says what's one season out and refuses to be impressed when I fret, and Pauline fumes and says you can't afford to stop, everybody will forget you." Of course she could continue choreographing and fully intended to

do so. Hall Johnson asked her to stage a voodoo scene for his musical play *Run, Little Chillun,* and Doris was fascinated by his dancers
who knew authentic rituals full of savage, primitive movement. Her
job was to arrange these for the proscenium stage, an intriguing
challenge. Even more important was an offer from the Theatre Guild
for her and Charles to stage and perform the dances for a production of Molière's *School for Husbands.* The opening was set—dan-
gerously—for April, but this was their first chance to break into the
best of the legitimate theatre and they could hardly refuse. Doris
hoped the costumes would be voluminous.

By the end of March she was still asking her parents for a run-
down of weekly expenses so that she could try to help, but she also
had to set money aside for hospital and infant expenses. Leo was
now on the *Queen of Bermuda* and had been promoted to first officer, but his pay was no higher—still about $100 a month. Doris
knew the Humphreys felt a strong sense of obligation to their creditors (she was like that too), yet she saw no reason for Leo to pay
either their debts or her own. As it was, she was running about $25
short each week.

Mama-San sensed hints of guilt between the lines, assuring her
daughter that there was no need to justify her desire for a child.
Why should the younger generation sacrifice for the older? She
grieved that she had to depend on Doris who, in turn, felt the obligation so keenly. Most of all, though, she regretted the lack of open-
ness in their relationship:

> You always so carefully delete all note of anxiety from your
> letters that it is hard to tell. Our great trouble always has been
> that we say too little and leave each other to conjecture all sorts
> of non-existent attitudes of mind.

For both economic and artistic reasons, Doris felt she could refuse
no opportunity, and by early spring she was rehearsing the company
for Lewisohn Stadium concerts that were scheduled for the second
week in August. She had to compose a new opening number which:

> . . . is a plague to me constantly. It must set the right keynote
> of dignity and vigor, it must not be a royalty piece, must be a
> suite of dances—or at least have a program—and of course must
> be written for orchestra, must include a part for me, not too

strenuous but telling. I finally decided on Suite in F by Roussel—antique dances in the modern manner. These must be conceived and composed next. Charles will help me—and after I get them sketched out will go ahead while I am occupied with my biological composition.

Even the Roussel nearly posed a financial threat when the copyright owners demanded $100 a performance. Doris managed to get the fee down to $35, but then she still had to buy costumes and a Maypole for the last number. Desperately, she asked for an advance on her teaching salary from the Dalton School, and got $160. Though the check had to be dated October 1, the doctor considerately said he would accept it.

Fortunately, *School for Husbands* was postponed, with rehearsals to begin in September.

By the end of June the doctor was suggesting that Doris take some long, bumpy car rides. Charles and José obliged by driving her on several, but by July 2 she was still "feeling much too fine and healthy." For a change, she stayed home and puttered about the house. The delay was creating fears that she confided to her family:

It looks as though the N.Y. Stadium will [be] out of the question for me, and unless something happens soon I won't even be up to direct, and that's most unfortunate. If I were inclined to be superstitious I should think this bad beginning a foretaste of continual trouble between my child and my art.

On July 8, 1933, Charles Humphrey Woodford was born in Lying-In Hospital. He weighed seven pounds and had curly blond hair.

Family Life

WHEN Doris first brought the baby home to West 12th Street, she was pleased with her new role as mother and kept her letters of congratulations in a baby book. But it took little more than a week for the delight of novelty to wear off, as the Stadium concert was looming: "It's very annoying to be kept down when everybody is needed at the front, and I am not at all the sweet devoted little mother, busy and happy with the home tasks."

On August 9, with the baby just four and a half weeks old, the Humphrey-Weidman company drew eight thousand people to Lewisohn Stadium. "Better than Beethoven," remarked Pitts Sanborn in the *World Telegram.* "It is considerably her choreography which makes this evening of dances probably the most freshly entertaining and clever of all the dance programs ever given there," wrote Henry Beckett in the *Evening Post.* Doris danced only the Sarabande in the *Roussel Suite*, a performance sanctioned by the doctor —or so she said. Eight days later she danced again in Philadelphia's Robin Hood Dell. When the concerts were over, she had to admit to her family that the last few weeks had been the hardest she had ever known. Yet, though aware that problems lay ahead, she felt content with the choices she had made:

> I won't be the solo dancer I was for a long time yet, and bringing up a son at the same time will make things go slower. But I don't regret it for a minute, and I doubt if I ever shall. I suppose most women would only regret having waited so long to produce a child. I'm really surprised that I was so determined con-

sidering that I had no encouragement for the project except from the man. . . . At the end of two years we are more devoted than ever, not in the prosaic way that married folks usually are, but as sweethearts. I have had vindication of all the fine qualities I saw in him at the first look—lucky us! The marriage contract of which I was so afraid has had a negligible effect on us —at least on me. . . . So far our chains have rubbed no wounds for which we may be thankful.

Early in September a German woman named Lise Alida Hein was found to care for the baby. Doris needed the help desperately, for she had already gone through a frantic experience one day when she could find no one to stay at home with her son and had to take him to a nurse on her way to class. She was teaching now, both at the studio and at the Dalton School, in addition to rehearsing *School for Husbands*. At the same time, she was moving into a new apartment. For three weeks she didn't have time to write a single letter home.

The Woodfords, Pauline, Charles, and José had been thinking of finding a place where they could live together in order to pool their limited financial resources. Since the rent had to be reasonable, the space large enough for six inhabitants, and the location close to the 18th Street studio, they had to search for some time. The one they chose, at 31 West 10th Street, was on the third floor of an elevator building, and it had seven rooms with two baths. The Woodfords had a room of their own as did each of the other adults, while the baby shared his with Miss Hein. The "family" was to live there for seven years.

Each of the occupants brought his or her own furniture. On the mantel above the fireplace were two Cambodian headdresses, which Charles had acquired in the Orient, and his Gauguin painting of Polynesian women, which Doris especially admired for the beauty of the hand gestures. She contributed her Shaker bench to the living room. Later, after he had made some money in Broadway shows, José bought an organ which was also housed there. Pauline, who was managing the company and would soon be handling the formidable job of booking cross-country tours, thoughtfully kept the files in her bedroom.

Financial conditions permitting, a cook prepared the meals, but much of the time conditions did not permit and the members of the family had to take turns at the stove. On lucky days the lot fell to Pauline. Everyone was on the Hay diet. Devised by Dr. William Howard Hay of Pocono Hay-ven, the rules called for alternating days of all-protein and all-carbohydrate meals, with an emphasis on vegetables; white sugar and bread were forbidden. Since Charles and José both had enormous appetites and were concerned that they might wake up hungry in the middle of the night, they always kept a little cheese and a few apples or oranges under their beds. The gas stove had seen better days and sometimes backfired. Nevertheless, Pauline made some famous spaghetti dinners for the company parties that were frequently given for holidays or to celebrate the end of a season.

Though they were not aware of it for some time, Miss Hein kept a picture of Adolf Hitler in her room. In Der Führer's friend Ernst Hanfstaengl she found a nickname that seemed just right for the youngest Woodford—Putzi. This the naïve family heard as "Pussy," and Pussy he was until he was five and a more grown-up name became appropriate. Humphrey was chosen because there was already a Charles in the family. Thereafter, anyone calling him Pussy had to forfeit a nickel, and the young man soon had enough coins to start a savings account.

By November Doris was still pleased with the baby, who was nearly ready for the sweater and bonnet Mama-San had made for him. But he had given his mother some trouble, for the doctor had failed to warn her against dancing barefoot, and she had painfully injured her metatarsals. Fortunately, *School for Husbands* was performed in shoes, but she had to be careful about concert work—an obstacle that she accepted stoically.

At this time she was also coaching Cornelia Otis Skinner in period dance style for one of the actress's distinguished one-woman shows, *The Loves of Charles II*. Miss Skinner was distressed that she had to leave New York just when she would have liked another lesson in the branle (a dance better known to the loves of Queen Elizabeth, as a matter of fact). She found her instructor "most kind and forebearing," though the situation was, she felt, "like the humming-bird teaching the ostrich to fly." She had seen the Molière play: "You are by far the best thing in it," she told Doris. "It is a joy and delight to watch you."

In the audience one night was another famous woman, who wrote to Doris and Charles:

As the evening wore on I swelled up nearly to the bursting point as I gazed upon my two artistic children. Not that for one moment I feel that I ever have encompassed either what you are doing in this delightful bit of nonsense or in the nobler and more austere beauty of your modern developments; all I mean was that I was filled with a loving pride that I had at least been half of your art parent in the earlier days.

The letter was signed: "Ever affectionately, Miss Ruth."

Another offer came to the Humphrey-Weidman group when a smart supper club, the Palais Royale, asked to have some dances for its new show, which would open on December 22—just seventeen days after the repeal of Prohibition. The auspicious timing, along with the prospect of work for the dancers, encouraged the directors to take it on. Sharing honors with several of Charles's lighter numbers and Doris's *Life of the Bee* were the singing trio, the Boswell Sisters—and a much-promoted turtle soup. Doris did not have to perform herself, though the project gave her an idea: "My ambition is eventually to give an all Bach program in a night club. . . . For contrast I direct angels and shepherds at the Dalton School." The Palais Royale was not a success for Humphrey-Weidman.

By January the baby weighed eighteen pounds, which was just right, and Doris decided to go on the road with *School for Husbands*. As usual, she needed money. Mama-San had given her the accounting for 1933: Daughter had sent her parents $570; they had received $112 from other sources; they still owed $33. She spent a week with them in Vermont, taking the baby along, before setting out for Pittsburgh. From there the Molière play was booked in Philadelphia and Washington. A concert at Mount Holyoke College on February 21 was followed by the opening of a course at the New School. The weary dancer did not know how she was going to manage it all.

In March, Horace Humphrey died. Doris could not stay very long with her mother because she was preparing two new dances for the next concert, but she tried to write more often. The schedule was getting terribly full and Leo was becoming irritated:

I wonder what you'll confront me with this time. The last I remember the dentist loomed large as a *successful* rival for your attention. Let me tell you, I don't mind being made jealous of your work, but I'll be damned if I admit a dentist as a serious contendent for your favours, even if he wins.

In April Leo was ill and home for a while, but Doris was so busy she hardly saw him. The concert fell on the fifteenth, with *Rudepoema,* a duet for Charles and herself, coming out as the most successful premiere. Mr. Martin told the next day's readers of the *Times* that its idiom was "crude peasant, almost primitive movement, imaginative and beautiful."

The following month, Mama-San came for a visit, and Doris suggested that she plan to arrive in New York on the nineteenth, when daughter could get her settled before going off to other commitments: "You can pinch hit for me with Leo who has several days in town and no me for the first few few days."

For their vacation this year, all three Woodfords went to Charles's farm in Blairstown, New Jersey. He had bought the 176 acres of land with José the year before, when his choreography for the Broadway musical *As Thousands Cheer* had brought him some welcome funds. Now he was furnishing the house with marvelous antiques he had picked up at various auctions. In the beginning, they had plumbing but only kerosene lamps; electricity came later. José laid stones and mortar for a patio as well as for a tool shed. The country was beautiful, the house had plenty of rooms, and the only disadvantage they found was the presence of a few rattlesnakes, which worried Doris when Pussy began to run around on his own.

The farm was to offer a haven to the 10th Street family for some years to come, as they would be spending numerous week ends as well as vacations there. For these occasions, the cooperative routine of the Manhattan apartment was transferred to Blairstown. Each day, one person did the cooking while another washed the dishes— though one guest cleverly arrived with a supply of paper plates. Members of the company were frequently invited to visit. Leo came whenever he could, though he sometimes resented the lack of privacy, wishing that he and his wife could have a vacation alone together, but knowing that financial considerations made the farm the logical place for them to go.

On July 30, just a week after Leo had to return to the *Queen*, Doris set out for the Bennington School of the Dance, leaving Pussy in New York with Miss Hein. So idealistic was the Bennington project that when Pauline first heard of it she reacted in her character of Cassandra Legree: "There must be a hitch," she told Doris. But there was none.

The program had been conceived by Robert Devore Leigh, president of the new women's college in the beautiful hills of southern Vermont, and Martha Hill, director of his dance department, soon joined by Mary Josephine Shelly from the University of Chicago. The idea, born that past winter, was no less than to found the first center for modern dance in America, combining a school, led by outstanding artist-teachers, with a concert series, utilizing these same artists as performers and choreographers.

Backed by knowledge, taste, and enthusiasm, the Misses Hill and Shelly were determined to attract the finest faculty in the field. They wanted all the best and they got them all: Martha Graham, Hanya Holm, Doris Humphrey, and Charles Weidman. For good measure, they added Louis Horst to teach music and John Martin to lecture on dance history and criticism. In the first year the ranking choreographers presented only "recitals" in the small college theatre (previously the attic) of the Commons building. But the full-blown festivals at the Bennington Armory, replete with major premieres enhanced by the innovative designs of Arch Lauterer, were not far off. The modern dance was young, the venture was bold, aspirations ran high; they were setting out to make history.

Doris's turn at Bennington came three weeks after the school had opened, for each of the stellar faculty had been engaged for a separate portion of the six-week term. She was pleased with her suite, which had maple furniture and pink curtains. The administrators, she found, were thoughtful and charming. But at times she wished she were back in New Jersey with Leo and Pussy, for she was encountering some problems at Bennington:

I've just got up after an exhausting evening in the theater. As usual it seemed pretty unsatisfactory to me—I feel blind about these concerts, never know how they really look, but with a general idea that they are unfinished and messy. The heat and humidity were terrific, but the audience was large and loyal. At least to Charles. You see he had just finished a week's work here and I'm sure half the girls are in love with him and as I was in the distasteful position of the chosen one—the partner, the lover even, they would not be very pleased with me. Please get off the stage Miss Humphrey and let me imagine myself as the inamorata of the romantic young man with the dark eyes. Isn't he divine and so cute too. Anyway *our* love dance—The Two Ecstatic Themes made a big impression. Some of the ecstasy that was and is ours must be in it.

It is raining and raining and Charles and Pauline have gone back to New York leaving me in the rain with ninety physical education teachers in the rain all frustrated and yearning for something.

Nor was Charles the only source of her difficulties:

There is a permanent staff of Martha's [Graham's] votaries, so anyone else is at a decided disadvantage. Added to that our participation in the show business injures the delicate membranes of their nostrils. I haven't forgotten the shock Miss St. Denis gave me on the Follies stage in a like circumstance. So we are well aware that danger lurks and try diligently to forfend ourselves against it.

Leo reprimanded his wife for her preoccupation with what he considered petty jealousies:

What a waste of time and effort, and between artistic groups too. You can, of course, avert it by ignoring it, if you are willing to accept the consequences, which few people are. But among artists whose common misery is patent I would think it could be submerged by the realisation of a common struggle against larger issues than personal aggrandisement in the State of Vermont.

"Ice and Fire," John Martin had called Doris and Martha. The former never exploded, though she could be stubborn. Martha, abetted by Louis, let her flamboyant fury flare at any apparent slight. In one weak moment, however, she made a confession: "Doris is really a choreographer," she admitted. "I'm a dancer. Doris knows how to put a dance together and I don't." They were each to have their share of successes and failures at Bennington.

For Doris, the session in Vermont was followed almost immediately by the teachers' course in New York. By now an accepted annual event in her life, it still gave her little pleasure and was often something of a tribulation for the students as well. Doris simply did not like teaching technique, especially to those who had practically none when they came to her. She preferred to take classes for dancers who were already skilled, so that she could try out her choreographic ideas on them. She also liked to use classes as occasions to give talks on theory, a custom that frustrated the young who wanted to work up a good sweat and disliked standing around listening to speeches, no matter how inspired. But they kept coming, for in the end they recognized the value of what Doris had to offer and they spread the word that garnered fresh recruits for the following year.

This year the company gave three concerts at the Carnegie Hall Studio to show their pupils what the finished product could look like. Doris's chief contribution was a dance on the theme of Orestes to music by Milhaud—a project she had been working on for some time and which she hoped would become one of her major repertory pieces. (Unfortunately, she needed a large and fine orchestra to present *Orestes* to a theatre audience; despite her persistent efforts to interest musical directors, the full production was never realized.)

The company's leading men were doing well. José was dancing in *As Thousands Cheer*. Charles's *Life Begins at 8:40* would open soon and would be a hit, though Doris had reservations about it and about him:

> Really he must decide where to lay his eggs in the future. This commuting to Boston [where the show tried out] from summer courses is disintegrating. I haven't seen it and am a little afraid to. I hear Albert Johnson [the designer] has smothered them in stage sets.

For herself, Doris disliked both dancing in shows and directing them, nor did she see how any artist could like them. Art came first; anything else was a necessary evil—necessary only to earn money to support the art. Once, when Letitia Ide asked for a leave from the company to appear in a musical that she said she would enjoy, Doris was puritanically shocked: "You're not supposed to enjoy it," she exclaimed.

Actually, Doris felt that money-making activities were practically incompatible with being an artist and she expected her colleagues to feel as she did. What could she do with money? She didn't care about clothes and hardly ever bought them without Pauline's goading her to do it. She would just as soon wear the same gray suit every day and frequently did. Absorbed in her work, she was all but oblivious to her physical surroundings outside of the studio and the theatre; worn furniture or peeling plaster she could simply ignore. Food did not interest her—lunch was usually coffee and a milkshake; dinner whatever she had time for. In restaurants, she ordered the fifth item on the menu—whatever it was. She was superstitious about the number five; besides, the method saved the time needed to make a decision, and the consequences were immaterial anyway.

Security, however, she did want. As her husband later commented, she wanted only the freedom to pursue art and to produce it. If she had financial worries—and she always did—they were related primarily to the upkeep of the studio and the production of new works. After fulfilling her obligations to her parents and to her son, art was her sole concern. Her attitude was bound to cause friction with company members who felt differently.

This fall, Doris took on a musical for the usual reason: she needed the money for the company. These Broadway ventures were almost always trying for her, and this was one of the worst. She simply could not compromise, so when Howard Dietz and Arthur Schwartz asked for extensive changes in her dances for *Revenge with Music,* she balked. Unlike Shubert, they refused to give in and hired the Russian ballet master Mikhail Mordkin to replace her. All of Doris's sixteen dancers stayed with the show because they needed the money. Since preparations were under way for a company tour, the situation was serious:

> We've been busying ourselves the last two weeks in making out a plan for the Group for next year which will keep them out of shows and working together on concerts. We've just sent it out and we're waiting to hear whether they will all come in or not. It demands considerable sacrifice in money and time. Most of them will be taxed fifteen per cent a week to provide a fund to carry them through next winter, so we'll see whether they want money or art the most. If the majority come in we will replace the others and go on with the plan.

As she anticipated, the group proposal caused something of a furore, most of the members disagreeing, not only with the directors but with each other. After a month of discussions, each member of the company finally said "yes," but some changes had to be made in the plan. As a result, Humphrey-Weidman could afford only two pianos for accompaniment, which would leave just enough to pay the dancers minimum Equity wages and their train fares on tour. Doris and Charles got no wages at all.

Doris got nothing also for staging Bach's Christmas Oratorio for a charity evening. But Lillian Gish was the Madonna and the sponsor was a rich man who cared about the arts, so Doris felt it might lead to something.

Always uppermost in her mind was the next work. For, apart from presenting an additional need for financial security, the coming of Pussy had made little difference in Doris's life. While she was occupied with classes and rehearsals, which was most of the time, he was in the care of Miss Hein. And in the absence of the nurse, it was most often Pauline who took over her duties. Yet current child psychology favored noncoddling mothers and, although he showed insufficient interest in food, Pussy seemed to be as content as any little boy growing up in a nonprofessional household.

He now had a mouthful of teeth, which was news to brighten Grandma's otherwise melancholy Christmas. During the summer she had returned to Oak Park, for after Horace's death, she had grown lonely and restless, lacking outlets for her energy in Vermont. She needed to be usefully active, she knew how to manage the school, and Ethel needed a manager. Meekly, Julia asked her daughter for suggestions about making financial arrangements with Ethel, and Doris projected a plan on a percentage basis. Now settled with her friends Grace and Lewis Blackman, who provided her with a basement room ("not damp"), Mama-San satisfied her need for service with bookkeeping at the studio.

And she had something to look forward to. In January she would see her daughter, for Chicago was one of the early stops on the first tour of the Humphrey-Weidman company.

Pioneering

DORIS wrote to her husband:

> Well, we're off on our great artistic adventure. So much depends on our reception in these new places. People thought the concert very good on Saturday, but I remember doing a solo dance in Canada after which not one clap broke the stillness.

At the beginning of 1935, the modern dance was anything but a household word to middle America. Few had heard of it; even fewer had actually seen it. Ballet was somewhat familiar, for Pavlova had toured in the 1920's and the Ballet Russe de Monte Carlo began its American travels in 1933. But Isadora Duncan had performed rarely in her own country, while the Denishawn tours had taken repertories of exotica, amply adorned with colorful sets, costumes, and picturesque paraphernalia. When audiences did see modern dance, even in its Broadway form, they didn't seem to recognize it. Doris kept a review of *As Thousands Cheer* which commented that "the Charles Weidman Dancers, headed by Letitia Ide and José Limón, present some extremely colorful and exotic numbers in the new style of interpretive dancing." In the margin, Doris wrote: "Mary, mother of god!"

Humphrey-Weidman set out on its crusade with uncompromising ideals of high seriousness. The repertory was—the repertory. And that was what the public got. They took *Bee, Alcina Suite, Shakers, Water Study, Dances of Women, Dionysiaques,* and *Rudepoema.* Though some engagements took the company to legitimate theatres, most of their dates were arranged through college physical education departments so that the routes came to be called "the gymnasium circuit."

Five years earlier, Doris had stated that "the dance is the thing, not the costumes, decorations, music, or drama," and she stuck to it. The attitude was practical for touring. Some time before, she had devised a functional, economical scheme to cover every possible need for décor. Stemming from the idea she had first used at the Brooklyn Little Theatre in 1928—when she had employed screens in place of a cyclorama and a set of platforms and steps to enhance the placement of groups of dancers—was her concept of the famous boxes. In principle they were similar to Gordon Craig's "architectonic" scenes, which used mobile screens to create abstract forms that became evocative of mood as they were filled with light and motion. In her own individual and imaginative way Doris chose boxes of various sizes, ranging from 1½ by 3 to 3 by 9 feet, which could be assembled in an almost infinite number of ways. The individual modules, held together by hinges and completely collapsible, were easy to transport, easy to set up and take down. She used these simple pieces with virtuoso brilliance.

From the Texas Special on its way to Dallas, she wrote Leo:

> Your heartening letter reached me in Chicago. That was a warm touch in the middle of trial and tribulation. I can hear you say, Of course she's a worrier, everything is probably all right. Well, this is my impression. Managers are timid, they will not advertise us properly. Moreover we did not supply them with the right copy about us. In Chicago they emphasized Charles as a Nebraska boy and me as a local girl. So many things must be watched it seems impossible to get them all done properly. Audiences are cordial. The Chicago one gave us an ovation. But another cross to bear is the fact that all mention in the press and social functions is riveted on Shakers and Water Study. It's just as though Charles and I hadn't danced at all. My big healthy children are beclouding me. The house was so bad in Chicago they would only give us half the money contracted for. Now is that trouble, or isn't it?

Then, leaving Toronto, José discovered he did not have the right papers for re-entry to the United States. Frantic phone calls to his father in Los Angeles. Charles had two new boys in the company,

slow learning and not promising. But male dancers were hard to
find, so one took any that were willing and not physically incapaci-
tated, and worked like the devil to turn them into performers. Problems, problems. But: "I read Elie Faure's book 'Rhythm in the
Forms' and was so rejuvenated and invigorated that I can live and
work for some time longer."

Back home in February, Doris and Charles choreographed a
production of Gluck's *Iphigenia* for the Philadelphia Opera Company. There was a lot of dancing in it, so Doris enjoyed the work:
"I like to compose better than anything." Louis Horst found "most
of the nine dances . . . of rare excellence. Especially fine were a
solo done by Miss Humphrey with a kind of archaic madness, a
charming duet with Mr. Weidman, and the finale of the big ballet in
the second act, which was built toward a grand and stirring climax."
Stokowski was again the conductor and the work commanded considerable prestige. But difficulties still rankled:

> Charles is having even more trouble with his boys than I did
> with the girls. He needs six in this thing. The two he wants in
> addition to the four we had on the road will not leave their jobs
> in "Revenge." . . . José the corner stone is in a precarious physi-
> cal condition with a rupture or something like it. And so we're
> taking blows all around sorry to relate. Criticism on the road
> was on the whole bad and the home press too but to offset that
> audiences everywhere were vociferous in appreciation. Possibly
> it comes from only a few who shout and clap loud enough to
> seem like the whole crowd. What the Chicago critics said was
> mild pap to the American Dancer Magazine man who declared
> it was all a deadly bore and trite to nausea. You can't help
> listening to them and wondering, because the same people make
> comments on other dancers which seem exactly right. So we
> wonder, watch everything with a sharp eye, tighten the belt and
> say on with the dance.

Matters were none too rosy at home either. John Gassner asked
for the $92.50 still owing him for his commission on *Americana* from
October, 1932. Several of the girls complained: they had stayed in
shows for financial reasons, but they had accepted the group plan
and were contributing to it. From Doris's letters they gathered that
she no longer considered them members of the company. Why?
Then there was Leo:

If only you can pay enough attention to convincing me that you consider me in the same way [that I do you], then I shall be content enough. Today it seemed to be so, hence I came away happy. But sometimes you don't make it clear, and then I'm miserable and worry all the voyage.

I know I give little enough assurances of my affection—not supported in any way by those material things which would be much more practical definitions of support in these trying days. . . . If only I could get close to you . . .

Yet he was proud of her success with *Iphigenia*, for the press had given her rave reviews:

But do you suppose she is satisfied? Indeed no. It is not her best work and it appears that she doesn't care for praise of the casual . . .

At times he felt happy about everything concerning her:

It's really Olympian of her to attempt the tasks of being an artist, wife, and mother, but she does them all, keeping up the standard of her work, entirely crazy about her child, and keeping her husband in love with her.

On March 10 Leo was operated on for an infection of the lymph glands of the neck. Four days later he wrote to Doris in Boston, wishing her well with the concert that night and adding that he would be in Roosevelt Hospital another week. On the nineteenth Doris was in State College, Pennsylvania, but she may have gotten back to New York in time to welcome him home.

Losses on the tour had been considerable. Even the profitable engagements in Boston and Philadelphia were insufficient to meet the train fares and salaries. So Doris was pleased when William Kolodney, the new director of the Education Department at the 92nd Street YM–YWHA, approached her with his plan for creating a dance center at the institution. He had asked John Martin to be chairman of the dance committee, with Martha Graham, Doris, and Charles participating. Here was a most welcome offer of a small but steady salary for teaching.

Temporarily relaxed, Doris wrote her husband, reviewing the joy of their meeting, but her description only made him melancholy:

> I wondered if that letter was a symbol of your realisation that the thing had passed. . . . In my most lucid moments I realize that I was only the insignificant medium whereby you attained an emotional climax. And of course it hurts. . . . Try to remember that I am no longer a lover, but a parent. There was a period when I could have seized and held you. Now there is no more chance. You move purposively in your own individual direction.

On this trip he was headed for South America, so they would see little of one another for a while.

By the time he returned, they had planned a family vacation. At the age of two, Pussy could travel to Bermuda free, which was a considerable inducement, so Doris booked passage for June 6. Even then, she had to borrow on her insurance to pay the fare. They stayed at the St. George Hotel and had a fine time.

Then she was ready to face the problems of the summer. Her course at Bennington began on July 20, and she found a room for the baby with a family in Wantagh where he would go with Miss Hein. "Poor little Pussy boy to be so disposed," sighed Leo. "Still, he's better anywhere than in the city."

After the leisure of her vacation, Doris felt pleased with her marriage:

> It makes me very happy to think that love still wraps us round after all these years. I am glad that the dark winter has given way in time to make this anniversary as sweet and fond as ever.' Only space separates us darling and that's a very little thing between lovers.

Was this happiness, perhaps, one of the sources of the great flowering that was *New Dance?* Though premiered at Bennington, the work had actually been composed in New York in July. The music was commissioned from Wallingford Riegger—who never knew that Doris had choreographed some of the movement to Roy Harris's *When Johnny Comes Marching Home*, which she used as a substructure later to be removed. The famous 7–7–10 variations that were added the next season—three-phrase units performed in solos, duets, or trios against a background of dancers moving in a steady 4/4—were, however, choreographed only to counts. When the entire dance was finished, Doris called on Riegger, who then wrote

Top: *New Dance*, 1935; Doris Humphrey at right. (Collection Walter Terry.) Bottom: *With My Red Fires*, 1936; Doris Humphrey, center, as The Matriarch. (Photo by William Black; collection Walter Terry.)

The Matriarch in *With My Red Fires*. (Photo by Martha Swope from original by Barbara Morgan; collection NYPL.)

melodic lines that he handed over to Ruth and Norman Lloyd with the request that they "write my kind of chords for this."

New Dance, Doris declared, represented "the world as it should be, where each person has a clear and harmonious relationship to his fellow beings." Certainly, its joyous affirmation of the state, where the individual contributes positively to his group without sacrifice of personal identity, must have cheered her in the atmosphere of Bennington, which "never appeals to me because it takes on the nature of a contest and is highly disturbing to my peace of mind and ask me when I ever had any."

Later she admitted that the new work had been "praised"—an understatement considering John Martin's first review which called *New Dance* "one of the most exciting pieces in the modern repertoire. . . . Certainly a more authoritative piece of creation in the dance has not been seen for many a day."

Afterward he elaborated: "Certainly Miss Humphrey has found in this larger medium an impetus to create quite the most beautiful and distinguished work of her career. Her 'New Dance' . . . has an impeccable unity and builds to its climax with inevitable logic. Its mood is one of tremendous animation, energy, joyousness of spirit." Margaret Lloyd found *New Dance* "the first pure example of the abstract symphonic ballet. . . . Its communication is made by overtones of implication in the movement and not by direct musical, literary or scenic appeal." Joseph Arnold Kaye asserted that "this piece will go down in dance history. It is certainly one of the greatest compositions conceived by a dancer in our time. . . . Doris Humphrey appears in it as one transfigured. This writer has never seen a dancer so filled with the ecstacy of the pure dance as she was, or one so able to communicate this feeling to those who watched her." The work, indeed, represented a culminating point in Doris's technical mastery of intricate group composition and in her use of movement to express her ideas of man's potential to conquer his environment and fulfill his destiny. Even on tour *New Dance* enchanted its audiences, though one provincial critic found that, as an essay on social problems, it was far less clear than a college professor's lecture.

After the premiere, Doris was free to leave Bennington. She picked up Pussy in Wantagh and took him to the Blairstown farm where she joined him on week ends. He was "blooming with health and beauty," she asserted. Though he refused to speak to or shake hands with strangers, he was very affectionate with his friends, behaved nicely at table, and was never noisy in public places.

The critical acclaim for *New Dance* did nothing, of course, to alleviate the financial strain that constantly hovered over the family on 10th Street. They were trying to reorganize their lives to hold down expenses, but they all found it difficult. Doris had her own sense of priorities: "Beyond the rent saving I don't know what else we could do as other things must go on, like sets, costumes, pictures, publicity for the works, and dentists, doctors, food, toothpaste, shaving soap, laundry for us." While she tried to economize, Charles was buying red glass at auctions because he fancied it for the farm. Hardly endowed with his partner's conscientiousness, he borrowed from anyone in the company who happened to have a cent to spare, proudly displaying his antiques and ignoring unimportant matters like debts and impending taxes.

This year, the pioneering tours were curtailed:

> Last year, only the old dances were successful and we can't do them anymore with enthusiasm. . . . We're going to concentrate in New York on recitals, and give only the latest things out of town on the few occasions when we go out. They won't like it anyway but we might as well keep on growing ourselves. . . . The ballet is fatal competition. Also people like Ted Shawn who sell their companies so cheaply.

That fall she was able to place Pussy in the Bank Street School, which kept him occupied and cared for from nine to three. Tuition there was adjusted to the parents' income, so the principal apologized to Doris that they had no scholarships to offer. At least the nurse would now be needed only afternoons. Doris got up early to make breakfast for her son and see him off to school. Then she took a nap before going to teach at the studio. Though Pussy was shy—after all, she realized, he had had little contact with other children—he seemed to get along very well with his new classmates.

While Doris prepared a revised and enlarged version of *New Dance* for a concert at the Guild Theatre, Leo looked on:

> Dear God—How long? Will she ever relax? I'm on vacation and am virtually living in fear and trembling under the kitchen

table. If there were a cellar I'd live in that. . . . The poor saps around here think she's a famous woman. She's not. She's a great woman.

Although the Leonard Elmhirst Committee had given the company $750 to cover the anticipated deficit of the October concert at the Guild, Doris was unable to pay her insurance premium in December. Still she found the financial problems relatively insignificant, as the October reviews had been ecstatic and the January concert fared equally well.

> Well here's the "Times" latest word on my last effort—and what an effort. The Theatre Piece is intricate and long, about forty-five minutes and it took everybody working full time to get it together. This was an entirely new form for me to attempt—a sort of ironic-comedy-drama, which showed, I hope, among other things that I have a sense of humor. . . . With [Charles's] Atavisims and Theatre Piece we stick pins into about everything outside except possibly politics. I, however, offer a solution in New Dance. Of course it is a very little view of the world, and does not attempt to be a complete analysis of what really is—you can't put in everything—but our generally [sic] feeling of contempt for stupidity and hatred of vicious competition is what is there and we mean it. Incidentally, these themes give an opportunity for movement and satire which is extremely rich in bite and humor—a grand new field for me.

Though Mr. Martin called *Theatre Piece* "devastating," the critics were not so unanimous this time, Irving Kolodin telling readers of the *Sun* that, though the choreography was ingenious, the piece was "overburdened with special pleading."

In February, there were demonstrations at colleges—Smith, Swarthmore, and Hood, as well as concerts at Temple and Hampton. Pussy was left in the care of a new nurse, Miss Hein's sister Marga, whom Doris found "grand." *Theatre Piece* and *New Dance* were repeated at the Adelphi Theatre in April. Shortly thereafter Leo was promoted to chief officer on the *Queen*, with a better cabin on board and better pay. This gave hope for a little more financial security and held other advantages as well. Doris was pleased that he could now host passengers at meals which would give him some contact with a wider range of people, broadening his "now exclusive diet of dancers and seamen."

Now she was teaching classes also under the auspices of the WPA, having been appointed in March to the staff of the dance unit of the Federal Theatre Project, headed by Hallie Flanagan. The unit director was Don Oscar Becque, and her choreographic colleagues were Gluck-Sandor, Felicia Sorel, Tamiris, and Charles. The budget allowed for the employment of 185 dancers as well as for costumes and sets for eight productions, a theatre, orchestra, and staff. If Doris had any particular feelings about the political significance of the project, she made no mention of them. Unlike Tamiris, who withdrew from all other commitments to dedicate her efforts to WPA, Doris simply added this activity to everything else she already had, apparently considering it just another dance job. Though she fully agreed with Leo's liberal leanings, she never had time to become involved with the specifics of politics. At one time, when he was questioned about her possible leftist tendencies during this period, he replied that his wife would have given a concert under the auspices of Satan himself—as long as he put up the production money and did not interfere with artistic decisions.

In June the ever helpful Pauline took Pussy to the farm while Doris prepared for concerts at Lewisohn Stadium and for the impending session at Bennington. This summer would be especially busy, for it was Doris's turn to direct the workshop, a new project introduced the previous year when Martha Graham had been placed at the helm. It involved rehearsing a number of advanced students in a new work—the idea being that they would learn in the process something about how a dance is formed. The rehearsals were held in the evenings; each morning Doris had a two-hour technique class, and each afternoon a two-hour class in composition. Fortunately Mama-San accepted an invitation to come to Vermont to help take care of Pussy, and her grateful daughter gladly paid the train fare.

This summer Bennington looked to Doris like a Corot landscape: animals grazed on a soft meadow, dark trees spread their large and verdant branches. She exuded happiness, for a new dance was brewing. It had, in fact, been formed in detail as she and Mama-San traveled north:

> The drive was long and uneventful but it gave me my first consecutive hours for thinking about the new work temporarily

called "Romantic Tragedy." First a hymn to Aphrodite, or Priapus or Venus, anyway to the excitement, the greatness, the rapture, the pain of, frustration that is love. A voice will speak of that from a temple and the ever willing victims will respond with flutterings, stabbings, listenings, impatience, fire in the blood (I know I'm not as good as Whitman). Next the process will begin. Put the force to work, seek out the mate, rush from one to the other, buffet the rest out of the way. Yes, there are two lovers at last, the end is all but achieved, the heat and thirst quenched. But what and who is that beckoning in the window? It's a woman—old—she's beckoning to the girl lover —she's the mother—she says it's late and no time for young girls to be lugging around with unknown young men and good-ness knows who he might be or what sort of a family he comes from. Come in this moment, your virtue's at stake, the world will say you're a bad girl. You won't? You will do as I say. Sew the seam, mop the floor, walk like me, talk like me, come away from the window—How can I mop the floor and sew the seam with my lover outside? I have danced in the Hymn to Priapus and I belong to my love—The old one is quiet now in the house, steal away through the window to the waiting lover. In the shadows find him, wrap him round. The old one has missed you, she's screaming now from the top of the house, the alarm is spreading, people are running, shouting, they're on the mor-bid scent, they gleam with virtuous hate. She's run off with a nobody? Which way? To the town, to the inn? No, here by the wall. Tear them apart, the dirty things. What shall we do, old one, marry them with a gun and giggles or run them out? See that they're well battered, punish, pinch, tear, beat, and I shall shut the door. So—let's take them over the rocks, up-down through the rocks, leave them at the Priapic stone. Moralists point the finger
thrifty lift your eyes
sentimental ones weep over young love's
    impetuosity
Scandal mongers laugh.

She went on to give Leo news of Pussy's birthday party—delightful with many presents. Katy Manning would meet his train at Albany next week—Doris couldn't, since she had to teach till six:

To my love in the Whitman manner—priapic, caressing, cajol-ing, patient, impetuous, tender, thoughtful, well-worded, too-sensuous, lazy, beginner-not-finisher, aesthetic lover, enduring lover—behold the man!

At the premiere of *With My Red Fires*, the audience broke into applause even before the flight of the lovers had finished. John Martin was mightily impressed. As Julia Humphrey watched her daughter portray the domineering matriarch, did she recognize the signs of her own past possessiveness? Or—perhaps—Pauline's?

After teaching an unpleasant summer course in New York, Doris went with Pussy to Coonamessett Inn in Hatchville, Massachusetts. Pauline, whom the small boy had named Pumba, went along to help care for him so that Doris could get some rest. She needed the time to gather energy for the rigors that lay ahead, for the concert schedule would take her out on the road in October. With the kind of routine she had to maintain now, help was essential and she was grateful to have Marga that fall:

> Our business is as involved and difficult as ever—and as we have no gorgeous Bennington staff to make it all run smoothly, we're pretty well distracted. We're getting ready some lecture-recitals for a small group to take to Cleveland, Detroit and Ohio Wesleyan next week. These always have to be done over every time with different people and different numbers. In between I teach, see a woman who wants to combine drayma with the daunce, have two sets of pictures taken, write a contract for Mr. Hurok [again, nothing came of it], see the representative from the New Dance League about [promoting my system of dance] notation, call up Riegger to see where the devil the score for the New Dance is, read a couple of ballet synopses from a lady poet in Cleveland which are too dreadful for words—audition thirty girls who want half-scholarships at the Academy [of Allied Arts] which we are offering this year and so on & on every day. I haven't quite forgotten my nice vacation—although the physical effects have pretty well worn off now.

Marga had turned into something of a mixed blessing, since Pussy resented her stern discipline. The mother tended to agree with the nurse: "I think the progressive idea is only a partial preparation for life. We must be prepared for the fact that some things have to be done whether you like it or not." She might have been horrified, though, had she known how strict Marga was in her absence. Because Pussy was so thin, Marga forced him to eat until he sometimes vomited—and then spanked him for getting sick. But he liked his school, and his teachers said he was doing very well.

For Christmas, Grandma knitted him a sweater, and his parents gave him an auto repair shop. Leo had been home since the end of November with a broken ankle acquired in a scramble to put out a fire on the ship. Doris had another teachers' course to contend with and a big concert coming up at the Hippodrome. Mama-San hinted: "If you don't have time to read this, give it to some one who will tell it to you between acts. Sometime you'll write to me again, won't you?"

The Hippodrome concert attracted an audience of some five thousand, with *Red Fires* coming in for the greatest praise. Though the orchestra made some bad mistakes, throwing one dance completely out of rhythm, the public seemed unaware of the problem. The *Trilogy* as a whole evoked such praise as Miss Lloyd's: "not only the greatest dance composition, but the greatest artistic expression of present-day life in any form that has come out of America."

Leo was recovered by now but still home, since the ship's doctor refused to take him back until two months after the accident. To Doris's delight, he brought her breakfast in bed and took in most of John Martin's lecture-demonstration series on modern dance at the New School. The time was most opportune, for on February 23 the company was to start a tour of the Middle West that would take them to nine cities in two weeks.

Most of the dancers were happy to tour, the reasons being principally financial. Performing in a New York concert paid them $5 or $10 after months of unpaid rehearsals; teaching yielded $2 to $5 a class. Even in 1937, this was barely a living wage, so most of them took part-time jobs. They taught tap or ballroom dancing; some of the girls modeled. But no one lived in luxury. One of the dancers recalls a time when three members of the company had thirty cents between them. They bought a soup bone for twenty cents and spent the remainder on vegetables. Just add water and —voilà—meals for three days. But on tour it was better. Since local enthusiasts frequently invited them out to eat, most of them were even able to save a little of their $35-a-week wages.

This year the company had two performances in Chicago, but Doris had no time for a visit with her mother. The pioneering struggle had its drawbacks:

Leo has gone back to his glamourous romantic life on the high seas carrying America's lower class bourgeoisie back & forth to Bermuda. Charles and I try to convince the rest of America that the modern dance is something too, both activities quite depressing for different reasons.

Leo was depressed, and not only about his voyages. He was bored and lonely. The pleasantness of his weeks at home with his wife had only made him wish he could have more of them and made him increasingly resentful of the art that took her away from him so much of the time. Yet he questioned the validity of his attitude:

> Your task takes on such a hopelessness in the face of it all that I am almost persuaded to say "Give it up." Self interest plays a part here too. This I realize, so I am cautious. I have to be careful about my own motives.
>
> How would it effect me if you did give it up? Would I finally throw off that element of aimlessness which is in me and admit my responsibilities? I wonder, now and a little voice whispers to me, "Listen, this woman is not yours completely, she's not surrendered herself to your care entirely. So you should worry. Be as aimless as you please my lad. The aim of a man's life is possession, personal in goods, mutual in love, and in your love there is an element of non-possession which you cannot overcome until she stops giving herself to the public. So just drift along my lad and wait." . . .
>
> Meanwhile nothing but admiration for your courage is in my mind. But somehow I feel that as a woman you have a right to be loved and cherished wholeheartedly and without reserve and by nature the right to give yourself to the man who awaits your pleasure with impatient anticipation.

In March the company set out again, starting this time in Georgia where Doris found the reception most enthusiastic. The tour ended in Boston on April 12, leaving less than a month to prepare for the concert at the Guild Theatre on May 9. And the program for the summer was going to be grueling. . . .

At Bennington this year José had a fellowship in choreography which stipulated that he use the time to prepare a work of considerable length and substance. He already had two short pieces, *Canción y Danza* and *Danza*, in the Humphrey-Weidman touring repertory, and Doris was keeping a sharp eye on his current project, *Danza de la Muerte*, a symbolic comment on the Spanish Civil War. She knew that he was gifted with a fine sensuous feel for movement and with great sensitivity. Also, he shared her scorn for oppressors and her faith in the ultimate triumph of human aspiration. These feelings bound her to José in a way she had not been bound to Charles, whose instinct for comedy and satire complemented her cosmic visions but did not parallel them. His "In the Theatre" section of the *New Dance Trilogy* had given the work an incisive element of contrast; as usual, his repertory balanced hers. Even his serious, dramatic *Lynch Town*, premiered the previous season, depicted a specific social situation where Doris would have stressed the theme as an abstract statement.

Ideologically, she was close to José; only his inexperience and a certain lack of objectivity about his own work separated them. His imagination seemed unbounded; Doris had once copied a passage from G. K. Chesterton: "Art is limitation; the essence of every picture is the frame." She knew how to apply this rule to herself, and now she applied it to José. What he most needed was the critically firm yet sympathetic editing that only she could give him. She gave unstintingly of her time and of her taste. He was most agreeable. "Yes, Doris," he would say, "Yes, Doris." After the premiere of *Danza de la Muerte*, John Martin predicted that Limón was a composer to be reckoned with importantly in the future. Rather than staging a new work herself this summer, Doris remounted the *Trilogy*.

The Bennington season was followed by the usual summer course in New York and a pleasantly uneventful August of teaching at Perry-Mansfield. But as soon as Doris was home, the pressures began to mount: two new dances, *American Holiday* and *Race of Life*, to choreograph; sessions with fan dancer Sally Rand who wanted a "Snow-Bird" number. ("She's tough and likeable and a hard worker"); preparations for a holiday season called Dance International (a marathon of performances by ballet and modern dance companies with participants from forty nations); planning for eight weeks on the road:

> The net result is an extremely intensive life, exciting & adventurous with an economic background as stable as quick-sand. Pioneering exactly says it in one word. Forcing your way, with Indians & the elements to battle with, and the uncertain re-

ward of soil that may be fertile or barren but in either case will have to be cultivated strenuously after you win your right to it.

That fall Doris entered Pussy in the Friends School on East 16th Street, where she taught in return for his education. She found it a great improvement on Bank Street: "The atmosphere of the classroom is more controlled and that's a good thing."

This winter only one of the new dances succeeded. *American Holiday* tried to represent the influence on the living of the ideals of a dead hero. Mr. Martin reasoned that the choreographer was attempting to break through the general obscurity of the modern dance by employing both spoken words and explicit stage action, but he found the result platitudinous. *Race of Life,* however, was greatly enjoyed. Long a fan of James Thurber, Doris translated his cartoons into a comedy of a woman determined that her man will reach the top (symbolized by a mountain made out of the ever-useful boxes). In *American Dancer* Albertina Vitak wrote of her delight in seeing "the usually exquisite Miss Humphrey" turned into a "lumpy and gallumphing" caricature.

The tour that began in January was extensive and strenuous, taking the company all the way to the West Coast and involving forty-two performances—some full concerts, others lecture-demonstrations—before they returned to New York in April. Pauline had booked some of the dates through regular commercial channels, others through college organizations or local dance enthusiasts. Since this was the biggest tour ever undertaken by a modern dance group, her task had been tremendous, and she had accomplished it with incredible efficiency and skill. From her "office" on West 10th Street, she made contacts, "sold" the company, deciphered train schedules, sent out publicity, arranged programs—did a dozen jobs that brought glory to other people.

How she did it—while designing and sewing costumes, playing piano for classes and rehearsals, lighting concerts, to say nothing of cooking—no one could understand. Then there was Humphrey, for it was Pauline he turned to whenever he needed solace and Pauline —eyes still on her bookkeeping or on an unfinished costume (due to be worn on stage that evening)—who would snap, "Don't show me anything that isn't bleeding." But she looked at anything if he asked her. Pumba, Cassandra Legree. With her sharp tongue and her boundless devotion, she was indispensable. The company was her life as it was Doris's. But Doris had a husband. For Pauline there had been some men, but none of them had lasted very long. Now there was José, but she did not expect that to last either. For Leo, who wanted his wife home with him and their child, she had little sympathy. The important thing was Doris's career, and that meant on with the dance—on tour.

On leave in New York, with only Pussy and Marga to keep him company, Leo was grateful to find a letter from his wife. She had told him about a dream, and he appreciated the unusual candor:

> It implies a trust and confidence more convincing than the recitation of a credo, and tells me just how far we have travelled towards our mutual blending into each other. I know you hate it—fight it with every effort of your trained and conditioned prejudices, but it is a corollary of safe navigation.

Yet this assurance of her trust could not compensate him for the pain of her absence. He dramatized his conflict for her with a dialogue between "complaining unreason" and "stoical reason":

> C.U. My girl left me. I don't see why. She must love dancing more than me.
> S.R. Ah, shut up, stupid. Of course she loves dancing more than you. Why the Hell shouldn't she?
> C.U. But she says she loves me, and nobody can love two things at once. So that she can't love me.
> S.R. Well! She probably believes she does. That's because she's both a woman and an artist. When she's a woman she's with you, but you run a poor second when she's an artist. . . . Your love (and hers), we suppose, grows and flourishes in direct proportion to the separations and disappointments you suffer. If there were no art, no sorrow, you would have no love. Let that be your consolation.
> C.U. I am unhappy.

Apparently she did not respond as he had hoped, for a little later he apologized that his letters had struck her as overlugubrious. He had only wanted to tell her that she was loved and he was lonely. Their attitudes could not be the same: "How you balk at complete surrender. I don't! I would have you every minute of every day." But her replies frustrated him: "One of the most extraordinary things about your letters is that you completely ignore mine."

Mama-San was also feeling the brunt of her daughter's reticence:

> I was a little disturbed about our last conversation. Why is it, I wonder, that we can never say things to each other. It's all so constrained and careful and afterwards my main impression seems to be of the things which by superhuman restraint you refrained from saying. I suppose I succeed just a little in making myself natural and conveying what I really want to. If it didn't matter so much I presume it would be easier but it's a pity, isn't it?

Doris could reply only with factual comments—financial matters, current activities, plans for the summer. Her work for the WPA Dance Project, a new production of *With My Red Fires,* would provide some funds and she could soon send a check for $40 to Oak Park. And, though no money was involved, she had received the Dance Magazine prize for group choreography this year. It was awarded for *To the Dance.* Doris found it ironic to be recognized for this comparatively slight "opening number" after slaving over much longer and more intricate dances. The citation read: "To the Dance, composed as a curtain-raiser, yet contains truer dance quality and much finer choreography than any other work of its kind seen this season. It was conceived in terms of dance, without philosophy or ideology, and can be readily appreciated by any kind of audience."

On May 28, Doris and Pussy sailed for two weeks in Bermuda —he was still small enough to go free and Leo had rented an inexpensive cottage on St. David's Island. It turned out to be alive with roaches and spiders, but the weather was beautiful and Doris found the vacation perfect.

Home again, she faced a new work for Bennington to the Bach Passacaglia and Fugue in C minor, then teaching at Perry-Mansfield. Leo worried: "You see I believe that you are capable of killing yourself with that wretched will of yours." At this point she was worried too, though not for herself. José was teaching in Greeley and would be late joining rehearsals. There were complicated schedules to make out and new student dancers to absorb into the group. With luck, she found a student to take care of Pussy, but there was the usual atmosphere of rivalry that she detested:

The first thing we heard here was that yes, we had a wonderful tour but why did we want to jazz up our dances in order to be successful—because that's just what you left Denishawn for. . . . So much for the dirt. . . . I'm still in love with you—& I hope that will help to ease the long absence—by now I think you believe it and I am deep in your heart & you in mine.

Her letter both comforted and perplexed him:

For a man asks, "How can a woman want him so and yet separate herself? It hurts the pride—the ego grumbles unbelief. . . . It's something to know that your work is going on well, but poor Dear you never seem to achieve peace of mind, do you?

He analyzed their contrasting points of view:

The constant living and loving of one woman is a thing so profoundly scored into my nature that I am convinced that I cannot achieve any tranquility until that is accomplished. And without such peace I fear I shall never accomplish any work of any importance. You who are more or less egocentric have no sympathy for this attitude. I'm sure I don't know whether my psychology is right but I suspect that since you had formed the habit of creativeness long before you formed any deep affection for anyone (I'm admitting, in writing, that it exists) the mechanism goes on anyway, and brings with it certain satisfactions and pleasures which are not for me. It only complicates the whole problem that I want you to have them.

Doris did indeed find satisfaction elsewhere. This summer it was in the music of Bach, which was always a source of inspiration for her. The tranquility that Leo could find only in their love, she discovered in the *Passacaglia*. Her program notes explained that she had treated it:

. . . as an abstraction with dramatic overtones. The minor melody, according to the traditional Passacaglia form, insistently repeated from beginning to end, seems to say "How can a man be saved and be content in a world of infinite despair?" And in the magnificent fugue which concludes the dance the answer seems to mean—"Be saved by love and courage." . . . [The dance was inspired by] the need for love, tolerance and nobility in a world given more and more to the denial of these things.

The initial critical response was qualified. Mr. Martin had reservations about the use of the music, while *Dance Observer* remarked that the abstract patterns were of questionable significance to an audience concerned with what dance had to say to them. At a subsequent performance, however, the *Times* man found his objections overweighed: "It is indeed in every way a beautiful and authoritative creation and shows itself both in its lofty content and its mastery of form as the handiwork of one of the most richly gifted of contemporary composers." Later, *Passacaglia* was a success on tour, where a California critic found in it "the real triumph and dignity of modern dance. . . . The surge of humanity, the ordered, upward trend of life and the strength which faith gives, were all mirrored in motion."

Before setting out for Perry-Mansfield, Doris spent a few days with Leo in Poughkeepsie where he was training the English crew for the international boat races. The Italian crew won, but the English came in second. With the bonus he received, they bought a double bed—after years of having one only slightly larger than a single.

In Colorado, Doris's full time was taken up with classes, and she was bored with hearing that she was such a good teacher: "Some day I'll get violent about this, but it will probably be too late to recover the dancer I might have been except for the blood suckers."

In the fall Doris and Charles enlarged their studio, taking more space on the same floor of the 18th Street building. Mama-San's school, however, seemed to be gradually disintegrating. The old students were leaving and new ones were not arriving. Much of this Julia blamed on herself, feeling that her methods were too old-fashioned to appeal to young people. What she feared most, though, was the prospect of becoming a helpless invalid and a burden to her daughter: "My whole aim now is to readjust, fit in wherever I can, meet whatever life may still have for me gracefully and without a long face."

Doris replied that she was sorry the school was in trouble, but the Humphrey-Weidman studio was losing money too—about $200 a month. She used outside opportunities to make it up; witness her strenuous teaching schedule this year, at Columbia and Temple

Charles Weidman and Doris Humphrey — a portrait study at the height
of their careers. (Collection José Limón.)

Top: José Limón, ca. 1935. (Photo by Martha Swope from original by Helen Hewett; collection NYPL.) Bottom: *Rudepoema*, 1934; Doris Humphrey, Charles Weidman. (Photo by Martha Swope from unattributed original; collection NYPL.)

universities as well as at the Friends School. She sent her mother a check for $25, apologizing that it could not be more. But she really had nothing herself; in fact, she couldn't attend an important party for the Ballet Russe because she had nothing appropriate to wear. Her family had to come first. Humphrey (no longer to be called Pussy) had had a Halloween party. Mommy could not be there because she had to rehearse, but she heard the children had a fine time.

Leo came home one night in November to find a note from his wife, telling him that she was in Baltimore but would be back in the morning: "Well, my darling, you *would* have a dancer who goes off on her toes just as you arrive. Never mind, shall be back on both feet & *you* can welcome *her* for a change." Probably he saw little of her when she did return, for a concert was coming up at the Guild and she was worried about the reception of *Passacaglia*.

Doris wanted to be a good wife and she was trying, but this time the obstacles seemed almost unsurmountable. It was, she confessed, "the first serious clash between my career on the stage & in the home":

> Pauline wants to book the company during May and June in the west between the end of the tour and the summer engagement of the Bennington School of the Dance at Mills College in July. But I announced long ago I wouldn't go away for more than two months at a time. The tour has already extended to three as it is. I am accused of preventing sixteen people from working by refusing to stay out there. . . . I'm not ready to say that it is impossible to live the two lives I'm attempting but it looks very close to it at the moment.

In the end, the immediate problem was resolved when the extra West Coast dates did not work out.

A three-weeks tour of the Northeast began on January 9. Pauline had decided that the economical way to travel was by bus, so she hired one that started off for Middlebury, Vermont, in a violent snowstorm, with no shovel and no chains. Once they went off the road, broke a wheel, and waited for hours to be rescued. A little later the bus could not make it up a hill, so everyone had to get out and push. They arrived at seven forty-five. Before the eight o'clock curtain, they had to unpack, set up the boxes, press costumes. . . . Through it all, the dancers recall, Doris was imperturbable; she didn't blink. She was able simply to detach herself, to retreat into her own thoughts, oblivious to the panic surrounding her. But when the company set out for the West Coast, Pauline supplied them with railroad tickets.

Trying to think ahead so that everything would run smoothly at home, Doris left an order at the market to deliver enough groceries to keep the family for a week, explaining that she would send new lists each week that she was away. But with the constant pressures of touring, she forgot, and the store simply supplied the same order week after week. When she got home, the refrigerator was filled with cabbages.

She felt badly about leaving her family but, at the same time, felt that this was what she must do:

> Of course I hate leaving home as long as this—but there seems little else to do about it short of stopping entirely. After having worked all these years for a chance to dance it would hardly be sensible not to when the opportunity comes—nor would it be just to deprive Charles and the rest of the company of their opportunity either.

They started in the South, where Doris found the public cordial if not very knowledgeable. There were some nice receptions for the company: "At almost every gathering of this kind someone asks me if Martha Graham is in our group, but this time a girl asked me if I taught in her school."

The South held further hazards. The trains, largely of no recent vintage, crawled along, stopping at every tiny hamlet for what seemed to be arbitrary periods of time. Sometimes chickens were brought on, and often the train was devoid of that civilized appendage, a dining car. The company was essentially a congenial one, but the long hours bred nervous tensions and occasional quarrels. Doris remained aloof, uninvolved. She could sleep through almost anything. And she could use the enforced idleness of the waits on station platforms. Later she told her choreography classes: "A dancer should never be bored because wherever you are, you can watch life going on, can watch people; you always learn, you are always fascinated."

Naturally Pauline, the ever solicitous, was there to take charge and to see that Doris was ready to come out of herself and meet the public in a manner proper for a great artist. As the train neared their destination, she would cast a disapproving eye: "You can't appear looking like that!" Pumba knew exactly what fabrics and what colors were most becoming to her charge, and she saw that Doris was wearing her Fortuny gown and picture hat as she descended to the platform to greet her local fans.

From the South they went to the Middle West and then on to California. The cross-country reviews showed a range of reactions. In many places the company found sympathy, understanding, even enthusiasm. But a number of writers admitted to bewilderment; they figured that something significant was intended by the choreographers but they couldn't imagine what. Others admitted that they knew this "self expression" was supposed to be "sublime" though they found it "ridiculous." One called it "grotesquely impressionistic"; another, insisting that jazz and tap dancing were the only real American idioms, asserted that the Humphrey-Weidman group was shockingly decadent, half-mad and fearfully dangerous (though he did not specify what it was that they endangered).

The company got home in early May, when Doris looked forward to a vacation with Leo on the farm. She had been feeding him ideas for the theory book and he had been writing the first chapter at sea. "We should meet occasionally if only for the book's sake," he told her. But he was also concerned about Humphrey: "You miss too many days—weeks of his life."

Doris felt guilty about this too. Busy with teaching after the brief respite on the farm, she arranged for Pauline to take the child to visit Mama-San. When he got violently ill on the train, Doris blamed herself for having taken him to a restaurant she knew was not too good: "I never should have taken him in there. The whole thing was because both Pauline and I were too busy to cook." She saw her mother briefly while en route to Colorado State College, and she took the kind of presents Humphrey especially liked—soap from each hotel where she had stayed on the last tour.

The temperature in Greeley never failed to reach 100 degrees, and this was not its exclusive unhappy aspect:

> Looking at it objectively I should say that there is no one on
> the campus who has made the original contribution to art I

have, or to anything else, yet I am unknown here except to the pupils in one small section of the despised physical education department. The physical education section is something like a combination of a circus and a drugstore. It keeps you healthy and occasionally provides amusement. Everybody likes to see the animals perform, but when it comes to the serious business of culture you lock the football players and the dancers up in their cages. In my case it's not really so conscious as all that, they don't know I exist at all and wouldn't care if they did. My rage is not personal so much, as despair over the stupidity of the whole thing and especially of the position of the dance.

There was an important compensation, however. Every day a Mrs. Robinson, "the most devoted admirer one could wish," drove sixty miles from Denver just to see her classes. Helen Mary Robinson, known to her friends as Hay, had trained as a dancer in Los Angeles and New York. She had had her own ballet school in Denver, supporting her lawyer husband through his early years in private practice, until his partner advised her that it was not proper for a rising young attorney to have a wife who taught dancing. Now with two small daughters to care for, Hay sought the company of dancers whenever she had a chance. She was to become not only Doris's fervent disciple but her closest friend.

This year the Bennington faculty was transported to Mills College, and Doris went there directly from Greeley. Since no formal concerts were scheduled, most of the staff found the California session comparatively relaxed, and they easily managed to visit the Golden Gate International Exhibition. But not Doris; she was overworked as usual. Her wise and patient molding of the choreographic talents of José was taking more of her time now, though of course this was not officially part of her responsibilities:

> José and Katy Manning are giving part of a concert next Friday, and it takes the entire family to get it together. José has bitten off a huge chunk of his native land to exhibit—portraits of five kinds of Mexicans—the Indian, the Spanish invader, the peon, the landowner and the Revolutionary. He's really very curious about his dances. He always scorns the dancers he knows for wanting to be dramatic—but he invariably goes for it himself. Now this is not a natural talent with him. Consequently Charles & I try to help when he is obviously looking stunning but not saying anything. One of the dances is excellent—

really a remarkable piece of work for one not to the manner born. Katy is doing a Bach Suite with him—an old one revived. This is another headache, as, to begin with, styles have changed since he composed it. It was done in a flat mirror style—you know, two dimensional, which is something juiceless that we all outgrew five years ago. Katy is doing them quite well, but it's a long process as all the movements have to be molded by hand.

Since Mills had a playschool for faculty children, Humphrey came along, living with Pumba who had brought him out. The only incident the boy suffered on this trip was a sudden near-midnight nosebleed. Reaching in the dark of the Pullman for a handkerchief, Pumba managed to find a piece of cloth to serve the purpose—only to discover in the morning that it had been her brassiere.

At the end of the session, Humphrey brought back a report that said he did not take enough responsibility with his possessions; was easily discouraged if his efforts did not meet with immediate success; was doing well in music; enjoyed being with children and needed plenty of company his own age. His mother was particularly pleased that he had learned how to swim. He also indulged in some extracurricular activities. A favorite pastime was picking flowers from the numerous beds around the campus and selling them to the girls in the dormitories.

The season at Mills ended with a demonstration program given by the faculty:

> Martha was the first with something that looked very much like American Document, only gayer & more lyric. No more hard angles or glum faces. They smile, they run, they skip & leap. How these gals do change. Hanya too—I must say we're the only ones who appear to have made up our minds about dancing once and for all, as to theory, movement, style, focus, everything. My group did very well and I was proud of them. For one thing they were more accurately trained than any of the others.

From Mills, Pauline took Humphrey to visit her sister in Los Angeles. Doris left immediately for Steamboat Springs:

> It's rather a mess here, as Charles, true to his nature, came one week, and threw enough difficult technique at them to floor a professional company. I've at last made up my mind that he

cannot be let alone to do just as he pleases, because he lacks judgment so—It's hard on me to be the only one with sense, but I'll have to accept it. In his demonstration at Mills he had again the same characteristics as always—the winning charm, the irresistible humor, the messy, illogical technique, much too difficult & too long for his admiring and frantic group.

For the coming season, Charles agreed not to do a show, which was fine for artistic purposes though it meant a serious drop in his personal income. He was considering leaving 10th Street to get a room by the week or month so that he would not have to bear the burden of paying rent when he was out of town. Also, there had been some friction between him and José. Doris dreamed a bit about the pleasant possibility of an apartment for just the three Woodfords. But that would be expensive, and who would do the cooking and the housework and stay with Humphrey in the evenings? When Charles decided to remain, she had to admit that the only economically feasible course was for the whole family to stay together.

Leo was becoming increasingly worried about the world situation. If war came, it might be years before he saw his wife again. Suddenly, on August 26, he wired her that the *Queen of Bermuda* was under orders that made him decide to quit immediately; the ship had been recalled to England where it was to be used as a transport for war goods. The only 10th Street resident who had a steady income was now out of a job. The long unstable edifice was beginning to crumble.

Threats

Aᴛ the farm for a brief rest, the Woodfords worked on the theory book and completed the first chapter. Then Leo began to look for a job. His prospects were limited for, while he had applied for American citizenship, he would have to wait three years for his final papers. It was December before he found a position with the United Fruit Company on a ship carrying bananas from Cristobal in the Canal Zone and Puerto Barrios, Guatemala. Though demoted to third officer, he was relieved to have work.

For Doris, Christmas was especially busy with three concerts in the studio in addition to a teachers' course. Life seemed to consist of nothing but work. However, she admitted, it was hardly fair to complain "as I asked for it all, and must pay the price." She sent Humphrey's current report card to his grandmother:

> Even if the school can find no fault with him, his Mommie thinks there are a few flaws which have been overlooked. For instance, he doesn't like to play games with boys at all, and prefers playing house with the girls, announced that he had married two little girls last week. This seems to be much too much and I think I'll have to get them to encourage a tougher attitude, or shall we say more masculine.

Undoubtedly Doris's fears for her son were augmented by the predominantly feminine atmosphere of the dance world to which he was so much exposed, but she made efforts to counteract its influence. She had him earn money for skates by mopping and dusting the studio.

Leo was in Baltimore, where his ship was in dry dock for a week, and he urged her to come for a visit:

> Nobody would describe you as being a cheerful person ordinarily, but that is different from being cheerless which is how I would have described your attitude last Thursday. I know that you are indescribably harried and worried, also tired from the Christmas activities—but you have been all these things before without producing such a deadly chilled effect. Leave your affairs in what order you can and come out and spend a weekend with Doctor Woodford—or have I lost my healers degree? I don't have to tell you the directions in which my mind runs when you are like that.

She did go, and by the time she got back to New York, she was feeling much better and had gained some weight:

> Pumba was so impressed with this that she has taken over, so to speak, and leaves orders for Susan [the maid] to bring me breakfast in bed. The kind of breakfast the rich and glutonous have, including real cream. I am not deceived into thinking that she really cares so much about me—but I am her booking property, and like an entry for a cat show, must look as sleek as possible.

She continued to glow over her visit:

> I thought it was a heavenly change and rest, and such a joy to be with you. I am certain now that it can always be this way, but I know you doubt, when you come home and find me distracted and busy, that we can ever restore our true relationship —or *some*times you doubt. But I know it's all there still, and I hope you can live to believe it.

Prentice-Hall had given her an advance on the book, and she tried to encourage him to work on it: "There's so much to be done— and certainly work is the best filler-in for loneliness—although I have heard that riotous living has its points!" Then she set an example for him by relating how Eugene Loring's *The Great American Goof,* just premiered by Ballet Theatre, had stimulated her thinking on dance theory:

> My impression was of a wandering and pretentious piece about as dramatic as a day at the beach. "First I played a little with

a dame, and then I got hungry and had a hot dog, but this gave
me a stomach ache so I threw a sand ball for a while and then
I met a guy who thought the world needed reforming, so I
said 'I guess that's right.' " Curtain. (This is *not* the story!)
Maybe it's life but it isn't drama. The good points were the sets
—forms were thrown in colored lights on gauze pieces to sug-
gest the different scenes (there was one for riotous living). And
I must admit that the dialogue [by William Saroyan] was very
good—and disturbs me because it did not follow the rules I had
decided on for voice with action. The lines were natural in
language, they were said by the dancers, the sentences were
short, but included all the words required by grammar. At the
same time the dancing—or better rhythmic pantomime was
highly stylized. I do wish you could see it.

But the theory book had to be postponed as plans proceeded for
the next concert at the Guild. Mrs. Dorothy Luckie, whose daughter
was in the company, had offered to cover the deficit, and Doris was
thinking of Roy Harris to write the music for her new dance. Her
thoughts ran in the same, single direction all the time Leo was
ashore:

I realize, of course, that you were concerned about the whole
thing when I was at home—but even yet it is difficult for me
not to interpret your attitude personally—and you know what I
think then. Never will I understand that heart of yours which
carries your work with you all the time—sleeping and waking.
To me, it is a form of illness. Perhaps, considering that you are
incapable of separating yourself from it, it is just as well that I
am away most of the time. Looking back—it does seem significant that as soon as I left, you began putting on weight and
looking more blooming. It may be that the constant presence of
a lover is more of an embarrassment to you than the worth of it.
After all it does demand attention, even in such an unassuming
one as I. Of course you can't admit that, even to yourself—but
the physical evidence is quite convincing. Probably our friend
Pumba instinctively realizes this when she says that *I* am happy
at sea—meaning that *you* are better off with me there.

Doris replied: "As for my having my problems constantly on my
mind, this is just the way it is—and by this time I'm surprised that
you can be surprised about it." She had her complaints about him
too; but she didn't tell him, she told her mother that apart from his

single day in New York between trips, "I don't know I have a husband as he is never here to enter into any of the life or the problems."

She had stopped to see Mama-San, who looked bent and decrepit, when the company was on tour in the Middle West in March. For twenty-five years Julia Humphrey had managed the studio, and now Ethel was planning to close it. This would make little financial difference, but it left no outlet for useful activity. The visit was depressing for both of them.

On Easter Sunday this year, Doris took Humphrey to church to expose him to religion. Having none of her own, she could not bear to give him any instruction herself, nor did she want to impose any particular beliefs on him. Her idea was to let him see several services of different kinds so that he could make up his own mind. Apparently it did not occur to her that a boy of six was hardly ready to make up his mind about the relationship of God and man. Humphrey was unimpressed by the service.

In April Doris changed her insurance policy to get some extra cash. She needed it, for something was wrong. Several months before, she had fallen down a flight of stairs, apparently with no worse a result than taking the skin off both shins. Yet one of these had become infected, and now her left leg was giving her considerable pain. The doctor thought the condition might have been caused by the accident, but was not entirely sure what it was, nor did he know how to treat it. If Doris was seriously alarmed, she gave no indication of the fact, though she did admit concern about anything that interfered with her dancing. She had to dance.

However, she did not go to Bennington this summer. This was not her turn for a new production, and she felt that the teaching could be handled by members of the company with Pauline as accompanist. In early July she worked with Thomas Bouchard on a film of *Shakers*. Then she took Humphrey to the farm. Charles was there with a new friend and student, Charles Hamilton Wiesner. Renamed Peter Hamilton, he would join the company in the fall. And Hay came with her car, so it all began happily. Humphrey enjoyed the country. Charles was in fine form, and trying to train Hay to enter into the spirit of their Bohemian way of life. She, however, was still appalled at some of his jokes, and never entirely succeeded in covering her shock at his risqué stories.

As usual, Doris did her share of the cooking, and as usual, her efforts were not much appreciated. There was the day she baked a chocolate cake, remarkable for its texture—like hard rubber. Valiantly chewing, Charles and Hay looked at each other and started to laugh, a misdemeanor that made the cook order them to leave the table.

Probably her mind was elsewhere than on the stove, for the fall held exciting if somewhat frightening prospects. She and Charles had decided to move to a new studio at 108 West 16th Street, where they would have their own theatre. It was a dream she had cherished for years. The space, which had been used by the painter Winold Reiss, needed considerable remodeling, so they were worried about the costs. But wouldn't the Humphrey-Weidman Studio Theatre be worth it?

From Bennington Pauline sent questions: Had Mr. Reiss moved out of 16th Street yet? How was Charles getting on with his drinking? Was Peter Hamilton working? She was worried about Doris's walk and the twisting of her back, but "tell me about your new dance so I can start thinking about costumes." And two days later:

> Let me know the dimensions of the studio. Do you really think I do things badly and slipshod? I don't—I have "gifts"—the gods have been kind to give me the magic word—I'm really a witch—you're jealous because you're not a witch.

And three days later: Had Doris given notice to 18th Street? What about the wiring for the lights in the new theatre?

After the summer course in New York, Doris went up to Bennington to see the festival with the objective view of an outsider:

> [It] considerably strengthened my belief in myself, at the same time terrified me—for how shall I ever be able to carry on the modern dance alone? If this sounds egotistical to a fantastic degree, all I can say is—you should have seen it. It was thin, it was barren, it was boring. Even the critics who commonly rave were downright disappointed. I also saw some moving pictures of a good many different dancers, which depressed me further —although Charles & I were good. Can you think it's me say-

ing these things? Lincoln Kerstein [sic] gave a lecture in which he predicted doom for all of us—with a possible hope in joining an opera company. I would usually leap at his throat, but after the concerts I saw, I have an awful feeling he is right. And moreover that no opera company would have it either. It was all extremely stimulating and just what I needed—only I would like my vibrations stirred sometimes by going *with* instead of *against*.

Leo was home briefly but pleasantly. He was worried about Humphrey, though. Perhaps they should think about moving to a community where there were children and space for them to play; it was time for his son to start acquiring some toughness and endurance. Doris sent Humphrey to a beach in New Jersey, where Marga was now caring for a boy just about his age. Doris could not take care of Humphrey now. She had gone to the Hay Sanatorium in the Poconos.

Again, the diagnosis seemed to be that the condition resulted from an injury, possibly the fall on the stairs. The lower back was badly out of alignment and she must have osteopathic treatment. But after returning home she had little time to give to thoughts of her health. She was hearing glowing reports of José's summer at Mills College, and planned to take his new dance into the Humphrey-Weidman repertory. She had her own studio-theatre; she had a new choreographer. . . . Then a letter came from José:

> I want to tell you many things—chief of which the reason why I cannot continue our long and wonderful association.
> Truly I regret this—painfully—I really had planned to go on working with you until I dropped by the wayside—but I want to explain why this is no longer possible . . .

Doris already knew what he was going to say. There was no doubt of his sincere desire to remain with the woman who had made him into a dancer and was in the process of turning him into a choreographer. The trouble was with Charles, whose attentions to Peter had created such emotional tensions that José felt he could no longer work in the same company with them. The situation had finally erupted in a stormy scene. While Pauline tried persistently to talk the men into reconcilation, Doris despaired that the conflict could ever be resolved:

The psychological atmosphere is still highly charged, in fact the late "incident" will color relationships around here for the rest of our lives. Pauline grieves and grieves, and even beats herself for being a failure—a different note for her.

Fighter that she was, Doris was nearly felled by the blow. Characteristically, however, she drew on that tremendous store of determination that had seen her through previous crises:

> I, at first felt that the success of our project would be so uncertain that I'd better give it up—but we all know that no one person is indispensible, so I sent the deposit on the studio, & am continuing without knowing how I'm going to do it. I suppose you'll say, of course you'll do it, but our dancers are the vital part of our equipment, and it is possible to die in default of enough vitality in the cast.

Leo suggested that she consider abandoning the idea of having men in the company. And he reminded her of the presence of a further threat—the draft might get them anyway.

But *Song of the West* was choreographed to include men, and she had to go on with it. She thought it would be good when broken in and she liked Roy Harris's music—the center section for voice, flute, and piano was lovely.

For the time being, what was left of the family came back to 10th Street. It was miserable. In addition to having psychological problems—Doris said they were all living "on the edge of a volcano" —they were under rather worse than usual financial strain. Since the rent was considerably overdue, both the gas and electricity had been turned off. Until the bills were paid, they cooked on Sterno, used flashlights and candles, and plugged the iron and a radio into a light socket in the hall outside the apartment.

For the November tour, Doris left Humphrey with Charles's father, Grandpa Weidman. She spent Thanksgiving with her mother. Writing from Texas, she told her husband:

> I am feeling quite well, the road is easier than the New York life even though it is in fits and starts. There are some long mornings for sleep once in a while, and I am being conscientious about food. I have a thermos and lunch box outfit which is a

treasure when I have to stay late in the theatre before a performance. I do notice the hip more, dancing isn't good for it,
but it's no worse than last year.

This was her first mention in some time of her physical problem.
Perhaps she did not want to burden him with it. Or, equally possible, she was still managing to keep somewhat remote from it herself. There were so many other matters for her mind to dwell on . . .

With the help of Mrs. Luckie, who contributed $2,000 to the
enterprise, and of some other loyal supporters who took out "mem-
berships," the studio theatre was evolving into a nearly ideal setting
for the company. Doris had seen a newspaper advertisement an-
nouncing "theatre chairs at a bargain." They turned out to be up-
holstered ones from the Metropolitan Opera, which was being remodeled, and she bought 150 of them at seventy-five cents each.
"So our audience will have plush bottoms whether they are so
equipped or not!" But the renovations were extensive, and Doris
did much of the work—such as taking the shellac off the floors—
herself.

She was in a period of alternating moods of elation and despair.
The theatre would be beautiful. But *Song of the West* was not quite
right. And she had lost José. Hay tried to console her:

> Queer that he is the first person for whom I have heard you ex-
> press a need in words. Pumba said maybe that need was the
> reason why your new dance wasn't what you wanted. . . . You
> make José into a dancer and he fails you when you need him. I
> think he will be back. I don't believe ten years of friendship
> *can* end that way.

The first performance at the Studio Theatre took place the night
after Christmas, but Doris managed to have a tree for Humphrey,
and they all had dinner at the home of their friends Adele and Max
Brandwen. Hay's presents were a special delight, for they came in a
large box that, when untied, revealed numerous small parcels, each
marked with the time of day at which it should be opened.

The opening night audience was delighted with the appearance
of the Studio Theatre. While the building sat on a drab street next to
a Chinese laundry, red draperies warmed the foyer where the guests
entered. Tasteful displays of photographs, sculptures, and flowers

brightened the setting. The space widened as they passed into the auditorium which extended to the width occupied in the front by the laundry. Steep tiers of bleachers, holding the Metropolitan Opera chairs, had been raised above the floor, leaving a stage area some 25 by 50 feet. Folding gray screens served as wings while a blue curtain masked an ugly window at the back. Though the full complement of lighting equipment had not yet been installed, Pauline did wonders with what she had.

The critics were pleased with the opening season. Houses were good, filling the 150 seats every night. A few neighbors attended too—a good sign, for building new audiences was important. Charles's new dance, *On My Mother's Side,* was a hit. Still unsure, Doris postponed *Song of the West* until January, when she presented it in two sections: "The Green Land," a lyrical solo of joy in the earth, and "Desert," a tense group ceremonial of primitive worship of sun and space. One reviewer found the first part a remarkable tour de force; the second "brilliantly effective theatre . . . a thoughtful poem with many layers of implication."

For March, she planned a revival of *Life of the Bee,* partly a practical choice, since no male dancers were involved and the draft board seemed ready to pounce at any moment on the few she had left. Yet she was worried about *Bee:*

> [I am] trying to build it better than it was originally. These revivals are always chancy—they have been good so far, but I never take it for granted—what if a dance about Bees just seems too silly now? The whole point is to build up the choreography sufficiently so it will not matter what it is about.

Bee was a success on tour, but *Song of the West* was not:

> Cecil Smith on the [Chicago] Tribune said the Green Land looked alarmingly like early St. Denis (nasty) and the Desert had absurd headdresses & was monotonous. These are the moments that try the courage and determination more than others. . . . He went on & on about the Square Dances, it was gay, ingenious, beautifully costumed, retained the social character of folk dance, etc. Now I have to pick up the pieces and try to improve Song of the West—the most difficult thing one can do after a bad reception. There is too much evidence from everybody that I have not expressed what I intended in them.

(The following season she added another group dance, "Rivers," which Mr. Martin called "a most distinguished composition . . . it never loses a kind of majestic sense of the inscrutable dignity and timelessness of nature.")

While on tour Doris had seen her mother who, at seventy-five, was "just a little bundle of bones," but seemed healthy and proud of her endurance. Doris urged her to apply for an old-age pension and tried to keep her from feeling humiliated for having to depend on charity. At the same time, she sought to justify her own course of action, which she feared was at least partially responsible for her mother's condition:

> You were only unfortunate in having a husband who was a poor provider, and a daughter in a pioneer profession which is badly paid. I have asked myself many times whether this latter was justified and every time I come to the hard conclusion that I can do no other way. I have thought of getting a job in a college dance department, with no expenses of group, studio, advertising, etc., but I know that I would fail. It would probably mean moving from New York, which I could not do to Leo, and even if I did attempt it the atmosphere of tightness and amateurishness and pedagogy would drive me nuts in short order. I hope you will understand as you are the chief sufferer from such a situation.

On the home front, Humphrey had the measles. And the Woodfords were seriously thinking of moving. The 10th Street apartment was a shambles. The rugs had been taken up as too dirty and too expensive to clean; the furniture had been clawed by the cat. "Also we have come to the end of a cycle in our relationship to each other." Leo was urging that they try to get Humphrey away from the world of the arts and into contact with "working people who have to meet and overcome physical realities."

Doris had been reluctant to invite Humphrey's contemporaries to visit him on 10th Street, perhaps because she recalled the reactions of the "normal" families of her own classmates to the situation at the Palace Hotel. The living arrangements of the Humphrey-Weidman ménage were, to say the least, unconventional, and she may have feared that her son would be embarrassed in front of his friends by the presence of so many people in a single apartment.

Top left: Mother and son, winter 1933–1934; right: the Woodford family, ca. 1936. (Collection CHW.) Bottom: Son and mother, ca. 1935. (Photo by Martha Swope from original by Edward Moeller; collection NYPL.)

Top left: Charles Weidman, photoportrait by Marcus Blechman; right: Pauline Lawrence, unattributed photoportrait. (Photos by Martha Swope from the originals; collection NYPL.) Bottom left: Doris Humphrey at the Blairstown farm, ca. 1938; right: the three Woodfords at the Limón farm, ca. 1952. (Collection CHW.)

Humphrey, on the other hand, while aware that his home was different, enjoyed his large, informal family, and had formed happy friendships with his schoolmates in spite of his parents' fears.

Yet the move had to be considered carefully, since it would mean abandoning Pauline. In the years since her marriage, Doris had become simultaneously more needful of her and more antagonized by her. It was a relation of hostile dependency. Hay remarked at this time that Pauline was so careful of Doris's bodily wants and so careless of her emotional needs. Without Pauline, the tours would have collapsed, the studio classes would have been hopelessly disorganized. It was Pumba who made the arrangements, set up the schedules, kept the books, played the piano, designed the costumes and the lighting, saved the choreographer from any number of petty annoyances. Her cat had to be sleek for the show. But this meant prodding, and Pauline was by nature outspoken. She said what she thought whenever she felt like saying it, and often this was when Doris least felt like hearing it—even when she knew Pauline was right. Insensitive to Doris's moods, Pumba persisted with unasked-for advice about food and clothing and money and choreography. There were reminders here of "mother knows best," a problem Doris had encountered before and had no wish to have to cope with again. Yet Pauline loved her. As Hay remarked: "She would curse you with her last breath, but she would die for you and we all know it."

Now, however, life was changing. With the Studio Theatre at Doris's disposal, there would be less touring and less complicated schedules. Perhaps because she could see what was coming, Pauline became even more demanding. Torn between lingering loyalty and growing irritation, Doris hesitated while Leo tried to convince her:

> The tone of your letter is alarming—so tired—so fearful. If only I could get you somewhere where you could relax and renew yourself. I don't see, however, how you must abuse yourself for running away, as you call it, from an intolerable situation. If it were things or conditions it could be called cowardice—but to merely remove yourself from the everlasting presence of ill-nature and incompatibility is a social privilege. Furthermore— if the situation is sad, it is your duty to yourself and to us, your entire nature might easily crack and wreck us all. It seems to me that you have every reason to feel encouragement about your work. Isn't thirty-odd performances in New York a considerable

advance over three or four—Of course the Black Widow is more intolerable because of the "Decline and Fall" of the "Great Touring Business." The provincials can come to you now—if they need you so much, and let them come with gold, frankincense and myrrh. If they don't, it doesn't matter. You are not a travelling salesman. You're an artist.

Worries were taking precedence over other matters that Leo wanted them to be concerned about. He had hoped that they could get back to work on the theory book, but the cause was beginning to look hopeless. Doris was fretting over the prospect of the new dance she had to do for Bennington this year: "It hangs over me like a black cloud as I can't make up my mind what to do. The world situation continually urges me to make some sort of comment. Yet the whole thing is so vast that any statement seems silly."

With Leo, she had a brief vacation at the farm. He found it disappointing—there were too many people, they were never alone, and when they were, she was distracted by thoughts of the new dance: "I hope the problem of composition resolves itself, for you are too remote for my fancies when the creative itch is bothering you. It's all right when you settle down to construction, but the tentative stage is hard."

Yet new works had to be created. Even if it were not for a commission, like this one of Bennington's, Doris felt compelled to make dances, and the task inevitably held for her both joys and terrors. She once told an aspiring choreographer: "I feel sorry for you. You've bitten the apple and now your life will be hell. You'll be driven. It doesn't make any difference how many children you've had, you don't know what you're incubating this time—a beauty or a monster."

This particular incubation period was especially hard on her. Finally the theme was formed. It was to be a biography of the Humphrey-Weidman company from 1930 to 1940, the struggle of pioneer art in a world geared to profit: "We should be able to do that with feeling." Unfortunately, she did it with too much feeling. Painfully aware that the era had ended, she let an unusual tinge of sentimentality pervade *Decade*. It was a failure.

Though she carefully made no mention of it in her letters to her mother and her husband, Doris was increasingly troubled with the pain in her left leg. Hay drove her from Bennington to Albany to see Dr. Mildred E. Perkins, who reported that the X-rays showed a mild degree of arthritic roughening of the bone. She sent the patient an elastic bandage to wear pinned to a narrow elastic belt that would take some weight off the leg and protect the joint in action.

While she was working on *Decade* in Vermont, Doris left Humphrey at the Buck's Rock School in New Milford, Connecticut. Primarily, it was a camp for refugee English children, many of whom were seriously disturbed at having been ousted from their homes. Distracted by so many other concerns, Doris neglected to explain the situation to him, and he was miserable at first, though in time he came to like the camp. In September she sent him to the farm while she went to see her mother. The visit was not a success:

> What a pity that your generous gesture in coming so far to see me should seem to end in futility after all! I seem to have failed you at every point, even, or perhaps most of all, in establishing sympathetic understanding which I long for more than anything else in the world.

Yet on the occasion of her daughter's birthday, Mama-San assured her: "You have given me happiness and pleasure, comfort and pride from the moment I first saw you. . . ." But then they were separated.

At the end of September the Woodfords had moved to their new apartment at 145 East 22nd Street. They had two and a half rooms in a new building that faced a factory. The bedroom, which looked on a courtyard, was given to Humphrey, while his parents slept on a studio couch in the living room. Doris saw no cause for complaint, probably recalling that her own parents had slept for years on a Murphy bed. Leo was tremendously relieved:

> It's hard to define the exact feeling on finding my family, at last, in a place of our own. . . . I know that your burden is now doubled due to the evacuation of Pauline, though I feel that that will pay psychological dividends bye and bye. You will feel a freedom you have not felt in years. You will be a happier woman and a better artist for it. . . . It still has many problems. The one of Humphrey moving about alone in it is important, though as yet no solution suggests itself.

It was the beginning of a lonely time for the youngest Woodford. While his earlier mode of life had been unconventional, he had en-

joyed having so many friendly people about him. Now he was to
spend much of his time alone. Most often his father was at sea.
Coming home from school in the afternoons, he would find an empty
house, for his mother would be teaching or at a rehearsal. Sometimes
he went over to the studio where he would watch the activities
for a while, though in time they bored him.

Humphrey enjoyed being helpful himself when he could. At
the studio, when the scholarship students who usually assisted with
chores were occupied with classes, he would answer the phone and
take orders for concert tickets. For the third grade, Doris sent him to
the Dalton School, which meant a long bus trip to 89th Street each
day. He disliked it intensely, and the next year he went back to
Friends Seminary, which was just a short walk from the apartment.

While scholarships were always rather easily arranged for Humphrey's education, many expenses could not be cut. Leo urged his
wife that they would simply have to make out a strict budget and
stick to it. His minimum salary at the time was $166.75 a month,
and he figured that home expenses—rent, gas, electricity, food, and
necessities for Humphrey—could not come to much less than $130.
Out of the remainder of his salary, he had to pay about $20 into the
retirement plan and for such items as laundry, cigarettes, and toothpaste. They would have to do without a cook. In fact, they would
have to do without whatever they possibly could. Under the circumstances, though he understood Doris's need for the studio and for
productions and he wanted her to have them, he was alarmed at the
financial drain they were causing:

> Actually the desperate situation you are in is only just becom-
> ing evident to me now. I have not even grasped a complete pic-
> ture, but from time to time, and more frequently now, I hear of
> $100 here and $150 there. The whole must amount to a tidy sum.
> I think it imperative that one of us be kept solvent, for sweet
> credit's sake, in case of need.

The problem of Pauline, at least, was resolving itself. She set out for
California to see José, intimating that she might even marry him.
She did, on October 13, and Doris was relieved: "I'm sure they'll
both be happier."

They managed to arrange a November tour without Pumba. The performances went well, but Doris had forebodings: "I, personally am doing better, with more rest and more strength I can cope with my work. It is terrifying, though, to be unable to do the works, as at first, and to wonder if I have at last worn myself out beyond the point of rebound."

Yes, the tour was going well—in some respects. As usual in the years beyond the pioneering stage, the company met with critical acclaim from much of the press and appreciative applause from a small number of admirers, while financial failure continued to follow them. In the Dallas *Morning News,* John Rosenfield called attention to the "excellent group" and the audience's "enthusiastic response," but remarked that the box office had yielded not even one-sixth of the contractual fee. To say nothing of the physical hazards, for there was no floor cloth on the stage to protect the dancers' bare feet from splinters, and the lighting equipment was poor. The performance, he asserted, constituted a lesson in trouping.

Doris managed to see her mother in Chicago and Hay in Kansas City. The latter meeting was especially gratifying, for Doris had never—at least in her adult life—formed such an uncomplicated relationship with another woman. Hay had become her confidante and advisor, sparking her letters with bits of female wisdom and wry humor that must have helped Doris through some periods of intense anxiety.

It was Hay that she turned to in December when she suddenly discovered that she was pregnant. Should she go through with it? Probably Leo would like another child. As it was, however, she hardly had time for Humphrey. And there would be the added expenses. Yet abortions were illegal. What could she do? Wisely, Hay did not try to sway her decision, but she did offer advice on means of securing a safe abortion should Doris decide to have one. Leo was as supporting as he could be, though he felt helpless and frustrated:

> It is horrible and brutal for me to have to leave you to settle it alone, and to struggle through whatever the decision, also alone. I can only say that I am an unwilling victim. I do not happily escape, as many would . . . [but I am] entirely with you, whatever your actions, right or wrong.

She decided not to have the child.

So life and work went on. Doris had revised *Decade* and now felt that it was a success, though she soon dropped it from the repertory. But she had the pleasant diversion of playing a comedy role in Charles's take-off on silent movies, *Flickers.* She gave hilarious performances, both as the skinny pioneer woman, felling Indians right and left with a rake, and as Theda Bara, for whom she stuffed the arms and thighs of her costume to look voluptuous.

For Christmas, Hay gave a radio each to mother and son, while the former also got a subscription to *The New Yorker.* Like many Americans, Doris was suffering from the wartime shortage of cigarettes, and Hay could not bear to see her in want. She wrote to the company that manufactured Parliaments, explaining that there was this great artist who liked their brand and needed them desperately. They agreed to send her a carton every ten days.

The war was having more serious effects on Leo. The United Fruit Company now made its headquarters in New Orleans, so that when he was in the country at all he had to be either there or at Mobile, Alabama. Because of the censorship, he destroyed Doris's letters in preference to having them confiscated. In March he found time for a trip to New York, traveling all the way from New Orleans on day coach. He arrived in time to see her dance the Matriarch in *With My Red Fires:*

> I'm afraid that I was so overwhelmed by your performance in the murder that for the rest of the evening I was unreceptive— numbed—or shall we say, just plain scared. Of course, I am not obliged to accept you in your characteristic role, but I usually do. My living with you makes me perfectly aware that you have a drop of everything—saint and sinner—God and Demon. But, to see one of the less acceptable elements brought out, exaggerated, dramatised, given all the trappings of authenticity and performed with such power and vigor, is, to say the least of it, overpowering. Yet the character is not by any means repulsive. Quite the opposite. The body under that beautiful vicious face is full of fire and grace, serpentine in its fascination—vulgar yet hypnotic.

Performing had begun to pose a problem for her, and he went on to discuss it:

I see no reason for a direct answer to your question as to whether you should give up the solo—the truth is that you will probably slowly ease yourself out of it, as they become more difficult. You are an intelligent woman, quite conscious of yourself. You are in no danger of being a "Radha" [Miss Ruth's first role and one that she danced for decades] to the end of time. You grow out of one thing and into another with the fluency of a river flowing towards its inevitable fusion wtih the sea. Still, you are yet beautiful in your own right, & as a dancer, able to perform with great dignity and authority. It would be a loss to break away from the dance proper. Even after you reach the point of being unable to perform certain technical feats through sheer physical inability, it would still be a loss if you took yourself away as the unifying element in the group—for the authority is still there—the pure animal quality of group leadership.

Leo's visit was followed by Humphrey's spring vacation, which gave Doris another problem. What to do with him all day? When they just kept one another company at breakfast and dinner, she could "manage to give him a fairly stable feeling of having security and affection in his home." But she was simply not equipped to cope with vacations.

Pauline provided news and observations from San Francisco. The draft board had classified José as 1–A, but they were trying for a deferment:

He mustn't go to war—he is needed with the living. If he is drafted, I will tear down the country to get him in entertainment or teaching Spanish, etc. . . .

I am a wonderful help to José—I think this is the best thing that ever happened to me and José too. I am really completely happy now—though I miss you all terribly—but I bet you are glad I'm not there. Is that true Doris? What's more I think perhaps he loves me. I'm not sure but I rather think so.

Doris responded with news of the studio and the company, on which Pumba could not resist commenting: if they got a new manager, they must have a guarantee; they needed new tour routes; they should commit themselves to nothing without consulting a lawyer— or Pumba. Would Doris care to explain the new dance so she could send costume sketches? José was safely doing camp shows, and the draft board really wanted to change his status. They were "impressed by José as a man and as an artist, and even out here they don't come as good to look at." He was soon reclassified as 3–A, which allowed him to perform for servicemen. He was giving concerts with May O'Donnell, a former soloist with the Martha Graham company, and her musician husband Ray Green. Did Doris want Pauline to get what dates she could for the tour? Pumba would gladly do whatever she could as long as she could stay with José:

> [We] get along just beautifully. Why didn't you help me to get him long ago? I am the one for him, there is no doubt. . . . I must wait here with him—he needs me and you can surely wait till August. I have been with you for so long and did my best every minute of the time though you didn't always like it.

Doris mentioned that, since Bennington had not offered her a production this summer, she had decided not to go there at all. (Actually, the Bennington School of Dance closed this summer because of the war and did not reopen.) Pauline was quick with suggestions —how about a summer course? "If you need me, I'll come right away." Of course José needed her too, for the enrollment at his studio was not good. However, she was wary of overstepping: "I shall have to take a hand soon, but how shall I do that? He will start to hate me as you and C[harles] W[eidman] did. I shall have to be very careful for which I'm not suited."

The next letter from New York was interpreted as a cry for help: "I've decided that you may not really *want* me, but I think you need me." Next season's tour had to be planned at once. At this point, it would be terribly hard for Doris to break in someone else. Maybe Pauline could help with the April repertory season too. For the bookings, she thought they should offer *Shakers,* a solo each by Doris and Charles, and Charles's *Flickers.* She concluded: "If you don't want me to come, wire at once." Two weeks later, she was back in New York.

The two women still needed one another, and some—though not all—of the tension in their relationship had been eased by Pauline's marriage, which gave her another human being to protect and defend and promote. Leo wondered if the Black Widow was turning into a White Butterfly.

He called Doris from New Orleans, but she could not come to

the phone. He tried to understand that she could not leave a rehearsal, but admitted that he was deeply hurt. Yet, much as he resented her absorption in art, he could not encourage her to give it up—even when times were blackest:

> The problem of the boys and the draft is, of course, insuperable. I see that there is no repertory and no time to build one—and it would be impossible to support that studio without one. . . . I don't envy you the problem—no[r] the alternative which is to close down for the duration. I can't even bear thinking about that myself. For strange as it may seem to you I sympathise entirely with you in your terror of a life of just sitting waiting for me to come home—That is unthinkable. The tragedy of it, though! and the ever present threat of destruction—that's what must hurt. . . . The years and years of patient building threatened. But you are a fighter, if ever there was one and I know you'll come up before you're counted out. Think of all the times before when it looked as if the end of the world was coming, and yet you managed to survive.

Then he announced that he would be away for a long time; Doris might as well plan on a vacation without him. She heard practically nothing from him till a cable came in September, telling her he was in England.

Both Hay and Pauline had kept Doris company in New York that summer while José taught in Greeley. A Greenwich Village apartment was waiting for him when he got back in the fall. Then Olga Frye, the good friend from Denishawn days, came to help Doris with the studio, as Pauline was gradually easing herself—also being eased—out of the Humphrey-Weidman picture. Now that she had José—her Eagle, as Hay called him—this was not difficult. But Hay was perceptively aware of both sides of the conflict:

> I have wondered if for much of the twenty years [of your knowing Pauline] she has found your disinclination to share emotions (except in movement) as unbearable as it was for me so many times this summer. Could be that she has had to develope [sic] an immunity against such pain. Thats what has to happen to people and perhaps it happened to Pumba. Of all the worshippers at the feet of God she is the only one who does not stand in awe of you, nor say Dear God, gimme. And you want her approval. Interesting?

Humphrey had spent a happy summer on the farm—his last. The family relationships had altered and there was no point in trying to restore them; they all knew the effort would be futile. Only memories were left. . . . There was the birthday party when Pauline had called Humphrey out to look at a bush in the garden. Its boughs were full of marshmallows which she said had grown there overnight. There was the evening that Charles served dinner in the style of a Chinese dancer, and everyone laughed and laughed. There was the time they had all spent hours picking fruit in the orchard because Charles had obtained a large vat at an auction and they were going to make apple butter. They spent a lot of time preparing it; then sat down to enjoy their feast. But all their effort had been wasted, for the vat had been used for making soap.

They had been fun summers. They were over.

At the end of October, Charles took the company out on tour while Doris kept the school going in New York. The choice was her own and was probably related to her health, though she was also concerned about leaving Humphrey alone, especially now that his father was away for such a long time. She did want to be a good mother and was not beyond seeking advice on how to go about it. Someone referred her to a Dr. George W. Crane, who wrote her a nasty letter from his office in Chicago:

> Whether or not you give up your studio work means very little to anybody else in the world except yourself, but it will mean a great deal to your son, and possibly his wife and children if you were to give up your studio work and really resolve to become a normal mother and try to bring your youngster up in a normal home environment. . . . I would frankly call you a maladjusted woman, and base my diagnosis on the very fact that you are hanging on to this dance studio in contrast to doing something fundamentally necessary and vital in the world, such as rearing a good son.

He enclosed his "Test for Mothers." Dutifully, Doris took the test and gave herself a rating of "superior."

Leo got home in time for Thanksgiving dinner at the Limóns, for yes, as Hay had predicted, José was back. Then Leo was off again, and Doris returned to her routine. Would you, she asked her mother, like to know what I do on a typical day? Let's say Friday:

Humphrey calls me at 7^{30}—After a year without anyone to help
me with the first event of the day, I am not used to it, and I still
pull myself together with great difficulty. He gets dressed, I
get breakfast, we have it in the kitchen and usually play the
radio, sometimes he has a poem to go over or other homework. I
look over the arithmetic (the cycle repeats itself) and help with
spelling etc. This child never has to be driven to hurry to school
for he is the one who always wants to be a half hour early for
everything. . . . After this I have some coffee (when I can get
it) [coffee was rationed]. I'm not hungry yet, and play one program on the radio which is amusing and requires no concentration. Then, if I am particularly tired I sometimes sleep another
hour. This Friday, however, I did the housework, made beds,
washed dishes and made out the grocery order. Then I dress,
which always bores me, as I still think the female has to bother
far too much in order to be presentable. Oh yes, and feed my
kitty Butchka. . . . Then I take the grocery order to the corner
store and go in the A & P for a pound of meat for Baby [also a
cat] who now lives at the studio. . . . By this time it's about ten-
thirty and I have some breakfast in a coffee shop on Third Ave.,
as I hate cooking for myself. Then I buy a N.Y. Post to see what
my favorite columnist [Samuel Grafton] has to say about the
war, and also to take a look at the daily puzzle. . . . I hop on a
crosstown bus, transfer to another and arrive at the studio at
eleven. I depend on scholarship help in the office during the
day, and sometimes there is no one there to answer telephone,
etc., so I do that, and look over the mail, write notes to various
people as to answering it, also notes about lots of little things,
repair this, see to that, buy a money order (I do not have a
checking account), telephone so and so about so and so. . . . Next
I light the gas radiators which I put in this year as the steam
ones do not keep the place warm, also fill them with water. Friday the man who has been repairing the floor came in to get the
o.k. on his job and collect his money. People like that are usually very nice, they invariably take an interest beyond their jobs
—delivery boys, baggage men, repair people of all kinds, stand
and gape at the classes dancing, and go out with a new look on
their faces and frequently come back to see a concert. At twelve
o'clock José comes in for a rehearsal. We're working on an all
Bach program, he's doing the famous Chaconne as a solo. Very
good indeed it is too, also he is opposite me in the Passacaglia
and some Choral Preludes. This plan was all made when
Charles was called in the draft, but it was this very Friday
when Charles called me to say that he had finally been rejected.

. . . I worked that day on José on his various numbers, we get on very well, he thinks I'm wonderful and likewise. By now it is three o'clock, and I have some lunch, usually alone and not enough either as I'm bored with all the places around there. At four o'clock I have a class, four to six—the advanced students, many from the company. I never enter a class with anything but reluctance, but usually am interested before it is over. Friday night was my turn at N.Y.U. That is a class taken by one of my assistants. I go over every third lesson, 6^{15} to 7^{45}. That really does give me a pain, mostly because of the horrible gymnasium it's in. Then I grabbed another bite in a coffee shop and returned to the studio for a rehearsal. Olga was there before I left and has now a stack of notes for me—what about this and that. In the meantime she has very kindly gone over to keep Humphrey company for dinner, although she really does enjoy him as companion, it's a favor too. I work on the G-major Partita, Bach, which is a part of the new program and is coming along nicely. This is where I really enjoy myself for the first time all day, it's a group. I also have a part. Near the end of this, a woman comes in to make arrangements about a children's class, then I answer Olga's notes—close up the studio and go home in a taxi in a state of exhaustion about eleven-thirty. Next morning the sweetest voice in the world says, Time to get up Mommie, it's 7^{30}.

With the Bach program Doris had not, after all, tried to comment on the war-torn world. "Now is the time," she said, "for me to tell of the nobility that the human spirit is capable of." The *Passacaglia* was her supreme statement of this conviction, but the program was not limited to high seriousness, for it included the courtly playful *Partita* with its gentle air of balletic delicacy and grace. The *Dance Observer* critic was delighted by *Partita's* "sweet formality" and "sure sense of style." Mr. Martin, however, reverted to his earlier reservations about choreographing Bach. The music was, he insisted, "not suitable for theatre presentation"; it was too self-contained, tending to dominate in feeling and in form. The idea of the modern dance, he reminded his readers, was to "make its own forms out of motor impulses." The music of Bach limited this essential freedom.

Some other reviews were no more favorable, with José's *Chaconne* (later recognized as one of his finest works) coming in for a good share of the beating.

It was a blow to him, and Hay feared that Pauline would blame Doris for his failure. Pumba was passionately protective of her husband's career—far more than she had been of Doris's. Now the draft board was threatening José again, which gave her further cause to be defensive. But Hay had to admit her admiration for Pauline: "I've seen her take things that are lots harder to bear than that and take them heroically."

Of course Doris mentioned nothing of these personal problems to her mother, nor did she say anything about her health unless it explained some lapse in activity. She sent a birthday gift with apologies for its lack of originality, "but I've been flat on my back this week with bronchitis, haven't been able to go out and do things. The weekly concert had to be postponed, which was a disgrace. I haven't missed anything like that for years."

The hip was getting steadily worse, and though she was still performing, Doris must have realized by now that her career as a dancer must soon come to an end. She tried to cover up, speaking to no one about the pain. But she could not hide the growing disability that had begun to make certain movements almost impossible for her, and once in rehearsal she fell several times, letting Pauline bawl her out rather than admitting that physically she simply could not do the step. Then one day she astonished Charles by looking about her studio-theatre—the fulfillment of a dream, realized at such great cost of money and labor and time and dedication—and crying out hysterically: "I've done all this—for someone else!" It was the only time he ever saw her out of control.

Doris was forty-seven. But then Martha Graham was still going strong at forty-nine. And look at Miss Ruth at sixty-some. As she fought any threat to her plans, Doris fought this one—fought it valiantly if, perhaps, unrealistically.

Then another blow: in April, José was drafted. What a joy it had been to have him back; now he was leaving again. Yet Doris was not alone in her regret, for José was keenly aware of the loss he was about to suffer:

> For the moment I want to tell you how profoundly grateful I am to you for the experience of the last four months. I believe nothing so far has given me greater satisfaction and a sense of realization—of having functioned fully—as far as my limitations

would permit. And if this perhaps proves to be the last dancing I shall ever do, I shall be well content in having done it with you—whom I have always admired & looked up to as a great source of inspiration—and as one of the great tremendous humans alive.

Mama-San came to visit in August and September, though her daughter had extended the invitation with reservations, since Olga had taken a defense job, leaving Doris to manage the studio alone, ". . . and the mama of the studio, like any parent, is always on call for emergencies [but] I think we could have a good visit in between." In the end, Doris felt that the time had been none too pleasant for her mother, who insisted, nevertheless, that she had enjoyed it:

> . . . my only regret in those last days in New York was that my prolonged stay made the situation more difficult and more expensive for you.
> I think the main trouble is that you are the centre around which we all revolve. All that love and devotion, precious as it is, creates bonds which sometimes become chains instead of leaving you free as the truest, most understanding love should always do.

Doris was not unaware of the trouble, and she was trying. Hay remarked: "I've heard you say you would like to do better with human relationships." But it was hard.

Back at home in the fall, Julia was happy to find that her old studio had been taken over by one Betsy Ross, who was in need of an office manager and willing to hire an older woman. Mama-San could hardly wait to get back to work: "It's a little like being raised from the dead and I begin to feel the stirrings of the old war horse within me." The pay was minimal, but that didn't matter; the important thing was to be useful.

In October, the Woodfords moved to 132 East 16th Street. Surrounded by high buildings, the apartment was dark most of the time, and the Third Avenue "El" rumbled through the night. But it had a fireplace, louvred doors, huge casement windows, and a terrace. Doris planted some window boxes and Humphrey had a victory garden. Fortunately, she liked simplicity, for she could not spare the time to work on the appearance of the apartment; her physical environment was never very important to her. She had some pictures that could have decorated the walls, but she kept them in a drawer, hanging only a portrait of her favorite composer, Bach. In the maidless periods, of which there were many, Humphrey did some occasional cleaning.

The new apartment was close to her son's school and an easy bus ride from her studio. Still she seldom got back to it during the day. When he returned home in the afternoons, Humphrey frequently roller-skated over to the studio for lack of anything better to do. If he did go home, he frequently found a note from his mother, asking him to meet her at a particular restaurant for dinner— meaning that she had no time to cook because she could spare only an hour from the studio. When she did get home to make dinner for her son, Doris usually had to take a nap first. She always, somehow, managed to arrange for a nourishing meal for him, even though she would settle for a milkshake, coffee, and a cigarette for herself. Leo was away for long stretches of time now because the United Fruit Company was taking goods to Europe. They hardly ever saw him.

Doris did her best to be a companion to Humphrey. One Easter they took an excursion to Long Island because she knew the boy liked trains and trips to the country. He enjoyed the outing even though it was so cold that all they did at their destination was eat sandwiches by the pot-bellied stove in the station. Then there was the traffic game which Doris invented. It went like this: When you walk out of the house, you decide whether you should turn left or right. If the light on the corner is green, you go straight ahead; if it is red, you turn in whatever direction has been decided on. If you come to a bus stop and the bus is there, you get on and ride for exactly twenty-one stops and then get off. Mother and son saw quite a lot of New York this way.

In the winter, Doris choreographed a new dance. *Inquest* was a work of indignation and protest, born of her horror of man's injustices to man. She based it on a chapter in Ruskin's *Sesame and Lilies,* which contained a coroner's report on the death from starvation of a poor "translator" of boots whose wife resold his pitiful handiwork for whatever she could get. Doris told her composer Norman Lloyd: "In a time like this, when millions are dying, all you can concentrate on is the individual." The one man, the cobbler, personified humanity.

The story was told by a narrator reading the newspaper report of 1865. Simultaneously the scenes were acted out by the protagonists in a small, lighted upstage area like a room. At times the illumination shifted to reveal crowds, in an open space like the neighborhood streets, reacting to the events in the home. The story told, the characters reiterated the tragedy, this time more lyrically, with larger movements giving their passion a heightened dimension. Edwin Denby remarked on the striking portrayal of the dignity of a devoted family: "The piece has pointed out that poverty destroys humane values we all believe in. We applaud it as a sincere and eloquent sermon on the theme of the freedom from want." However, he felt that though the work appealed to the moral sensibility, its aesthetic value was secondary.

Nevertheless, *Inquest,* both for its choreography and for Doris's performance as the wife, drew large audiences to the Studio Theatre. "I think the sweetest three words in the language are 'Standing Room Only' except maybe 'I love you.' "

The elation did not last long. There was no use fighting any longer; the struggle to continue performing was futile. The pain she could—and did—endure, but now all the will and determination she could muster were not enough to make her body respond to her demands. "Steel and velvet" they had called her; radiant "with the ecstasy of the pure dance."

A performance of *Inquest* at Swarthmore College on May 26 marked Doris Humphrey's last appearance on the stage.

In the Face of Misfortune

D ORIS wrote all kinds of notes on the back of old grocery lists. One of these was a quotation from Katherine Anne Porter's introduction to *Flowering Judas:* "In the face of misfortune, the artist cannot be destroyed." * It was a motto Doris was intent to prove. Though she could no longer perform, she could choreograph, she could direct; her mature creative powers were at a peak. Why should a mere physical handicap stop her?

Burl Ives and Alfred Drake were to star in a new folk-musical documentary on the growth of America, and Laurence Langner asked Doris and Charles to do the choreography for the Theatre Guild production. Sensing that this might not be just another Broadway show, but a piece with some genuine integrity, she accepted. She also anticipated that the royalties called for in her contract might well support the Studio Theatre for another season.

In July she sent Humphrey to camp in Maine, while she went with Hay to North Carolina where Black Mountain College was holding a special dance seminar, and from there to Providence for a brief vacation with friends. Doris was grateful for Hay's companionship: "You slowed me down so I could hear the soft purring noise of other people's motors a little."

She really needed Hay, though the latter frequently wondered

---

* She did not quote quite accurately. The introduction, written for the 1940 Modern Library edition of *Flowering Judas and Other Stories,* makes the statement within the context of a much longer sentence and asserts that it is the arts, not the artist, that cannot be destroyed.

why. At first she had been afraid of boring Doris, whose fine mind and sensitivity seemed to overmatch her own. Sometimes it seemed that Doris wanted Hay around just to talk with Leo or Pauline or anyone else who might otherwise distract the artist from her thoughts. Hay also learned that Doris could turn off, could "be where she was," whenever she wanted to do so, simply by shutting off the other person when the effort of sociability became too much for her to handle. In the beginning Hay had been hurt by this, and Pauline had caustically remarked: "If you don't like it here, you can leave. Doris wouldn't care." But Doris did care. In her fashion, she loved Hay as much as she needed her. With all the constant strain of professional questions and decisions, it was good to have this calm, sustaining, personal, sympathetic presence.

When Humphrey's camp closed for the season, Pauline looked after him. She had made a cheery and charming home of a one-room walk-up apartment on East 13th Street, which she had decorated in black and yellow, with a prominently placed picture by José's favorite painter, El Greco. She wanted her Eagle to be content; she would take good care of him when he got home.

Humphrey was back with the Limóns in November when his mother went to Boston for the tryout engagement of *Sing Out, Sweet Land.* It looked as if the show would be a success in spite of Pumba's characteristic forebodings: "I hope you are getting more pleased . . . but you really knew it wasn't so hot, didn't you?" She was enjoying Humphrey and, as usual, she had plans:

> He should be starting music now—if you send money I will rent a piano. He needs a raincoat, please send money for this.
> . . . How about letting me have a slipcover made for the red chair and couch?

Then Humphrey would need Christmas money. Pumba also announced the formation of Limón Productions, with herself as executive manager.

Contrary to her expectations, *Sing Out, Sweet Land* was a hit and, as far as Doris was concerned, for all the right reasons. A reviewer commented: "When the songs are good the entertainment is excellent, and when the dancers are on stage it is well nigh brilliant. More credit, we suspect, should go to Leonidoff who staged the production, to choreographers Humphrey and Weidman . . . to the dancers themselves than to the author." The welcome royalties provided maintenance for her mother, who was now in a nursing home, and were a comfort to Doris at a time that was otherwise bleak. Now that she could no longer perform, the atmosphere of the Studio Theatre depressed her; it felt like an empty shell, and she turned it over to Charles who formed his own school and company there. José was still in the army, and though he asked Doris for guidance on a concert he gave with Dorothy Bird and Beatrice Seckler during his furlough in May, he was simply not there enough for her to nurture and shape him into the fine choreographer he was on the brink of becoming. Teaching composition classes at the Y was small compensation for the tremendous losses Doris had suffered.

In October, Mama-San died and Doris went to Chicago to attend to the funeral arrangements. Julia Wells Humphrey was seventy-nine years old and had worked until nearly the end of her life. She had not seen her only child for two years.

For Doris, the year 1945 was devoid of artistic achievement. Since *Sing Out, Sweet Land,* she had choreographed nothing. The arthritis in her hip had worsened so much that she was walking only with a painful limp (friends remember it as an "heroic" limp) and was embarrassed to be seen. No attempt to relieve the condition seémed to help. Leo gave her massage and carrot juice and doses of vitamin D. She tried a number of doctors who offered X-rays and physical therapy, but she had no patience with any of them and never managed to stick out the full course of treatments. Resentful of the time consumed by visits to doctors' offices, she sought some kind of miracle cure that would take effect overnight, a cure that, of course, she never found. Frustration generated despair, and she withdrew more and more into herself. Apart from the sporadic attempts to relieve the arthritic condition, she showed no concern for her physical well-being. Lunch was still a milkshake and coffee, followed by more coffee and a cigarette. When Leo was home, he cooked for her, but when she was alone she ate out, hurriedly and in any nearby coffee shop, or not at all. If she were to survive, her life would have to take on a new purpose, a new direction. Obviously, she could not find it apart from dance. But how, under the circumstances, could she find it in dance?

It took Pauline—coaxing, cajoling, promising, threatening—to force her out of her seclusion. There was a means of salvation open to her; it was José. Soon he would be back in civilian life, ready to resume his work with her. What a magnificent instrument he was—strong, handsome, tall, equipped with the splendid technique she had given him, perceptive, sensitive, attuned to her way of thinking. She should choreograph for José.

If Doris hesitated, she had reason to do so. Though she was unusual in that she could—and most often did—compose mentally, she had still communicated her intentions to her dancers by demonstrating—she wanted a run in this direction, then a slow fall with the body like this, then a recovery at this speed with the arms moving thus and so. Now she could not show them. Could she tell them in words? Unlike the ballet, which had established steps and a verbal language to describe them, the modern dance had no vocabulary. And, apart from a few basic Humphrey forms, she wanted to evolve fresh movements to suit the dramatic needs of each new dance. How—without moving herself—could she describe the specifics of the movement she wanted?

Pauline had the answer: All Doris need provide for José was a verbal hint, a rhythmic pattern, a shape indicated by the arm—he would understand. Through him, Doris could not only live again as an artist, she could continue to grow.

In December José got out of the army, and Doris offered him a present. The present was a dance.

It worked; from the very beginning it worked. He seized immediately on what she gave him, translating her words and the gestures of her hands into dance. She gave him a mood, a rhythm, a spatial design—and saw the movement materialize before her eyes. Sometimes only a partial indication set his own imagination on fire, and he would fill in the outline with a larger gesture, with a turn or a fall. She saw the potential; encouraged it and shaped it.

As a fitting theme for José's new dance Doris selected a poem of Federico García Lorca, his "Lament for Ignacio Sánchez Mejías." The idea came from a close friend, Elizabeth Dooley, a dramatist

Inquest, 1944; Charles Weidman, Doris Humphrey. (Collection José Limón.)

Chorale Preludes, 1942; José Limón, Doris Humphrey. (Photo by Marcus Blechman; collection José Limón.) Bottom: *Lament for Ignacio Sánchez Mejías,* 1946; Letitia Ide, José Limón. (Photo by Martha Swope from unattributed original; collection NYPL.)

who had acted with the Provincetown Players before she turned to writing and who was an ardent admirer of the Humphrey-Weidman company. Doris was moved by the poem and decided to enlarge on the experiment of *Inquest,* combining dance movement with a spoken text, a form that had long fascinated her with the problem of matching degrees of stylization and the challenge of finding movement to enhance verbal meaning while it avoided literal duplication of that meaning in gesture. And the role of the bullfighter who enters the ring "with all his death upon his shoulders"—magnificent for José. Yet he tended to move instinctively, like a beautiful animal but without the probing for motivation that the creation of such a character required. Doris analyzed everything with him: "Now you are listening, now you hear the bull bellow, now you hear the trumpet, now you have a feeling of strangulation. What does it mean when you pull up your shoulder? How does it make you feel?"

The experience opened the vista of a new kind of fulfillment for Doris. At the same time, it changed José. It marked the beginning, not only of his true greatness as a dancer, but also of his real development as a choreographer, for his own works took on a new beauty and power nurtured by dramatic imagination. The development was a source of pride and happiness to Doris, who emerged from her isolation and depression, freshly awakened to the joys of choreography. Pauline was right; José was her salvation.

Margaret Lloyd came up to Bennington for the premiere of *Lament,* and Doris sent her review in the *Christian Science Monitor* to Hay:

> Maggie kyed and kyed [Hay's expression] all over the floor— you couldn't ask for more than that as a tribute, but then she follows with some very choice words on paper too. I haven't the faintest shame about reviews, I like them to like me. By the way, please return, as usual I have no others. My family is hardly flattering in these matters. When I said "I have two reviews," they said, "oh, have you?" So when somebody writes to say, "do send me reviews," I can hardly wait.

She was deservedly proud of this review, for Miss Lloyd was quite ecstatic:

> . . . Miss Humphrey lifts the subject into the realm of exalted tragedy, purifying and ennobling the personal theme into a

thing of universal implications. . . . There are arresting passages that startle one into sudden awareness of the extraordinary technique involved—Ignacio literally standing on his head while executing strange rotary motions with his legs. There are passages of symbolical significance—Ignacio pulsing with life under the red mantle wrapped around his face and body like a winding sheet—the Figure of Destiny's play with the blue-green rope. And there are passages that take one's breath away in which all is forgotten but the spiritual experience. And, indeed, that is the paramount experience of the whole.

The second Bennington premiere showed Doris in a mood she had not indulged since her Thurber venture of eight years before— satire. Based on a *New Yorker* cartoon series by Carl Rose, *The Story of Mankind* hit at the stupidities of civilization, with woman always pushing her sluggish mate toward her ideal of refinement. The couple persisted through history: from caveman to Greek, from medieval castle to modern penthouse. Then, as a news sheet announced "atom split!" the protagonists prudently retreated back to their place of origin. Pauline devised some most ingenious costumes, simple leotards topped with various accouterments to indicate period—a classical tunic (draped wrong), a jacket of monkey fur (the same piece used previously to represent a tent). "Simple horseplay," remarked one reviewer, failing to notice the didactic point.

Doris enjoyed doing *Mankind* but José did not:

> Of course I like it, or I wouldn't have chosen to do it, but comedy is something he endures. This particular piece has a bitter message which sweetens it for him, but even so! He reminds me of Gustave Mahler who is said never to have had a trivial moment. Certainly José is not stuffy like that, and certainly he has a lusty, if not Rabelaisian sense of humor. But to him that is something for relaxation over a glass of beer, and a man's work must be a profound expression of his immortal soul. We just happen to differ on a little point like that. For my part I am pleased with both the dances and he does them both magnificently. Having accomplished these two works has given me a happier feeling than I've had in a long time. Not composing was very hard on me.

Pleased as she was with the Limón company, Doris could not help feeling resentful of the tremendous success of the Ballet Russe, which she was taken to see on her birthday. She admired Alicia Markova and "passively observed the acrobatic skill of the rest of the Russians from Brooklyn." Meanwhile, she sighed, "we go on, in our naive way, opening a tiny crack with a mountain of effort." José had taken his group out on tour, and there were all kinds of last-minute crises that made Pauline swear she would never book out of town again:

> Pumba chews off her finger-nails, sure that it can't be done, and she's poised to cancel the tour and ruin her reputation. . . . José is dauntless in a crisis, unrealistic, she thinks, but he holds firm, and with my help, they kept all their dates and are on their feet.

A New York concert was planned for January:

> . . . a big venture, but essential. The whole situation demands a performance in a theatre acceptable to the rigid zoning of the metropolitan press, so the critics can legitimately review it. The New York review is a piece of merchandise which unfortunately makes all the difference between getting on and not getting on.

So involved was Doris with the challenges of the Limón company and so gratified by their resolutions, that—despite Hay's persistent questioning—any mention of her health was relegated to the very end of a letter. Her friend Eleanor Frampton had offered to assume the expense of some new treatments and perhaps, she told Hay, there would be good news to report on that soon. There was none.

Doris began toying with the idea of semiretirement, considering a move to the suburbs where she knew Humphrey would enjoy the outdoor life. But she soon realized that unless her retirement was complete the idea could not work, since, as long as she was at all involved with dance, she had to attend rehearsals and performances in the city and the trip was much too wearing for her to make very often. Certainly a total break with her art was inconceivable. Much as Doris wanted happiness for her family, she was aware that as a frustrated housewife she would have little to contribute to their contentment. So the Woodfords stayed in New York and she did the best she could for her son. If she could help little on the social side, she could offer assistance with homework. She did this in the evenings whenever possible, but usually it was at breakfast that she drilled him in French vocabulary and suggested endings for his essays. She had said: "A good ending is forty percent of the dance"; she was a master of apt conclusions.

But there was so much for her to do in those rare hours that she spent at home. She prepared for rehearsals there, playing the music for a new dance over and over on the phonograph, counting out the beats, making notes on phrasing, floor plans, movements. Accustomed to planning mentally, she never wasted her dancers' time by working through her problems with them; she had already solved them in the living room.

She also sewed, frequently making torn sheets over into pillow cases with a frugality derived from her New England ancestors. She mended Humphrey's clothes and did all their laundry by hand, using a washboard in the bathtub. She seemed to enjoy it—probably because she was planning dances while she scrubbed.

Early in 1947, Laurence Langner announced the Theatre Guild's sponsorship of a contest for ideas of "ballet-plays," productions that would combine dancing and speech. Since Doris was already intrigued by this idea, she accepted Langner's proposal that she assist him with the preliminary reading of the manuscripts, taking over the Studio Theatre for her work (though it hardly required that kind of space) while Charles found other quarters uptown. After several months of careful consideration, Doris turned in her choices along with an entry of her own based on the James Thurber–E. B. White book *Is Sex Necessary?* and waited for the Guild to proceed. She was awarded the prize of $500 for an imaginative script that presented the text in the form of an illustrated lecture using alternating scenes of lantern slides flashed on a screen and live episodes of "rhythmic action set to music." It was hardly characteristic Humphrey material, but she was a Thurber fan and managed to contrive some witty visual images to accompany and underline the bright humor of the spoken lines. In the end, however, nothing came of the project and the "ballet-play" was never produced. Involved with successful musical comedies, the Guild had decided to drop the idea. Disheartened, Doris told Charles he could come back to the 16th Street quarters, for which she no longer had any use. For her, it was the end of the Studio Theatre.

Another plan that never came to fruition was Lucia Chase's idea for adding one of Doris's works to the repertory of Ballet Theatre. This was discussed for months, with Miss Chase showing considerable interest in the acquisition of *With My Red Fires,* which she saw as a potentially exciting vehicle for her great dramatic ballerina, Nora Kaye. But then she began to hedge about the cost; the platforms that Doris insisted upon using seemed so impractical. Would *Inquest* be a better choice? Or what about something short and new—something to go after *Giselle* or before *Interplay?* They could not agree on ways and means. Margaret Lloyd approved of Doris's decision: "I am thankful that you will make no compromises but insist on showing your works as they should be or not at all."

The Limón company's January concert at the Belasco Theatre was a great success, and Leo was thrilled for his wife:

> The enthusiasm of the critics is beyond belief if we did not know what they were being enthusiastic about. They [the writings] must make those dancers and choreographers' skins sit up and take notice—or will anything penetrate their egos? . . . It seems that both critics [John Martin and Walter Terry] put José at the head of the male dancers of our time, and duly place the credit where it is due. I think this is a tremendous achievement of yours—greater even than making a dancer of oneself. I congratulate and am proud of you.

Terry, in fact, had given her credit for José and more:

> Through his own efforts and through association with Miss Humphrey, Mr. Limon has become a dancer of manly elegance, of dramatic power and sensitivity, and a dancer without peer in his generation of men dancers . . . she has performed similar miracles on other members of his company.

Doris was happy, not only with the progress but with the continuing challenge that José's company provided for her. After a concert they had given at Vassar College:

> Pumba telephoned me today "it was an unqualified success from A to Z." Four stars from the Spider on 13th St. is something. As a matter of fact, I worked very hard on the program, we all did —made a number of changes in "Mankind," improved the style and execution of [José's] "Vivaldi," likewise the "Lorca." One

cannot expect dances to "stay put," and even after every improvement has been made as to timing, style, choreography, etc. they must constantly be re-sensitized or they, literally, die.

Of course all life's problems had not vanished. Leo was now sailing between Cuba, Guatemala, and New Orleans, and was away for months at a time. He could pay only half of a $40 bill for Humphrey's piano lessons; more than $600 was due to the dentist. Doris continued to worry that she was not doing enough for her son; his father felt that she was pandering to the boy's wants, and he would just want more. Was she taking care of herself?

No, she was not. She was too preoccupied. Her joy, and when need be her solace, was in creative work. It was the subject, whether consciously or unconsciously, of the new dance that was giving her much pleasure. She had started it in January:

> I am coming on nicely with my new piece to the [Aaron] Copland "Sonata," although the third movement poses some very difficult problems, the result of using music already composed. The problem, how to surmount or fuse the design of the composer with the superstructure of the dance & drama, and not do damage to either. It's a naive piece of sentiment and simple people. I am prepared to hear that beholders, who find in it no murder, suspicion, neurosis or bitterness or guilt will think it unbelievably naive. We shall see whether there is anybody left who can savor a dish without a touch of arsenic for flavoring. The cast is excellent. I don't know which I admire the most, Letitia is wonderful, José is powerful & exciting, Melisa [Nicolaides] is charming, and Miriam [Pandor] young and lovely.

Seldom had Doris been so satisfied with her own work as she was after this May premiere:

> I am pleased with the dance, now officially titled "Day on Earth," each of the four people in it is extremely well-suited to his part, and although the ideas in it are very simple, I think the movements are fresh & convincing. I remember you [Hay] were there when I tried out the very first phrase with Miriam. You should see her do that now, she does it like a silver bird. My husband likes the piece very much, and he's hard to please. Reactions were mixed in Boston, some people were touched and weepy. Others professed not to understand it. This latter group must have been looking for hidden meanings and complications

Top: *Day on Earth,* 1947; Ruth Currier, José Limón. (Photo by Martha Swope from original by Gjon Mili; collection NYPL.) Bottom: *Passacaglia* (1938) as revived by Juilliard Dance Theatre. (Photo by Martha Swope from original by Impact; collection NYPL.)

Ritmo Jondo, 1953; Pauline Koner, José Limón, Ruth Currier. (Photo by Martha Swope from original by Gjon Mili; collection NYPL.)

that are not in such a simple work. Pauline has come up with another set of original costumes, with character and style. We are asking a few people to see it here on Sunday before we put it away for the summer. I predicted in the first place that the palate educated on "Suspicion," "Born to Kill," "Serpent Heart" and "The Lost Weekend," would miss the dash of arsenic absent in "Day on Earth." For the record, I like a little poison too, but not in everything.

Just a man and three women in his life—his first love, his wife, his daughter. As, one by one, they leave him, he finds peace in his work until death unites them all. No more than that. John Martin called it "one of her greatest works. . . . It is almost as if she had looked from some other planet and seen things telescoped into a simple, arduous pattern of dignity and beauty. . . . In a work about man's burdens and his short earthly day, one has come subconsciously to expect cynicism, for that is the easy and obvious approach. . . . It is a graver undertaking to convince us that we are possessed of an intrinsic virtue, and that futility is not of us. To be able to do that is to be a mature artist and a profound one."

In June, Doris signed a contract with Green Mansions resort in the Catskills. She was to assume charge of the dance group, create and stage programs with them, advise and assist with the musical reviews. There was to be a weekly program throughout the month of July, and she would receive $500 in addition to room and board for herself and her son. Most important was the freedom to select her own dancers and repertory. She chose a group of nine performers and, in addition to some works of her own, put on a suite of sea chanteys choreographed by Herbert Ross and some solos composed by Anna Sokolow and Beatrice Seckler. Before each program she made an introductory speech, which John Martin complimented, not only for the wealth of information she packed into it, but for her tact in keeping the audience from suspecting that they were being educated.

Humphrey had many young people to be with, and his mother enjoyed herself. It was, she insisted, much better than a vacation. It left her content: "On my birthday . . . I was glad that my son & husband are well, & that, although plagued by my infirmity, I am working and producing." That summer she had read Philip Wylie's

Essay on Morals and *How to Live with a Cat* by Margaret Cooper Gay—"both fascinating and now [that] I know about morals and cats, doesn't that take in the essentials?"

In the fall she assisted José with a program to be presented at the New York City Center of Music and Drama and taught her choreography class at the Y, where she was also now head of the Dance Center. Enrollment had doubled since last year, which was encouraging.

Agnes de Mille congratulated Doris on the success of José's concert:

> I came out of the theatre replenished and fortified.
> The Lament is a memorable and noble work and the other compositions were in their several ways evocative, stimulating and delightful. There was an air of high excitement in the theatre that I have been missing since the dance recitals in the early thirties. . . . Something must be done to make it possible for you to give more recitals. For the sake of the theatre as a whole this must be done.

That fall Kenneth Robinson divorced his wife. It was a terrible shock, but her friends expected her to cope with it. Hay—with her warmth, her bright wit, her endless sympathy for other people's problems and her marvelous capacity for bringing comfort to others when they most needed it. Surely she could surmount her own troubles. She could not. In December she sought refuge at the Institute for Living in Hartford, Connecticut.

In her own darkest hours Doris had found in Hay the moral support she needed to buffet the conflicting pressures of her personal and professional life. Now it was Hay who needed succor, while Doris, cheered and strengthened by new successes, was ready to give it.

Helping

Doris had found a new direction for her life. Unable to dance herself, she danced through José. Unable to choreograph for herself, she choreographed for him and for the members of his company, all of whom became so attuned to her thoughts and feelings that her slightest word or gesture could elicit from them exactly the movement phrase she wanted. The relationships—not without their periods of tension, to be sure—provided a fertile field for this rebirth of Doris's creativity.

The Limón company, from the late 40's to the mid 50's, was small but beautifully balanced; its members not only technically adept and versatile, but intelligent, sensitive, and responsive. They were all marvelous foils for each other: Letitia Ide, still as lovely as in her early days with the Humphrey-Weidman group, gracious and womanly; Betty Jones, steel-strong but soft as a flower, quick and bright; Ruth Currier, sharply precise but delicate and lyrical (she was later to resent being type-cast as "ethereal," but she had that quality); Lucas Hoving, matching José in height, quietly compelling with a catlike stalk; sometimes joined by his wife, the dramatically gifted Lavina Nielsen. Most important was the woman who had joined the group as guest artist in 1946—Pauline Koner. Already an established dancer, she had come to Doris for guidance in choreography, and her mentor had wisely sensed the immense value of her performing abilities. With a high-strung temperament matched by an infallible sense of theatre; both intuitive and astutely developed, she brought a vivid but disciplined intensity to every role she created for the company. Led by José, still growing himself in stature and artistry, the ensemble became an extraordinary instrument for an extraordinary choreographer.

In 1948 the winter classes in composition, already underway at the Y, were extended to summers at Connecticut College in New London, where the scheme of the Bennington School of the Dance was revived. For Doris now, helping the young became an increasingly important concern. She had to contribute, not only to the present needs of the modern dance, but to the insurance of its continuation as well.

As director of the Y's Dance Center, she went faithfully to every concert presented there. Many of them were dreadful—endless solos, sloppy group dances, amateurishly executed. Never mind the rain or the snow, never mind the taxi fares, the cost in time and energy, the constant, nagging pain in the hip. She went. And when they phoned—as so many of them did—to ask: "Please, Miss Humphrey, will you come look at my dances?" she never said "no." When she could barely walk on a level street, she climbed countless flights of stairs to poverty-stricken lofts to see someone's—anyone's—pathetic attempts at choreography. Perhaps there was talent there; perhaps she could help. She always hoped and she always tried.

If Leo was upset by the extent to which she acceded to such demands, it was only because of the toll he knew it took from her dwindling reserves of energy. She still needed to make new dances; shouldn't she be devoting her strength to them? Also, this volunteer work was expensive. She could travel only by taxi, and no one ever paid her for these consultations. But she knew what it was like to be a young choreographer—eager, ambitious, and broke. Not that it was very different for her as an older choreographer. The Woodfords never lived without financial worries. On the United Fruit Company's ships, carrying cargo to the States from Cristobal, Puerto Barrios, and Havana, Leo earned a salary that was only barely adequate to cover the basic needs of a family with a growing son and an ailing wife.

With the years, Doris's concern for young people deepened. She had never much cared for teaching technique, but she did enjoy her classes in choreography. Beneath her apparent aloofness and reserve was a genuine concern for the youth that gathered around her, and naturally the students adored her.

"Don't just sit there like little birds with your mouths open waiting to be fed," she told them. She wanted them to accept her principles, which were tested and proved; in the course of her independent career they had not changed in any essential respect, though they had developed tremendously in scope and sophistication. But she was happy to see them applied in new ways, wanting her students to think for themselves rather than become carbon copies of herself. Perhaps her new methods of choreographing had some influence on this, for she was seeing the dancers in the Limón company respond to her direction in their individual ways and was gratified by the results.

She did not dictate to the dancers—she suggested, she motivated. But she kept after them till the movement was right. Under her guidance, each developed in his own way, each sustained his personal identity, but within the frame of a company style. She had known for a long time that this was possible—hadn't she said so with *New Dance?*

She worked them hard, but less hard than she worked herself. She seemed never to tire; she never complained of fatigue and never of pain. But she did not apply such Spartan standards to her dancers. She knew when it was best to spare them, and when they had reached the end of their strength, she let them go. Long after she had dismissed them, she would remain in the theatre to work with the lighting director or to discuss details of costumes with Pauline.

The first summer at Connecticut College Doris created what her dancers remember as one of her finest and most interesting works. The Bartók sonata that inspired *Corybantic* suggested to her an expression of the conflict and drama of the time. An Agressor threatens, but the Defender's group, disagreeing on how to meet the danger, panic and engulf all in destruction. After lying apparently lifeless, they recover gradually. "They have learned through suffering to be wiser, more tolerant." Innocence brings tidings of peace and the group rejoices, but its celebration is excessive: "the Defender guesses that peace will not be so simple." The ambiguity of the ending, so untypical of Doris, disturbed many of the spectators who saw it at this first American Dance Festival. (Doris tried a revised version the following summer, but the verdict was that *Corybantic* "remains as confused as it always has been to us. It is full of invention of such complexity that it never becomes clarified.")

This year the Limóns bought a barn and twenty-five acres of land in Stockton, New Jersey. Humphrey, now fifteen, went there every week end, making the farm his second home and the Limóns his second parents. He enjoyed the country, which his mother did not. Unconcerned that her New York apartment was cramped and noisy, she was content to stay there, her mind occupied with dance ideas. She had no need for beauty in her domestic surroundings. But Humphrey felt restless and confined in the city. On the farm he helped José repair the dilapidated buildings. Together they remodeled an old pig pen into a cabin. Its one room was cold, for there was no insulation and a single fireplace provided all the heat. But they didn't care; they cooked outside, under the stars.

In March, 1949, Doris was awarded a Guggenheim Fellowship "for writing a book on choreography with special reference to sources and methods for composition of modern dance." The fellowship carried a stipend of $2,500, and letters of congratulations came pouring in. But much as she wanted to write the book, there were so many other things to do: she was at work on a new dance, *Invention*, with Norman Lloyd composing the music for her; there were the choreography classes to teach; there was José's company to keep constantly groomed and growing. So the months passed, and Leo pestered her—at this rate, she would never get the book done. She should be able to dash it off in a few days; she owed it to a lot of people who were looking forward to it. But then José was doing a new work, and he needed her.

He had told her that he wanted to do a dance on the theme of Othello, and she found the music for him—Sir Thomas Beecham's arrangement of Purcell, titled *The Moor's Revenge*. Some of the summer residents at Connecticut College watched Doris coaching him through the last minutes of the dance: What would be the most effective way? Could you try this or that? Then she would shake her head in disapproval or nod it gently when she saw that the solution was right. She never embarrassed him with verbal criticism in the presence of his company—she did it with a look, a gesture, that only he would notice. *The Moor's Pavane* was the great success of the August American Dance Festival, overshadowing Doris's *Invention.* She did not mind; she was happy and proud of José. And Doris Hering praised the artistry of *Invention* with its "long sweeping lines of undistorted dance, interestingly broken rhythmically. Yet, no matter how beautiful the designs are, one is always aware that some emotional interchange between the dancers is giving rise to the variations in movement color. One can look at INVENTION as the depiction of changes in a man's personality wrought by two women. Or the work can be viewed for its structural balance alone."

Then, after New London, there was another set of Limón programs to demand Doris's attention:

> The season at the City Center had flaws, but for José (and me) it was a success. He is absolutely top man, his two new dances are very fine indeed, and he dances with power and brilliance. The Times and the Tribune should be giving the whole thing a going over next Sunday. I'm afraid my "Shakers" didn't come off as well as it should have—mistakes in judgment on my part. There were other mistakes by, for instance, Charles, who had a new piece called "Rose of Sharon," which was unfortunate in casting and conception of movement. However, the management at City Center (rumor has it) is pleased, and that means a continuation of the project. [In the end, it was not continued.] This is greatly to be desired, as the modern dance desperately needs a home, and support.

The holidays were pleasant:

> It was a wonderful and exhausting Christmas, full of dancing, tinsel, parties, food, clap-clap in a theatre, red boxes, crowds in stores, rich, satisfying words in reviews, violins playing Purcell. The Limóns bit off two large "do's" at our house—Christmas Eve they entertained the company until three, and we wrapped packages until five, then there was the whopping turkey dinner for ourselves.

Such family Christmases had been a tradition since the days on 10th Street. Pauline always did the cooking, and dinner ended with Cherries Jubilee. Once Pauline decided they needed a change and re-created a dessert she had had at the Plaza: Orange Hilton, a hollowed fruit filled with ice cream and liqueurs. It froze so stiff that no one could cut into it, and the next year they went back to Cherries Jubilee.

Humphrey no longer woke his mother at dawn on Christmas morning. This year he gave her a bottle of perfume called "Command Performance" and a book of reproductions of Henri Rousseau, "almost my favorite of all painters." He asked for a record of Satie and a pair of ice skates.

Humphrey was not too appreciative of his mother's efforts as a homemaker—though she certainly never claimed any distinction for herself along that line. He recalled getting canned asparagus for dinner three nights in a row. And there was the occasion that he saved her reputation at a cocktail party when she seemed quite content to serve the drinks in jelly jars and he came to the rescue by locating some respectable glasses.

At the end of April the Limón company went to Paris, where they performed in programs alternating with the Chicago ballet ensemble of Ruth Page. Doris was pleased with the idea, but a bit worried as well: " . . . no major figure in American modern dance has ever appeared in Europe. I'm ready for any reaction, they'll either think he's a crude Indian, or they'll throw roses in his path." Neither reaction occurred: Miss Page got most of the attention in the press, and the French audiences were largely indifferent to American modern dance.

After a summer spent, by his own choice, at a Quaker work camp in Kentucky, Humphrey went to Mexico with the Limóns, a favor that Leo agreed was not too indulgent, though he wished his son would earn his travel the hard way. José had gone there at the invitation of Miguel Covarrubias, who had asked him to teach and perform for the Instituto Nacional de Bellas Artes in Mexico City. Humphrey said they were treated like royalty.

For a special treat, Leo was home for Christmas—the first time in thirteen years. But Doris still had a major problem: "I can't get as much done as I used to, so I haven't nearly finished that book and it's becoming a big black 'thing' on my conscience."

Her following summer at Connecticut College was a good one. The new dance was a success, and she must have been pleased that Humphrey wanted to hear about it. In fact, he had already advised her on the title: *The Dream,* he thought, sounded prosaic. She accepted the criticism, though it was some time before she settled on *Night Spell*:

> My Quartet really came off—in fact I think the response amounted to an ovation. That applause is the most intoxicating stimulant in the world and I was naturally very happy about it. Most people were thrilled, but some, like Ben Bellet [the poet Ben Belitt] were looking for fancy Freudian meanings which are not in the piece. Our Quartet players are wonderful, costumes ditto; likewise the dancers, and, I may say, the choreography!

Night Spell had, in fact, received an ovation and for all the reasons Doris had cited. It was one of those remarkable instances in which she had created roles wonderfully suited to the talents of her company: José, the noble dreamer, was tormented by nightmare visions of Betty Jones and Lucas Hoving, menacing with staccato stabbings, sharp and strong; then saved by the tender, unearthly ministrations of Ruth Currier. The movement was excitingly inventive, though the piece as a whole was admirable rather than moving.

The fall brought changes. Humphrey, though accepted at two other colleges, chose to enter the International Affairs Program at Lafayette, which was not far from New York and quite near the Limón farm. While he was away, Doris went through the traumatic experience of seeing the Studio Theatre dismantled. Charles, who had been drinking heavily, was unable to continue its upkeep and had to take more modest quarters:

> Moving from the Weidman studio was quite a chore, I didn't get the last piece out until Sunday. It was a double cube, and I took it by taxi to Juilliard, where they took all the blocks belonging to 'Red Fires' which I'm going to teach there. It was quite a shock to go over there day after day and see all the things collected with such effort and ambition being torn apart. I can still hear the crash and rasp of partitions being dismembered. Every stick and rag was taken away. "Here lies a stinking silence." *

However, time could not be wasted lamenting the past, for there was work to be done in the present—which, at the moment,

---

* The phrase came from Lorca's "Lament."

revolved around the dance department that had just opened at the
Juilliard School of Music. Headed by Martha Hill, whom Doris had
so admired in the Bennington days, the curriculum offered a full
four years of training in technique and composition on the college
level. Along with José, there were teachers from the Graham school,
and Antony Tudor was in charge of the ballet division. Doris was
appointed to teach both choreography and repertory, the latter giving her an opportunity to revive some of her most important works.
It was a stimulating assignment, for she was already anticipating the
formation of a performing group for young dancers—as if the Limón
company were not enough to occupy her time.

She did take a leave from Juilliard in December to accompany
the Limóns to Mexico, where she taught *Passacaglia* to the dancers
at the Bellas Artes. She found them less well trained than their
American counterparts, but they tried so hard to please her that she
grew very fond of them. It had been a busy summer and winter
"and successful I think."

After finishing his first year at Lafayette, Humphrey got a job
as assistant purser on a United Fruit ship, with "white uniforms and
gold buttons yet" his mother remarked. He made two trips to Central
America, and his father thought him "grossly overpaid." Humphrey
had his own aims in mind: José had taught him how to drive and he
wanted to buy a car with his earnings. He spent the end of the summer with the Limóns at Connecticut College.

His mother was there too, and he found her in especially good
spirits. Monahan, who possessed "the longest whiskers of any cat in
New York City," was with her; she had a comfortable suite and was
in the privileged position of rating breakfast brought in on a tray.
Mornings she liked to spend alone in her room, free of the distractions of social pleasantries, so that she could concentrate on preparing for her classes and rehearsals. Colleagues understood and re-
spected this wish for privacy, refraining even from telephoning her
unless it was absolutely necessary, while the administration carefully
scheduled her composition and repertory classes for the afternoons.

She was working on a new dance, the Mozart *Fantasy and
Fugue in C Major and Fugue in C Minor,* using the music's title.
"Don't cringe," she assured her husband. "It's quite solid, and not
lady Mozart, and I am treating it dramatically." Even Louis Horst,

generally so hard on the musicality of dancers, found her handling of the contrapuntal and fugal patterns "perfection itself." In the end, Doris felt the summer well worth all the effort she had expended on it:

> In that six weeks in New London it is necessary to concentrate on the work in hand, everything else is eliminated. They had to get along without me at the Democratic convention, and I couldn't put my attention on the Korean war, or peoples' birthdays or anything. The happy result, however, is success, if I do say it. José presented two new dances and I had one new one and two revivals. There were other dances from his repertory which had to be rehearsed, then of course classes every day to fill in the chinks. People ask me if I enjoyed it. Well, no, that's not the word. It's like being slightly delirious with a fever and having a fascinating puzzle to do in forty minutes, sort of exciting, but definitely an abnormal feeling. . . .
>
> Pumba is wonderful. She did the costumes as usual, and her eye for color, line and style are unsurpassed. In addition, she played for classes and managed to feed both José and Humphrey. José is his same magnificent self, doing the work of three men and beautifully.

She was thinking of going away for a couple of months, somewhere that she would not be distracted by telephones and committees, so she could work on the book. Maybe Jamaica?

She did not get to Jamaica, nor anywhere else. New York claimed her, as she should have known it would. Already José was writing her with plans and questions, for his mind was not idle while he rested on the farm with Pauline and Humphrey. They had to think about the December concerts at Juilliard. He did not feel ready to do a new piece just now, but perhaps the Revueltas he had choreographed in Mexico last year could be used; if she was doing a new variation for Lucas, could he do his old variation in place of Charles's in *New Dance?* He wanted his own choreography to be seen, but:

> You know I am always uneasy and guilty showing my pieces next to yours. . . . Also because your dances are so magnificent and make the rest of us look like plodders, with varying degrees of talent and competence, but without that supreme and inspired quality which yours, even the minor ones, posess [sic]— In any case, it is a great experience and a privilege to dance your dances always and I would be quite content doing that only, if

that were possible. I hope you are having some rest, with all
the ordeals of dentists and doctors. I wish always that in some
miraculous way they may help you. You are exemplary in your
courage and fortitude.

Naturally, Doris wrote nothing to her son or her husband about her
health. But then she was too busy to think about it very much herself:
"I told everybody, your Christmas present from me is at the Juilliard
School, come and get it."

While the audience cheered the dances, the Juilliard conductor,
Frederik Prausnitz, found special praise for the woman behind
them:

> I could not help but learn a great deal, professionally from ob-
> serving the way in which you combine a quite unrelenting per-
> fectionist attitude with such masterly timing of criticism and
> pacing of demands. To everyone who did not actually see you
> work, it would seem a paradox that the further along the re-
> hearsals progressed, the less you were apparently in evidence,
> but the more the artistic demands rose. You seem to have a way
> of working from within the performer's consciousness, which
> would be well worth any conductor's while to study.

It was a busy winter. There was her friend Elizabeth Dooley's
Poor Eddy, a dramatization of the life of Edgar Allan Poe, to choreograph for Charles, who mutely enacted the poet while an off-stage
voice spoke his lines. Each of the eight dramatic scenes was followed
by a choreographic setting of one of Poe's stories or poems, offering
Doris such tales as "The Masque of the Red Death" and "The Tell-
Tale Heart" that she would surely not have chosen to tackle on her
own.

There was also a new work to choreograph for José, and it became the hit of the April season of "American Dance" sponsored by
the Bethsebee de Rothschild Foundation. *Ritmo Jondo*, set to a commissioned score by Carlos Surinach, was an incisive portrayal "of
men, of women, of meeting and parting." To tantalizing Spanish
rhythms, a band of assertive males presented themselves to a group
of feminine votaries, courted them with sweeping abandon—and
left them to see to more urgent matters. Mr. Martin exclaimed:
"The amazing Miss Humphrey has given us here a piece, which,
except for its musical sensitiveness, its choreographic resourceful-

ness and its general excellence, is utterly unlike anything she has done before. . . . a superbly moody and high mettled drama in abstraction."

Then there was New London in the summer, when Doris scored her second triumph of the year with *Ruins and Visions,* a statement of "the need for avoiding personal wishful patterns of living and for meeting reality with courage." She based her dance on Stephen Spender's poem "The Fates," but embodied its abstract concepts in a series of dramatic situations. A protective mother isolates her son from the harshness of reality; at the theatre they watch unmoved as an actor-lover murders his mistress; in the street they ignore the newsboy whose papers announce war. Finally, when the son is brought back dead from battle, the various characters, united by grief, relinquish their artificial self-involvement to face reality together. The audience at the American Dance Festival found *Ruins and Visions* deeply moving, though many considered it somewhat inaccessible. Everyone delighted in the repeat performance of the openly exuberant *Ritmo Jondo.*

In the fall Humphrey, finding the curriculum at Lafayette College uninspiring, transferred for his junior year to the University of Hull in his father's native city. He liked the English approach to education and enjoyed the unfettered social life there. He heard from his mother occasionally, but there were some problems that she preferred not to mention until they were at least partially solved.

Always reticent to discuss personal matters and reluctant to complain about anything, Doris had said little to anyone about the mounting pain in her hip. But she had, quietly, been seeing doctors about it. When the operation was over, she described it to Hay in a kind of detail that was most unusual for her. She may have felt freer by this time, since the story—apparently—had a happy ending:

> The medicine men let me go home the day before Thanksgiving. It was nip and tuck right up to the last minute, they could not believe I could get around on my new leg. But I passed the test, I can walk steadily on both feet on crutches, sit down and get up from a chair alone. This is considered very good in three weeks. You're one of my few friends who I am sure will be interested in my 'operation!' It's similar to the one Arthur Godfrey had. They take the hip bone out of the socket, replace several inches of it with a metal (vitaliun) end, remove the calcium deposits from the socket, put the hip bone back in it, in the

proper position (it was partially dislocated) sew you up and there you are. After going around to Doctors for fifteen years with no relief, and hardly any had any treatment to offer at all, I finally heard about this operation, which has only been performed about five years. This was last January, but I was much too busy to do anything about it until now. I had two orthopoedic specialists and they both said 'operate.' I can't pretend I went into it with my chin up, I had a bad case of stage fright. Actually I imagined it all much worse than it was. In the first place when you hurt too much they keep you comfortable with narcotics. Of course I did feel as though I'd been run over by a truck the first few days and after that I suffered more from boredom than anything else. Oh yes, and claustrophobia. I was in a very small semi-private room. My friends kept me in a forest of flowers, letters, books, things to smell, things to eat. They were lovely to remember me, and Pauline came every afternoon to dig me out of the smothered feeling.

Leo and a friend of his came Wed. to take me home, and he will take care of me until I can manage alone. Some things I can't do yet. He's a wonderful nurse, cook, masseur and companion; I couldn't be luckier in that respect.

I might be off the crutches in a month, but in any case I have to go to rehearsals by that time to prepare the Limón Co. for a series of concerts at the Juilliard School.

My general attitude about all this is a fury. After being master of my body all these years, it finally turns on me, and I am the prisoner of it.

That Christmas the Limóns gave Doris a sheared raccoon coat. It was the first fur coat she had owned (discounting a couple of hand-me-downs from Dorothy Luckie), and she was grateful to have it when the winds from the Hudson swept past Juilliard. Because, of course, she was back at Juilliard. Likewise the Y. She had no time for a normal period of recuperation.

In March Doris received the Capezio Award "for her creative leadership in the modern dance and for the repertory of high distinction with which she has enriched it":

Naturally I was no end pleased and proud. There was a very elaborate luncheon for the presentation, with a hundred or more notables from the art and fashion world. My nearest and dearest aided and abetted me for the event. Pauline took me to a store and said "buy that dress and this coat," and they were, of course, exactly right and most becoming. Then Leo calmed my nerves and gave me courage in regard to my acceptance speech, which, I was told, was good. Oh yes, the award carried a $500 check, which couldn't be more welcome.

Her notes for the speech had been neatly organized. There were two main divisions: "influences" and "summary of formative factors." Under the former, she discussed her mother and teachers, the bowl of gooseberries that Madam Hatlanek told her she should always eat before she danced, and taking the wrong boat to the West Indies where she met her husband, "the power behind the throne." The formative factors included encouragement, exposure to creative ideas, "frustration to steel the will and desire," and "fortunate accidents to carve the path."

It was good to have Leo home, though his stay was due to labor trouble on the New York docks. With the help of a cane, Doris was going almost everywhere now, though she did draw the line at three flights of stairs. She still had some pain, but "that horrible limp" was gone. However, she had to admit that the doctors would not promise how near to normal the leg would ever come. None of this deterred her from working through her usual kind of summer at Connecticut College. She created *Felipe el Loco* for the company, while keeping an eye on José's choreography for *The Traitor*, which used only his men's group. This time the Limón dance captured the praise; Doris's study of the tragedy of Diaghilev's Spanish dancer was found disappointing. On the surface it would have seemed that the role was ideal for José: a fiery performer, torn from his native land to serve a company of ballet dancers whose lack of understanding drives him to madness. But José was a Mexican and a fine dancer; not a Spanish dancer. And even Doris Humphrey could not carry off the idea of suggesting ballerinas with pseudo-balletic movement.

In October word came suddenly to the Limón company that they could tour South America under the sponsorship of the State Department's Cultural Presentations program. They had only three weeks to get ready for a one-month tour of four major cities (Rio, Montevideo, Buenos Aires, and São Paulo), playing big theatres with full orchestras, and with a repertory of fourteen dances:

What they'll make of it I can't imagine, as I'm sure they've never seen any modern dancing. Probably it will be like pioneering here twenty years ago. I've always thought they would do better in Europe and it is possible that if the powers that be are pleased they may send them there later. It astonishes me that the Republican administration is throwing away the taxpayers' money on art—they are really slipping.

The tour went well, however, and Doris was glad they had gone.

Her next project was a new dance for the Juilliard Dance Theatre, the company that she and Martha Hill had formed to offer performing opportunities to students and young professionals. Doris loved working with the group, which was so full of fresh enthusiasm, "Still with stars in their eyes," she said. She selected them by audition and, if their technical skills were not consistently high, she nevertheless found in them individual qualities that she enjoyed drawing out and developing.

Composing for the new company kept Doris "happy and interested even fascinated with work and more work." She was disappointed that there was not more improvement in the leg, but the doctor assured her that it was doing well. Life was really good now. Her works for Juilliard were subsidized with money for production, orchestra, and all the rest—a situation "unheard of in the modern dance." After all those years, after all the work and the sacrifice and the frustration—could it be that now, as she was nearing sixty, there was a chance to work without constant terror of financial disaster?

In April the Juilliard Dance Theatre premiered *The Rock and the Spring,* which Doris based on lines by Dylan Thomas: "Shall I unbolt or stay/Alone till the day I die/Unseen by stranger-eyes/In this white house?" The theme was a curious recollection of her early concern with the conflicting desires for security and adventure, here dramatized in the person of a young girl on the brink of womanhood. Handled with great sensitivity and delicacy, this was hardly the material for a sensational triumph, though the critics appreciated its suitability for the youthful dancers and the skill with which the choreographer had woven the fragile strands.

At this point, her only real fear centered on Humphrey and the draft. In June he graduated from Lafayette, and it was just a question of waiting.

But suddenly the pain in the leg became so much worse that

Doris was hospitalized "with rest and ice packs." She was furious. Grimly, she refused to give in, leaving for Connecticut College a week later on crutches. She wrote to Hay from New London:

> I came yesterday, with the minimum of wear and tear, and after the first day's work I know much more about how it's going to be. You see I can walk on one foot only, on crutches, at least I think so, I'm much too afraid to do any experimenting. When there's not so much at stake I will be braver, but my first concern is to get through this session. The management has cleared a big living room in this building (a different one from last year) for my classes, which I can walk to without going up and down steps. All my meals come on a tray. I conducted two classes and a rehearsal right off, and am enormously relieved to find there are no ill-effects today. So I have some confidence that I can go on like that, spending in-between time on a bed.
>
> I'm afraid this is not a good summer for you to come. As you can imagine, I am very far behind, for instance in a new dance [*Airs and Graces*] that I started in New York, and had to drop until last night. Another thing that happened to me right after appendicitis was a major do in my mouth, so that, on top of the operation, delayed me in making a start in N.Y. Now I've got to concentrate like mad. I have a victrola right by my bed, and I listen to music and try to think fast enough to make up for lost time. Also there's all the class work, and repertory and planning for that. And the hours it takes me to do the simplest things about dressing. In other words I feel that if I take my mind off the work at all I'll never be able to finish it up. . . . I'd worry about you. And you know how the Limóns work too. I'm sorry this is such a tale of woe, you can imagine that the failure of the mechanism is an enemy to outwit, to defeat, which takes all my strength and will to conquer.

Airs and Graces certainly gave no hint of her problems. "A bit of fluff, sheer soufflé," she told critic George Beiswanger, who was delighted with her visualization of eighteenth-century musical ornamentations, which included the Double Relish, Bite on a Third, Passing Shake, and Quinta Falsa. The published reviews were not so enthusiastic; Doris Hering felt that "the work never really took wing."

By September it was clear that Doris's leg was not going to improve. There was pain now in the other hip as well, and the doctors suggested another operation to make her more comfortable. But while the surgery had relieved the pain, it had also curtailed her capacity for movement, and she refused the operation, preferring the pain to what might prove almost complete immobility.

Friends were urging Doris to move to an elevator building, and she had for some time been considering the possibility of a place closer to Juilliard. Finally, when Leo was home to help her hunt, they found an apartment in a residential hotel, The Ruxton, at 50 West 72nd Street. There was an elevator, a twenty-four-hour switchboard, maid service, a restaurant. Doris hated it. True, it had all the essential features, but it was just two conventional rooms with a kitchenette and bath. No fireplace, no French windows, no louvered doors, and no trees outside. In time, however, she had to admit that she enjoyed having a bedroom after fourteen years of sleeping on the studio couch in the living room. But the involvement with domesticity was trying:

> To have everything tightened up is good for a messy housekeeper like me. Not having bothered with rugs and dishes and curtains etc. for years, I'm appalled at the effort it takes and the time. I've been waiting for a slip cover three weeks and still haven't got it, and I have a running feud with Macy's over things that didn't come and things that did but were wrong. It's all so distracting that I can hardly think about dancing, but the season is hard upon me and I've been putting my wavering mind on it in a desultory fashion.

She and José were each preparing two new works, and they had to move swiftly, for he would be taking his company out on tour in February, returning only shortly before the April concerts at Juilliard. But conditions now were better than they ever had been: "It's a good, solid feeling to be part of a serious and stable institution."

The leg was no worse, but Doris had been so thoroughly frightened by its behavior in the summer that she was being cautious. At home she stayed on crutches, using a cane when she went out. For the time being, Humphrey was home, but since his mother had five evening rehearsals a week, she hardly ever saw him. Leo had sailed to the Mediterranean and would be gone for a long time.

As April approached, the pressures mounted. Choreographing for the Limón company and for the Juilliard Dance Theatre, along

After a 1950's performance of Limón's *There Is a Time;* in the central group, Betty Jones, José Limón, Ruth Currier, Lavina Nielsen, Doris Humphrey, Pauline Koner. (Photo by Gjon Mili; collection José Limón.)

Top: *Dawn in New York*, 1956; Joyce Trisler, John Barker. Bottom: *Race of Life* (1938) as revived by Juilliard Dance Theatre; Patricia Christopher, Durevol Quitzow, Harlan McCallum. (Photos by Stephan; collection Dance Department, Juilliard School.)

with reviving *Race of Life*, constituted only part of Doris's responsibilities:

> Endless detail to see to, about all parts of it [the season]—programming, costumes, sets, music, rehearsal schedules and of course, the dancing. . . . People forget, balk, don't answer the telephone, are late, have ego trouble, can't come when you need them, are tired, sick, bored, annoyed. And some of them are also magnificent like José, most of his company and Martha Hill.

As usual, Doris sat through the performances backstage, quietly waiting and smoking. She wanted to acknowledge the applause but was embarrassed about walking on stage with the cane. So she found devices. One was to have a chair brought on and to sit down on it while the curtain was lowered, then to have it rise on her seated there. Or José would lead her on stage, but then she would remain on the side, not risking even his support to try to walk to the center where she belonged.

The revival of *Race of Life* was greeted with enthusiasm, as was the new piece for the young dancers. For the latter Doris had turned again to the poetry of Lorca, pitting youth and spring and lyricism against the ugly, mechanistic structure of city life. Walter Terry called *Dawn in New York* "one of Miss Humphrey's most distinguished and compelling creations"; Mr. Martin found it "tender, touching and singingly true."

Theatre Piece No. 2, however, met with mixed reactions, most of the critics praising its experimental intentions but feeling that it had failed to achieve a unity of style. Described as a "Concerto for Light, Movement, Sound and Voice," it was, in fact, a richly innovative work in the mixed-media style that was to become popular a decade later. Beginning with the theatre of primitive ritual as man celebrated the wonders of the unknown, the work traced the decline of the art in "Satires from the Theatre"—a singer and a dancer in separate spotlights, self-absorbed in the intricacies of their own pyrotechnics; actors chattering nonsense. But ending, as Doris would, with a renaissance, "The Theatre Grown Heavenly," using the words of May Swenson's "Poems of Praise." Unlike the majority of critics, George Beiswanger found *Theatre Piece No. 2* both brilliant and profound:

Works of large affirmation, dances whose core is the theory of art and life, pieces that are philosophical and religious in meaning, have come at important moments in the composer's career. . . . What a fertility of ideas and what daring! . . . Miss Humphrey has reached that stage of artistic adulthood where she confidently dares to do what her inspiration conceives, regardless of its prospect. She is composing these days, I should say, not to others, not even to herself, but to the being that calls forth all things, even dances.

That spring Humphrey left for Newport, Rhode Island, where he had been accepted by the Navy for officers' training. The three years that he would have to spend in the service disturbed Doris, for by the time he got out he would be twenty-five and not yet started on a career. Knowing that many other young men were in the same position was little comfort to her.

She had happier news about Charles Weidman. He had rented a new studio and was preparing to make a stab at a comeback. Doris was relieved, for "although everything is quite improvisational and 'make-do' about his work, still it's a miracle that he's alive and doing anything."

One of Doris's additional duties at this time was serving on the advisory panel of the International Exchange Program of the American National Theatre and Academy, which disbursed money from Congress to send American artists abroad. The Limón company had been on the agenda for some time:

> This has missed fire several times due to managerial complications and some devious wire pulling. If they ever do go, I've promised to show up in the key places in Europe, although Spain is the only country I really want to go to. Very strange, this business about the Spanish culture, you know all the Spanish flavored dances I've done for José. It wasn't just because he looks the part, but because I have such an affinity for the whole style of the people. The French? too chichi, in spite of French modern painting which I love. The Italians? too emotional, too florid. The Germans? Well, there was Bach, but the rest have no taste . . .

New London was as strenuous as usual that summer. Neither Doris nor José did a new piece, but there were replacements to be trained for the old ones, and she revived *Song of the West* for her repertory class. She delighted in the work of her protegé: his *Emperor Jones*, premiered that June, was a "rip-snorting piece . . . a real melodrama, highly theatrical, in which José has done an exceptionally good job."

The early winter was taken up with preparations for the January concerts by the Juilliard Dance Theatre. The company had been plagued with illnesses, which complicated the usually difficult tasks of getting productions on stage. Yet:

> I was pleased with the result, thought my young company danced well, and very close to their full capacity. The x-rays on my new piece were not very good though—disappointing. This is a very innocent, young idea, aiming at freshness, youth and beauty. I guess they frown because they want us always to be deep, dark and dolorous—or something—anyway it wasn't what they were looking for. Who was it who said about realism, "A rose is just as real as a sewer?"

Descent into the Dream traced a girl's development through childhood, youth, and womanhood, each stage represented by a group of dancers who guided the protagonist along her dream journey. It lacked the fresh spontaneity of Doris's earlier works for Juilliard Dance Theatre. Doris Hering found it "intellectualized. . . . There was obvious symbolism—a girl sitting on a wooden hoop (snatched by one of the boys); a scrim separating dream from reality. And there were obvious movement designs—skittering about for the young girls, jumping for the boys, a slow promenade for the girls-in-womanhood."

The summer's premiere in New London was more gratifying, though its intention was simple: a bright, pure-dance, opening piece to balance the Limón repertory, which was largely dominated by dramatic seriousness:

> My 'Dance Overture' aroused cheers of enthusiasm and accomplished what I had intended, a rousing opening. I find that real success comes in about one in three proportions and this came along at the normal rate. Nothing sweeter in the world than that "I love it" feeling from the audience. José had a new dance [*Blue Roses*], much longer and more complicated than mine. It was beset with incredible difficulties in production and needs some seasoning and revision, but will be a very good piece after a while. [It was not revised; it was dropped.]

This was written in retrospect on board the RMS *Queen Mary*, for the Limón company had, at last, set out for its first European tour. There were nineteen works in the repertory and a company of fifty. How would they be received? "We have an unreasoning optimism about that. In the first place, I can't imagine people not loving and admiring José, can you?"

A Good Fighter

A calm and restful voyage followed a week of frantic preparations. Fortunately, Leo was home to help with shopping, packing, feeding, and banking. Doris had had trouble finding a home for Monahan. The first try was with a lady who had a Persian that stood for the visitor's ill-bred growls and spittings for just twenty-four hours. The second lady turned out better. She lived alone and allowed Monahan to be the master of the house—which was the style to which he was accustomed. By the time she got on board, Doris was thoroughly exhausted; she slept twelve hours a night and napped in between. A week later, Leo sailed on the *Queen Elizabeth* to join her. What a joyful adventure it was going to be!

After six weeks of travel and performances in Europe, Doris reviewed her experiences with mixed feelings:

> Such a jumble of impressions, some quite breath-taking and others downright hostile. To begin with the present Leo and I are in this Hotel [in Paris] from which he takes off tomorrow for New York, and I in a few days to rejoin the Limón Co. in W. Germany. At the moment we're miserable. He's in bed with Flu, and I'm marooned on the 6th floor because of an electricians' strike (no elevator). Besides it's damp and clammy and we don't know what to do with ourselves. It's easy for him, he's in a coma, but I was reduced to washing hair and doing some mending jobs—with all of Paris waiting to be explored! You see when we were here before, the performances and rehearsals claimed my attention so I barely saw a thing. I suspect, though, that Paris is not my cup of tea, it's too pretentious.
>
> The really grand excursion we indulged in was a trip to Spain.

I left the company for a week, and we both traveled around Sevilla and the southern part. You know that strong Spanish streak I have in me—it was a joy to see the country and the people. It has that fascinating combination of austerity and elegance that I like. We particularly liked Granada and Toledo, where we saw El Greco's house and his paintings. . . . Next to Spain I liked England best. . . . The English reception was quite chilly in the press, always comparing us to the ballet and to our disadvantage. The best audiences and press were in Berlin where Wigman and others have been educating them for thirty years.

So some of it had been rewarding. Since Doris had such difficulty getting about now, Leo had hired a car with a driver for the trips in Spain. In London he had gone with her to find the home of the "translator" of boots that she had depicted in *Inquest*. It turned out to be in such an out-of-the-way spot that even the resourceful London cabbie had trouble finding it. When they got there, they found that the house had long been deserted and was now inhabited only by chickens.

The performances in Paris and London had taken place under the most unfortunate circumstances. The company arrived before the city dwellers had returned from their summer vacations; they played small, unstylish theatres; their advance publicity was meagre, providing biographies of the leading dancers but offering no insights into the nature of their particular style of dancing, which was like nothing Britain or France had seen before. Not knowing what else to look for, London missed the brilliant technical displays that they liked in the ballet; Paris was offended because the girls were not all pretty.

The Humphrey repertory fared badly. Labor laws forbade their taking a child on tour for *Day on Earth*, so a new one had to be auditioned and trained and rehearsed in each city. Soon the dance was simply dropped. *Lament* presented a language problem, and was not understood. Doris's more recent masterpiece, *Ruins and Visions*, could not be taken because the swing in the first scene made it too difficult to mount. The "Variations and Conclusion" of *New Dance* and *Dance Overture* were found slight and uninteresting. Only *Ritmo Jondo* had some supporters.

José's works, however, appealed to the European public. Less subtle and sophisticated, more brilliant and theatrical, they were comparatively accessible to the uninitiated spectator. Though the Limón repertory did not enjoy an overwhelming triumph in Western Europe, it was liked. And, as the season went on, José enjoyed a considerable personal success. The audiences crowded backstage to congratulate and fawn over the handsome, virile, charming Mexican. They ignored the frail, delicate woman who stood off in a corner, leaning on her cane, alone.

Doris was shocked and deeply hurt. The press called to interview José; they did not ask to talk with her. Neither of the Limóns, busy with the endless details of company management and the required etiquette of cultural relations, had time to notice what was happening, and left their artistic director to manage as best she could. Valiantly, Pauline Koner carried Doris's suitcases, helped her to register at her hotel, and get settled in her room, escorted her to receptions. But nearly everything conspired to make her feel useless, unwanted. Helplessly, she called long rehearsals. One, simply to stage some new bows, took forty-five minutes. The bows were beautiful, but the dancers were exhausted and the redoing was hardly necessary. Like Mama-San before her, Doris had to be useful, even if the work was realistically unimportant and, what was worse in this case, unwanted.

Doris returned from Europe early and alone in December. Friends found her shattered. She looked as if her world had collapsed.

At the Juilliard concerts in April, José premiered his *Missa Brevis,* inspired by the dignity and courage he had found in the Polish people. As a customary courtesy, he invited Doris to one of the late rehearsals. She found the work stunning, but felt—as she often did with José—that it needed pruning. However, she said nothing, nor was her opinion asked. Leaving the studio, she admitted to one of the dancers: "I'd better keep my hands off. José doesn't want my advice."

Of course it had to happen. Over the past few years José had gained immeasurably in stature as a choreographer, while the European tour had done much for his confidence. And at this point he needed all the confidence he could muster, for Doris was obviously ill. The woman who had encouraged, guided, and promoted him for so many years would probably not be available to help him much longer. How would he manage without her? Whatever feelings of security he might have experienced as a result of past successes would have been of little comfort to him now that he could foresee the personal risk of continuing to choreograph for the first time without her. But *Missa Brevis* he had created alone, and undoubtedly it was a fine, possibly even a great, work. If he could hold on to what he had discovered here for himself, if he could develop this line of creativity that was actually his own, he would be able to survive her. This work was a test for him, a challenge he had to meet with courage and independence.

Doris had never been very adept in the handling of personal relationships, though the respect felt for her by family, friends, and colleagues had always worked to resolve previous crises. This time, however, José's entire future was at stake and, much as he loved her, he had to protect himself. She could not understand this. As she refused to recognize her constantly failing health, she refused also to see the necessity of José's lessening dependence. If she had been able to accept his position, she could have coped more easily with the many trials this year was bringing.

Still, Doris expected the season to progress as usual—choreography class, Juilliard Dance Theatre, Connecticut College. And she fulfilled all of her responsibilities in spite of what must have been an insistent awareness of failing strength, for an illness more serious than any of the preceding ones was now ravaging her body.

She tried valiantly. When asked about her health, she retorted quickly: "There's nothing the matter with my mind." To prove it, she devoted every minute she could spare from classes and choreography, every remaining ounce of strength she could muster, to writing the long-delayed book on composition. "I have the title for it now, *The Art of Making Dances*. What could be simpler? And that's exactly what it's about."

Leo had been six months in the Mediterranean, but Doris hoped he would get back in time to come to New London by mid-August, and he did. He arrived to find her obviously ill. Her abdomen was strangely swollen and she complained that her clothes did not fit. Before they left for New York, she had to attend the final faculty meeting of the year, when she announced her intention not to return

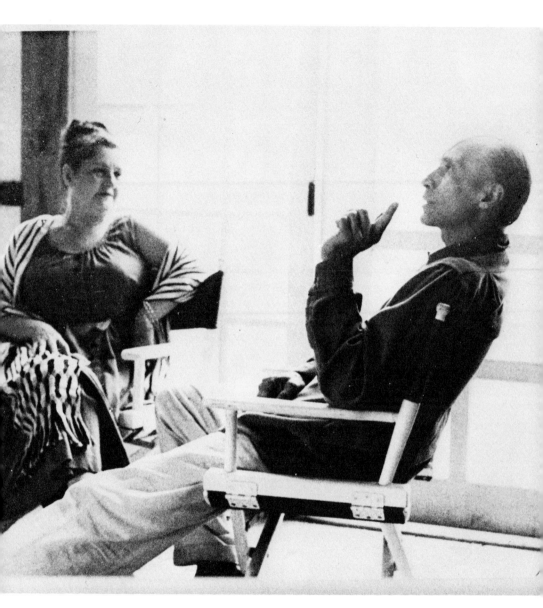

Pauline and José Limón at home, ca. 1955. (Photo by Martha Swope from unattributed original; collection NYPL.)

Doris Humphrey at Connecticut College, 1950. (Photo by Walter Terry; his collection.)

the following summer. The school, she claimed, had become too much of a closed corporation; new people should be coming in to teach in new ways. They were all getting into a rut, and she wanted to take a trip to the West Coast to see what was happening there.

While the school situation was disturbing, emotional tensions were plaguing her as well, for the rift with José had widened. He had done two new dances for the festival which had required so much rehearsal time that hardly any was left for Doris to work on her own pieces. In the old days, she would have made time for herself, but this summer she did not even try to force the issue. That, in the end, José's works were not well received did not lessen the pain of the rejection. That last day, as the Woodfords left the campus, José stopped them to say goodby. When he had gone, Doris —who hardly ever used profanity—muttered, "That beautiful bastard."

As soon as they got back to New York, Leo had to report to his ship, but phoned the Ruxton the first chance he had. She was not in the apartment; the switchboard informed him that she was in the hospital. Doris was told that the trouble was an inflammation of the intestine and she would be in the hospital at least two weeks. She asked if it was cancer, and the doctor said it was not.

He told Leo otherwise. An exploratory examination had revealed an advanced stage of cancer of the lining of the stomach. There was nothing they could do. Leo was not to tell her the truth. However, it was his job to break the news that she would probably be confined to bed for at least six months. He had to take a good, stiff drink of rum before he could face her with that.

Humphrey, who was now stationed in the Mediterranean, heard from his father only that Doris was desperately ill and that he should try to come home. Leo had taken an extended leave and planned to stay in New York as long as he could. But there would be hospital bills and after that a full-time nurse to care for his wife when she got home, so he could not remain out of work too long. Humphrey managed to get transferred to the Brooklyn Navy Yard, where he was given the position of security officer.

Notwithstanding the developments of the past two years—perhaps even more so because of them—the Limóns now devoted themselves to Doris, taking an apartment at the Ruxton in order to be near her. Pauline was wonderful, probably reminding Doris of her indispensability in the earlier days, but now without the harrassment that accompanied her helpfulness then. With Doris she was cheerful, but once she left the bedroom her face was drawn with strain and worry. In the evenings she and José sipped long drinks before they could face dinner.

Through it all, Doris worked on her book; first finishing the longhand manuscript, which Olga Frye typed for her, and then reading the galley proofs as they came from the printer:

> The rhythm is very strange; sleeping pills do not work beyond 4 a.m. so I sit up in bed then and write. Much later, in the middle of the morning, Leo brings me a cup of coffee and we have that and conversation from 6 to 7 a.m. Then he goes to work as I write and the nurse comes at 8:30. You know, you don't have to be crazy, but it helps. . . . I'm full of plans for people to carry on without me and am on the telephone much, directing the battle from well behind the firing line.

By December the bills had mounted alarmingly, and Leo knew he had to go back to sea. He sailed on the eleventh for the Far East via Panama. Doris was terribly lonely without him, for she missed those early mornings when she could greet him with: "I've done three pages! Would you like to see them?" Now there was only the nurse:

> . . . so I have instead of a husband a thermos bottle of tea. I have finished the book long ago, so now I write reminiscenses. I began in 1898, the year my parents moved in with me to the Palace Hotel in Chicago, and now, some eighteen chapters later I am only up to 1926. The whole thing will take me a long time, I must have the habit of writing now, because there's no particular purpose in the reminiscences. I vaguely think they might be the basis for a biography some time.
>
> Rinehart, my publisher, is very pleased with my book, and I am no end encouraged. . . .
>
> The news on the health front is not so good. I am very much swollen in the abdomen due to inflammation of the intestines, often with severe stomach aches. The doctor tries this and that. He comes with injections every other day which are a great relief, but seldom last till he comes again. He says cases like mine are very difficult to cure and I can't hope for a recovery before a year—that would be next August. By the way,

for this reason, and also because I've just been there too long, I'm not going to Conn. College next summer. It is likely that I am going to have to reorganize my life entirely in order to live with this thing.

I keep my hand in various enterprises in la danse by telephone. There's Juilliard which has many complicated problems, and a series of six modern dance concerts at the Y for which I am responsible. I'm getting very good at delegating authority and telling people what to do. I'm afraid that gets to be a habit too, and I'm quite complacent about doing nothing myself except writing. I'm going to make one big effort—put on my clothes and go see a run-through of some new dances at Juilliard on Jan. 5. Otherwise I just don't want to get out of bed—the tummy hurts more when I stand up. I often feel like an old-fashioned heroine in a decline, and I can't believe that this has happened to me.

Along with all the responsibilities she continued to shoulder, Doris found time and energy to write to all of her friends at Christmas. She announced that the book would be published in the spring and extended her best wishes for a happy year for people and cats.

On December 24, Doris entered the Flower and Fifth Avenue Hospitals for a routine draining procedure. But a clot developed in the bad leg, which the doctors—after briefly considering amputation—immobilized with ice. Then, in a last desperate attempt, they operated. Back in her room, Doris asked about the Juilliard Dance Theatre: Had the last rehearsals gone well? Would the dancers be ready for that run-through on January 5? She was not to see it. On December 29, Doris Humphrey died.

The next day, Leo flew home from Panama. At Humphrey's suggestion, the ashes were laid in the family plot in Illinois. Her husband chose the inscription for her gravestone:

"May her own works praise her at the gates."

Afterword

In the spring of 1971, Charles Weidman invited me to his studio to watch the beginning of a reconstruction of the entire *New Dance Trilogy*. We met on a rainy Saturday afternoon: Charles, Labanotator Ray Cook, and four middle-aged matrons who had once danced in a great premiere.

The obstacles were incredible. There was no musical score. In those days no one had money to pay for transcribing, so Wallingford Riegger's music existed in a single pencil copy, and no one knew where it was. Occasionally someone would hum a bit of a phrase, but for the most part they remembered only counts. Charles had some still photos and a few minutes of excerpts that had been filmed at Bennington in the summer of 1935. We looked at the pictures and watched the movie through three times. Then the agony began: one dancer starting a phrase and getting through perhaps two bars; another remembering the next two bars; then, most often, a long pause when no one could recall what happened next. Gradually, that miraculous faculty known as muscular memory began to function—not infallibly—but snatches of movement at least began to come back. Then—inevitably—another stalemate. Yes, we did something on a diagonal. But what? If only we had the score, if only we had a film of the whole dance, if only it had been notated . . .*

---

* The reconstruction of *New Dance* was performed at Barnard College on May 11, and at the Connecticut College American Dance Festival on June 30, 1972.

This had been the fate of *New Dance*—one of the most important works ever choreographed by Doris Humphrey. Only the "Variations and Conclusion," maintained in the repertory of the Limón company, has survived. Why did all the rest have to vanish? Why—long before this—didn't someone try to save it?

A few Humphrey works have been preserved: some have been filmed; some of the later ones have been notated,* most often from revivals that she staged herself for her repertory classes. But many of the greatest of them have all but perished—not only *New Dance*, but *Inquest, Story of Mankind, Ruins and Visions*— to say nothing of the many early pieces that some of her company members recall as among the most beautiful dances they had ever seen.

Doris was seriously concerned with the preservation of dances, having at one period devised her own system of notation, though she never found the time to develop it sufficiently to make it very useful even to herself. In the late 1940's she wisely allowed the Dance Notation Bureau to begin recording her works so that a number of them now exist in Labanotation scores. But these are limited to dances created or revived when notation funds were available from a sponsoring institution like Juilliard or Connecticut College. Fortunately, some of her finest works were done at such auspicious times, but many were never recorded in any way. The chief factor accounting for the loss is simple: money.

Equally distressing, if not more so, is the fact of the gradual attrition of Humphrey pieces in the professional repertory since her death. The Limón company, which knew a number of them, has kept only a few in its active repertory. On the other hand, the academic world has shown increasing interest, with colleges and universities staging frequent revivals based on the Bureau's materials. Yet, while some of the student productions have been—as Doris might have said—"very good indeed," they cannot replace professional performances. Regardless of their effort and sincerity, students can duplicate neither the technical brilliance nor the dramatic intensity of the dancers for whom the works were made. The Labanotation scores provide potentially invaluable resources, but as long as they are utilized primarily by amateur groups, they cannot do full justice

---

* A list of notated scores will be found following the Chronology.

to her creations. And they cover only a small part of her significant choreography.

Apart from the history-oriented, academic concern, enthusiasm has waned, for another revolution has taken place within American dance. Beginning in the mid-'50's, the climate of artistic taste started to turn away from the values associated with her era: away from dance as an expressive language; from dance as a vehicle for comment on the human condition; from dances structured with the clean, precise logic of conflict, development, and resolution. The young choreographers were concerned with dance as a self-sufficient entity, with movement as its end rather than merely its means of expression. They believed in comment, but on current issues rather than eternal ones, while the "well-made play," of course, was out.

Most revolutions thrive, especially in their early years, on their avowed purpose of completely overturning the current establishment. The point is made most clearly, most forcefully, when the establishment can be presumed wrong on every possible point. This, of course, is exactly what happened in the late 1920's when Martha Graham and Tamiris and Doris Humphrey were staging their own revolution. Then the reaction was directed against the classical ballet and their stand was extreme; they made anything associated with the ballet appear false and utterly outmoded. Actually, the objections were directed to the degenerate state of the ballet at the time, though the reformers did not bother to qualify their statements to that effect.

The choreographers who began to work along new lines in the '50's and '60's were involved with the same kind of tactics. Feeling that they had to make a complete break with tradition, they rejected almost the whole of the early modern dance. Again, they were somewhat justified, for much of what they were seeing, of what called itself "modern dance," was practically a travesty of the work done by the leaders of the '30's and '40's.

Doris was well aware of what had happened, for she sat through many a dreadful recital, seeing her long-established and lovingly taught principles distorted into inept caricatures of meaningful movement. The camp followers clutched at her by-word of expression, presenting plays, which needed words, without words. They grabbed at her mention of gesture but didn't stay long enough to learn about stylization, so they presented raw pantomime and called it dance. They glimpsed her moral purpose but put on the stage what belonged on the lecture platform. Doris lived to see herself blamed for the misuses of her ideas.

Seeing only the later versions and with most of the evidence of the earlier period inaccessible, the new generation easily called all the old ideas irrelevant. They were hardly to blame for the misunderstanding. How were they to know that Doris Humphrey shared their concern for viewing dance as an independent art—free of the demand to follow the structures of its musical accompaniment, free of overdecorative décor and costuming, free of the burden of storytelling and of personal displays of technical embellishments?

Of her generation in the modern dance, Doris was probably the most musical—the most sensitive to rhythm and phrasing, the most perceptive with regard to style. Her early work on Miss Ruth's theory of music visualization stimulated her interest, though she soon rejected the Denishawn idea of a one-to-one relationship of step and note as too simplistic. Her first independent ventures dispensed with sound accompaniment altogether, as in *Water Study* and *Drama of Motion*. Then there was the droning chorus of *Life of the Bee* and the curious system employed for *New Dance*—the use of a score intended for replacement. The experiments of these years led to the discovery of the three natural rhythms (motor, pulse, and breath) and to numerous highly sophisticated devices for counterpointing dance phrasing against musical phrasing.

The breath rhythms in particular gave a special kind of continuity and a distinctive flow to Doris's movement; they made the dancer appear on stage as a warm, vibrant human being; impelled not by rote but by a vital, individual power. The phrasing was remarkable—brilliant in itself, but always expressively motivated. In *New Dance*, the opposition of the soloists' phrases of 7, 7, and 10 against the ensemble's steady 4/4 (the assertion of individual identity) resolved at the end of each 24 counts (the individual in harmony with the group). In *With My Red Fires*, dancers moved in contrasted phrase units to underline their frenzy and confusion, building the dramatic tension of the pursuit of the lovers. She could be deceivingly simple, as in the telling application of unison movement to match the serenity of Bach. Yet, along with her abiding reverence for the German master, her musical tastes were catholic: witness her venture into electronics with *Theatre Piece No. 2*. The ideas never ceased developing.

For years she was intrigued with the problems of relating dance movement to the spoken word. She tackled it first in *Shakers*, with just two sentences, dramatically declaimed at climactic moments. The script for *Decade* is better forgotten, but possibly it paved the way for *Inquest*, where the literal recitation of the news story is first mirrored by the semiliteral enactment of the events and then juxtaposed to their more stylized retelling. Then *Lament* which so beautifully evaded the temptation of merely reiterating Lorca, with José "moving sparsely when the words are spoken, and freely during the musical interludes," developing the poem's kinetic imagery, "Up the stairs went Ignacio/With all his death upon his shoulders," with José striding boldly to meet his destiny. In *The Art of Making Dances*, Doris remarked that the use of words with dance was a whole area yet to be explored by young choreographers. They are still exploring it.

And she had modern ideas for décor. (The credits for costuming—and they are extensive—belong to Pauline.) Those marvelous boxes were used with such imagination, such theatricality. They could be grouped to represent almost any kind of natural or social setting; they could enhance dramatic focus or—more abstractly—they could provide tantalizing opportunities for the use of the stage space. But that was just one period. *Inquest* explored the use of lighting to define areas of action, focusing now on the home, now on the place that represented the town, now farther off on the outside world that was the entire world. Then later, for *Ruins and Visions*, just set pieces: in the first scene a swing for the mother and son, setting at once the Victorian period and the unrealistic frame of isolation established by the problem of the dance. She used only as much décor as was absolutely necessary, and she used it in every conceivable way—to establish levels of visual interest, to serve dramatic needs, to symbolize thematic concepts. Everything simple; nothing wasted.

Apollonian by temperament, Doris disliked excess in anything—in sound, in décor, in movement; constantly pruning, condensing, taking away until only the essentials remained. Many young artists think of their forebears as having overdecorated, overchoreographed, making their work busy and fancy. But, watching the attempts of a gifted novice, Doris was known to exclaim: "You're like a cornucopia— you just spill out movements. The first section alone contains enough material for the whole dance; just develop that." The attitude applied to both quantity and quality. Next to "Every dance is too long," Doris's most characteristic saying may well have been, "Don't just do something; stand there." When Pauline Koner choreographed a solo to verses containing the phrase "the earth reels," she thought of wild turns around the stage. Doris suggested otherwise: "Stand still and sway; feel the earth turning on its axis beneath you."

In *Shakers,* the thrust of the lower arm shook off all the sins of the world; in *Ritmo Jondo,* the girls' arms opening on a breath evoked their feminine readiness; in *Day on Earth,* the woman enters using the same movements as the man who awaits her—what simpler, what clearer way to show that they belong together? Such basic motifs Doris mined for every potential of design and significance— varying their spatial patterns, their tempos and accents, until every facet of their shape and meaning had been explored.

The dance was independent—free of music, of spectacle, of extraneous movement. For Doris, however, there were two areas where dance was not free: it was subject to the demands of formal, coherent structure and to the function of expressiveness. If *The Art of Making Dances* is taken at face value, the restrictions were rigid and inflexible. Actually, she used them with great flexibility, though she felt no need to stress this point in a book intended as a text for students—who should, after all, learn the rules before they break them. For herself she did not break the rules; she simply saw the breadth of leeway within them.

In life as in art she had to work around a form. John Martin recalls her in a restaurant, neatly arranging food on her plate. She recognized the activity as compulsive but insisted on working at the picture till the pattern satisfied her. The plate—like her working day, like her dances—had to be designed. Mr. Martin felt that her great virtue as a choreographer, the one that none of her colleagues could match, was this remarkable capacity to perceive the gestalt of a work, giving it that sense of completeness and inevitability which mark a classic.

Yet this same virtue, in certain periods of artistic evolution, can be considered a fault. When the Dionysian approach is in the ascendance, Humphrey choreography appears too rigidly structured, deriving not from passion—the proper wellspring of dance—but from thought. Unquestionably, she intellectualized. She liked to have her emotion under control; she never allowed it to burst through the formal design that she had so deliberately planned to project just as much feeling as she wanted to let go at any particular moment. Her choreography does lack spontaneity. Does it also lack passion?

No "good fighter" has ever lacked passion, but Doris's chief passions were for causes. In her works, she cared fervently about individuals, but not really about the individual; she was concerned with humanity, but not particularly about the human being. The feelings portrayed in her dances were always abstracted, heightened, sublimated—an approach that assured control. The majority of her dances are focused on generalized themes—the dignity of work, the nobility of aspiration (with its contrary, pettiness, for satire), the harmonious society. Frequently she set her ideas in contexts safely remote from her life. Though she admired the ardently dedicated and "the combination of austerity and elegance," she was not religious like the Shakers, and her experience of Spain was purely vicarious when she created *Lament* and *Ritmo Jondo*. Of course there were times when reality crept it, but usually she succeeded in disguising it. There is the persistent figure of the domineering mother—the Old Queen in *Life of the Bee*, the Matriarch in *With My Red Fires*. Yet both use formal ritual to make the revolt of the young, not an individual protest, but an act of necessity for the survival of a society. (*Ruins and Visions* lets the protective mother resolve her own conflict, but this came later.) *Day on Earth* was most precarious, for here was the intimate affection that Doris was so reluctant to admit in herself. Yet the problem was solved, partly by shifting the role to a male character, partly by falling back on the solace-of-work theme, partly by using the child as a symbol, again, of the inevitable cycle of generations.

Only the professional autobiography of *Decade* remained subjective and became sentimental—a unique instance of failure of control. More often failure came from excessive objectivity, when the abstracted emotion seemed forced and the beautifully structured design seemed wrought to no purpose. Yet in Doris's best works the craft perfectly serves the image of feeling.

She insisted that it so serve. All her movement had to function, to communicate; otherwise it was merely decorative—still at the mid-'20's stage of pretty, insignificant diversion. Even her "pure dance" pieces always had a definable mood or atmosphere; again the gestalt. At the same time she was in agreement with the young rebels who complained that the modern dance of the '50's had become too literary, a mere vehicle for the expression of ideas that could be better stated in words. Despite some claims to the contrary, Doris never—in her whole career—choreographed a "story" dance. When she did start with a written source, she manipulated it—interchanging temporal sequences, eliminating characters and episodes, shifting emphasis—until what she had was no longer a literary structure but a choreographic one.

From the beginning Doris's primary interest was in movement. Although a recurrent theme in her writings is "What shall we dance about?" she always considered this concern with subject matter as a springboard, a motivating force to get the choreographer going. After that, it mattered little whether or not the audience was aware of the specific content. As she asserted of her 1941 revival of *Bee*, the point was the choreography, the actual movement patterns perceived on the stage, not the insect behavior that had originally stimulated the composition in her mind.

Doris derived movement ideas from some of the same sources that inspired other choreographers. For *Ritmo Jondo*, she told her dancers to think of their arms as the branches of a tree; that way, they could move in free, natural patterns of infinite variety. Isadora Duncan told her students to think of the waves of the sea —again, nature. Doris built dances on primitive ritual (*Song of the West*) and on her American heritage (*Shakers*). Martha Graham used similar starting points. For Doris's exclusive contribution, we must look elsewhere.

We find it most importantly, I believe, in her use of the concept of the arc between two deaths. This is distinctive Humphrey and is not to be found as an essential, motivating force in choreography before hers.

The concept of the arc is remarkable in many ways, but perhaps most for its complete fusion of form and content. Drama is inherent in the kinetic idea, which embraces both the physical relation of the body to the force of gravity and its psychological relation to the environment. In the fall and recovery she found at once a basic impulsion to movement, generating spatial and temporal shapes and dynamic variations, while it kindled powerful emotional responses. There was no need to add dramatic significance to the motion; it was already there. The struggle for balance was the striving for the maintenance of life itself, constantly threatened, not only by the hostile forces without, but also by the insistent urges within that beckoned with the lure of daring the unknown. Then the suspension on the top of the breath phrase—the achievement, the mastery over darkness, turmoil, disorder. But even in failure there was triumph, for the will, though conquered, had tried, had made the most valiant of human attempts to fulfill its destiny and in so doing had set a model of courage and determination. The concept was ecstatic, heroic, tragic. It was simultaneously pure movement and pure drama. It did not refer to a particular person in a specific time or place; it was the abstraction of the nature of man.

Because the theory of the arc was inherently dramatic, it ran contrary to the rising trend of the late '50's, which some called "non-objective," some "non-literal," some "abstract" or—if derogatory—"dehumanized." But the idea, everyone agreed, was to reinstate dancing as the proper content of dance. No more plots, no more role-playing; just people dancing. Yet in the early days of the modern dance, it was Doris Humphrey who was fascinated with the potentialities of spatial, rhythmic, and dynamic patterns as the subject of dance. Who else was ever so intrigued with the contrast between a "circular descent" and a "pointed ascent"? Or with the "pleasures of counterpoint"? One innovative choreographer wrote in the 1960's that he thought of dance as the "drama of motion," apparently forgetting—or perhaps never knowing—that Doris had made a dance with that title in 1930.

In the '60's however, the approach had a rather different edge, for the choreographer wanted to let the movement "speak for itself."

The trend was to find movement anywhere—by improvisation, by chance, by systemic methods. The results were then allowed to take on whatever "atmosphere" happened to ensue, creating an open-ended structure susceptible to any number of unexpected shapes and any number of interpretations. By temperament, Doris could not be so permissive. While she wanted to expand the range of movement previously allowed the dancer, she wanted to expand it in her chosen direction. She had to control the atmosphere.

And here they did differ. For Doris, the fall and recovery, climaxed by the suspension, spoke the nobility of the human spirit. This was her faith; she would have it no other way. With the single exception of *Corybantic,* which seemed to state that man's warring nature could be only temporarily contained and that he would eventually revert to hostility, all of her works are resolved on a positive assertion, an affirmation that man can and will live in peace with himself and in harmony with his fellow man. (Leo asked her if she would ever find peace of mind; perhaps *Corybantic* revealed her personal conflict.) Even *Ignacio* "seems unendingly to exist with strength and grace in the memory."

In her later years, Doris admitted that audiences probably found her ideas overly simple and naïve; but she believed in them and she always had. In the draft for the first chapter of a book tentatively titled *What a Dancer Thinks About* (the typescript is undated, but it refers to *Passacaglia* and may be what she was working on with Leo in August, 1939), she wrote:

> . . . the mass pattern of the dance may hold the mirror up to humanity. It can indicate its vulgar grimacing images, scrambling and competing in wild riotous disorder. It catches the audience in the theatre in a sober and reflective mood and shows it the image of the drunken, orgiastic confusion which is optimistically called Civilization, and to which it returns once it steps outside. It is like playing to an alcoholic a victrola record of his previous night's indiscretions. Before the audience leaves, however, the dancer gives it an object lesson in the smoothness of line, beauty of form, and clarity of purpose a group can achieve by the coordination of its parts and the mutual cooperation of individuals composing the group.

Is it naïve, irrelevant? Doris once said that if we were to acquire tails, our sense of motor rhythm would change. We have not yet

acquired tails, nor have we lost those twin but conflicting desires—
to bask in the warm comfort of the hearth and to dare the cold
unknown beyond. Until such evolutions take place, her works will
still speak to us of a reality and an ideal that we can understand;
they can illuminate for us, as only great art can, a way to cope with
the reality and aspire to the ideal.

Doris Humphrey's stature as an artist is not fully recognized
today nor was it in her lifetime. Oh, there were tributes and even a
little money—but only a little and very late. Mostly there were
hardships, and many—though not all of them—were caused by
lack of money. Her husband once said that all she wanted was the
freedom to pursue art and to produce it. For that freedom she had to
struggle constantly. Leo added: "The mind went in one direction."

Speaking at Connecticut College in July, 1957, José Limón recalled the devotion that so consistently and so exclusively motivated
the person he described as "heroic":

> This woman had more guts than anyone I have ever known or
> heard of. Rebuffs, neglect meant nothing. The constant pain of
> a crippling disability was serenely ignored. The important thing,
> the core, the essence of existence lay in the dance, in the danc-
> ers, in the studio, the rehearsals, the passion, the form, the
> beauty and ugliness, the lyric utterance of the human spirit.

The commitment that enabled her to survive vicissitudes that would
surely have crushed one of less stoical disposition also made her feel
that sacrifice—of family, friends, leisure, physical comforts—was
simply a mandatory way of life. Yet sacrifice added the burden of
guilt. She wanted to give to her parents, her husband, her son, and
she tried. But the whip was relentless. Call it dedication, courage,
will, drive, neurotic compulsion—the name is of no consequence.
It brought forth masterpieces.

On the back of another one of those grocery lists, Doris wrote
a passage that she attributed to Oscar Wilde: "It is through Art and
through Art only that we can realize our perfection; through Art
and Art only that we can shield ourselves from the sordid perils
of actual existence." Through pain and deprivation, art was her
strength, her refuge, her joy. It is the legacy that she has left to us.

The Dance Writings of Doris Humphrey

MOST dancers are more articulate than the general public would believe, but even so, Doris Humphrey was extraordinarily articulate for a dancer. While most choreographers prefer to let their dances speak for themselves, she liked to speak for her dances.

Often she spoke about them to herself, jotting down ideas for movements and groupings as they came to her; after a work was completed, especially in the early days, she often made choreographic scripts for later reference and frequently devised program notes that set forth her intentions, sometimes in considerable detail. Her lectures were carefully prepared, the sequence of introduction, development, climax, conclusion all set down in very proper outline form. Sometimes she wrote out special phrasings or images that she wanted to be sure to use.

Statements were essential, for as a crusader she had to explain, analyze, spread the gospel. She had to publish. Her major work, of course, was that remarkable book *The Art of Making Dances*, which occupied her thoughts off and on for twenty years and was in press when she died. Beyond that, more than a dozen of her articles appeared in magazines or anthologies during her lifetime; and, had time permitted, there would probably have been even more, for her papers contain drafts of numerous pieces—some in a variety of much-worked-over versions—that she never completed to her own satisfaction. The finished ones, characteristically lucid and concise, are shaped with the dexterity of a master craftsman. Doris Humphrey worked at writing as she worked at choreography—thoughtfully, thoroughly, and with conviction.

Space permits that only a sampling of her writings be included in this book. The selections cover the full span of her choreographic career, and include not only published works but certain of her manuscripts as well.

THE PUBLISHED WRITINGS OF DORIS HUMPHREY

A. "Daffodils," "Greek Sacrificial Dance," "Will o' The Wisp." In Mary Wood Hinman, *Gymnastic and Folk Dancing*. New York: Barnes, 1916
B. "Interpreter or Creator?" *The Dance Magazine*, January, 1929
C. "What Shall We Dance About?" *Trend*, June-July-August, 1932
D. "Dance, Little Chillun!" *The American Dancer*, July, 1933
E. "Jitterbug, Jitterbug—Fly Away Home!" *The Spur*, December, 1938
F. "This Modern Dance." *The Dancing Times*, December, 1938
G. "A Home for Humphrey-Weidman." *Dance Observer*, November, 1940
H. "Reflections on the Humphrey-Weidman Season." *Dance Observer*, June-July, 1941
I. "My Approach to the Modern Dance." In Frederick R. Rogers, *Dance: A Basic Educational Technique*. New York: Macmillan, 1941
J. "Choreographing Bach." *The New York Times*, February 14, 1943
K. "America's Modern Dance." *Theatre Arts*, September, 1950
L. "Dance Drama." In Walter Sorell, *The Dance Has Many Faces*. New York: World, 1951; second edition, New York: Columbia University Press, 1966
M. "Advice to Young Choreographers." *The Juilliard Review*, Spring, 1956
N. Doris Humphrey Answers the Critics." [1957] *Dance and Dancers*, March, 1959
O. "Doris Humphrey Speaks . . ." [November 7, 1956] *Dance Observer*, March, 1962
P. *The Art of Making Dances*. New York: Rinehart, 1959; paperback edition, New York: Evergreen Books (Grove Press), 1962

GREEK SACRIFICIAL DANCE
[Music: Saint-Saens]

o   o   o
3   2   1

Entrance of the three central girls walking abreast toward audience.
Step-Three slow walking steps and three fast running steps. (Meas. 1 to
4) Repeat steps (Meas. 1–16) Enter in this formation, while the
chorus enters and dances. No. 1 and 3 down on knee away from
audience and arm away from audience in the Greek offering position (Elbow bent in and palm up) No. 2 stands up with arms up
and palms up elbow being a little bent.

1—Enter Chorus: 8 on a side and numbered thus.
  Right side 2,1,2,1,2,1,2,1 leader.–leader–2,1,2,1,2,1,2,1, left side
  Each leader comes in from opposite sides (Left and right) with the
  same step as above (Meas. 1–16.) Form a circle around the three
  central girls. Hands joined. Heads down. All circle to left with the
  same step as above. (Meas. 17–24) Raising arms and heads with the
  hands still joined forward five slow walking steps to the center (Meas.
  25–29) All turn to right and run 4 steps away from center and face
  out (Meas. 30–32)

2—Continue in the same direction facing out. Hands joined and Heads
  down. (Meas. 33–40) All "Ones" go in to center 5 walking steps
  gradually lifting your hands to the Greek offering position over head.
  All "Two's" go backward 4 steps kneeling on the fifth count, hands in
  offering position (Meas. 41–48) "Ones" now backward and "Two's"
  forward in their original circle and pause taking a hold of hands
  (Meas. 49–56) All raise hands over head slowly and heads back and
  then to side (Meas. 57–64) All move up to original leaders, forming
  a straight line. The two leaders facing each other. Each girl except
  the leaders place their hand, away from the audience, on the shoulder, next to the audience, of the girl in front. The leader's arm next
  to the audience in the Greek position (elbow bent in and palm up,
  level with your chin) (Meas. 65–68.)

3—Each leader leads forward (Meas. 1–16) left side leader going in
  front of right side leader. Make a sharp turn towards audience leaders again facing each other, and coming up towards the three central
  figures, one and three having arisen slowly while the rest are making
  a straight line, facing audience (Meas. 1–16.)

4—The two leaders and the three central girls circle arms out then in
  and up in front of face in offering position, over head palms up.
  (Meas. 69–70) One girl from each side next to the leader do likewise both moving at the same time (Meas. 71–72) continue on to

the end of the line each one raising hands up in 2 measures (Meas. 73–84.)

5—All lower hands slowly (Meas. 85–92) The end girl from each side leads out to exits away from center (Meas. 93–108) with slow walking steps, and the three center girls turn their backs to the audience and walk straight back and out.

Source: Mary Wood Hinman, *Gymnastic and Folk Dancing*, Vol IV. New York: A. S. Barnes & Co., 1916.

CIRCULAR DESCENT
Circular Descent – Medtner – count in six

Begin—

Move to left—circle through body [-] arms & back follow—bend body & left knee [-] six counts

Move same way to right six counts [-] right arm at end of phrase curved over head, head down [,] weight on right

Repeat first phrase to left with a deeper bend, wider circular succession.

Phrase to the right, both arms cross, right knee turned in, body bends right

Repeat opening phrase to left [-] come up slightly on "and" following six to prepare for turn.

Turn left on right foot, arms close—step feet apart facing left—move into succession like 1st phrase but to the right

Repeat turn & succession opp. direction & foot.

Body circle to right [,] arms follow over head & pause on accent.

Immediately follow with gesture down right

Four small body circles [-] side, up, down left [,] rising higher each time to perpendicular—and stop in original position

Music original phrase—with strong accent draw left foot to right, body in circle to left & finish right, finish profile left bending slightly side & back, arms [:] right over head, left around body in front

Turn slowly to left keeping weight on right [,] pushing on beat with left, arms and body stretch out to horizontal slowly. Half way round after six counts, recover almost to original position, continue turn with same movements to facing front in 4 more counts. On five, six stretch left leg to left in two pushes, and equalize weight on both feet, body bending right—arms as in diagram (bottom p. 2*)

Keeping same accent, throw weight on left, bending lower to right, right hand to floor almost, keep turning left [-] draw right foot up, face back [,] arms over head.

Continue turn to left, face front, step to left, move in circle to figure 4 (p. 1) straighten on end of phrase [-] arms straight.

Music, second theme increasing accelerando
Beginning here floor plan follows a semi-circle and back to center

On 1 [,] step across right, body moves back and circle to right, turn on right foot once round—arms together as in last figure, on count 4 step left, body bent forward and turn once on right (like pirouette) right arm breast high [,] left low around body in front.

Repeat this double turn a little broader & faster but step to side on one, cross on two.

Turn again like the first half of figure, then step right, left leg across back off floor, arms make double hourglass motions (in circles in front) [-] finish very low in knees [,] both ft on floor [,] body facing forward, sway back on right foot. Change weight to left and turn, circle in body (similar to figure 12)

Repeat figure 14 with circular motions of arms the same —also repeat low turn following it, but finish on both toes facing left, arms close around body [,] head back

Step backwards, and 1 and 2 and 3, like music, moving to center [,] turning half to right as you go. Fall on left knee facing front [,] body bent left (these gestures following not clear). [sic]

Sway on both knees, gesture to rt. [,] back to left, throw weight on left hand, face back on knees, throw right

* P. 2 of DH's holograph script—i.e., figure 9.—S.J.C.

arm over head and to floor [-] turn to face front on knees [,] arms far forward together on floor, draw up to position like figure 1 on knees

Music original theme
Make circular movements beginning to left like original, then right, with left knee off floor, then left with right knee up, head profile to right, stand slowly [,] arms making in and out parallel circles in profile right, finish facing front like figure 4.

Begin turn like figure 8 & 9 to left but stepping forward on left on beat [-] increase speed to whirl, arms horizontal—finish facing diag. left [as] in figure 6—but reversed with strong accent [-] immediately back with rt. arm to floor & right knee, body back—slip to lying down, sliding on hands, right knee turned in.

NEW DANCE

There is a great difference between the modern dance as it is presented today and as it was presented as little as five or six years ago. When I gave my first recital in New York apart from the Denishawn company, the stage was bare, there was only one pianist for the music, and costuming was at a minimum. Now, however, the modern dance leaves this period of barrenness and comes forward as a new theatrical form.

In the past two seasons, Charles Weidman and I have developed our forms away from the recital stage, where each dance was about five minutes long, and have composed long ballets, consecutive in idea. More significant than this is the fact that these new dances are the comment of two American dancers on contemporary life. This comment naturally brings them close to the theatre, but this is a theatre of movement rather than of words.

It might be interesting to describe one of them in some detail, since the manner of building will show how a large, complex theme may be presented entirely through movement, and, I believe, more forcibly than could be done through words.

I have composed a trilogy of which the general theme is the relationship of man to man. There are three long works which would take an evening and a half for presentation. One is in symphonic form and two are in dramatic form. The first, *New Dance*, represents the world as it should be, where each person has a clear and harmonious relationship to his fellow beings. The second, *Theatre Piece*, shows life as it is today— a grim business of survival by competition. Much of this is done in satire.

The third, *With My Red Fires,* deals with love between man and woman, and between two women.

Let me describe *New Dance* for you. It was to be a dance of affirmation from disorganization to organization. It begins with two dancers with the group standing on the blocks in the corners as audience. For this Introduction, since I wished at first to convey a sense of incompletion, I chose the Broken Form, by which I mean an unfolding continual change, with contrast but very little repetition. This is the same form that Mr. Weidman and I used in *Rudepoema,* where a movement was done several times and then discarded, giving way to new ones.

By this means I was able to present the main themes of the whole composition, which were elaborated in the remaining sections of the dance: First Theme, Second Theme, Third Theme, Processional, Celebration, and Variations and Conclusion. I used lateral lines, perpendiculars—in fact, as many varieties as possible to convey the sense of a jetting forth of movement as yet disorganized.

The movements used in this Introduction were by no means spontaneous. I had a very clear reason for them. They were mainly feet and leg themes; I consciously eliminated any free use of the hands, arms, head, and torso. My main theme was to move from the simple to the complex, from an individual integration to a group integration, and therefore I thought it best at first to confine myself to movement which was in a way primitive. The primitive urge for movement—in fact, all early dancing made use of steps and leg gestures but scarcely ever used the rest of the body with any emphasis. Therefore, until the group integration had been achieved, the feet and leg themes seemed more expressive.

There are two essential movements of the body: the change of weight and the breath-rhythm. After the various themes had been stated in the Introduction, I used this essential changing of weight as the basis for the First Theme. The Second Theme used the breath-rhythm.

The Third Theme, which was composed by Mr. Weidman, used both of these in a single section. My only function in this was to explain the general idea: that it must be a loose form, broken, unbalanced, not symmetrical, and it must have an inconclusive ending. Each of these themes was in this sense inconclusive, because each was only a part of a whole. I would never perform any of these sections as separate pieces, except the Variations and Conclusion which is a summation of them all, because there is a dramatic idea behind them of which each theme expresses only a fraction.

This dramatic idea played a large part in determining what movements and what forms were necessary. After Mr. Weidman and I, as leaders and integrators, had stated our themes together and alone, it was necessary to bring the women under my orbit and the men under Mr. Weidman's before they could be finally fused.

The Broken Form would do no longer. Those themes which were

stated had to be conveyed to a group, and a group never accepts immediately en masse. For the First Theme, then, I used the Cumulative Form. The leader molds the group; the women are gradually drawn into the movement. One dancer may cross the stage and return; when she crosses again, two or three more follow her until finally the whole group is doing that particular movement-phrase. This section ends inconclusively.

In Second Theme, the leader again tries to unify the group. The dance ends in a revolving pulsation, but is again not cohesive enough to make a compact whole. It is inconclusive because there are only women. In Third Theme, the men take the stage and are compelled and molded by Mr. Weidman as leader. Now all themes have been stated for the groups and to finish them the two groups must be brought together.

Processional uses the Cumulative Form once more and in movement brings the themes to a head; in dramatic idea brings the whole group to an integrated whole. I chose a slow tempo for this because that gives a sense of greater control and, theatrically, is obviously in sharp contrast to the preceding sections. The men never deviate from a perpendicular but the women are fluid and make a wavering line. It was here that I used symmetry for the first time as the best way to express cohesion and completion.

The groups have now fused and break into a Celebration, which is built in fugue form, joyous in character. The fugue was eminently suitable to express a harmonious chorus wherein no member was more important than another. It is a short theme and goes directly into a square dance, which is again consciously symmetrical. I could have used several symmetrical forms here, but chose the square dance because at a moment of climax forward movement is the most powerful. Other forms do not have that direct impact. The ballet, incidentally, has used the square a great deal but rarely uses all four sides. It confines itself to the side from the back of the stage to the front and then weakens that impact by almost walking around the other three to get back to its starting point.

Having thus unified the men's group and the women's group, one more section was necessary in order to express the individual in relation to that group. Too many people seem content to achieve a mass-movement and then stop. I wished to insist that there is also an individual life within that group life.

All previous action had taken place within an arena marked by masses of blocks along the side of the stage. Mr. Weidman and I had stated our themes in this arena before the watching crowd and had finally brought that crowd down into our field of activity. It was obvious, now that all were working in unison, that the arena was useless since there was no longer any conflict between those who do and those who watch. In order to focus the dance and fully convey that sense of unity, the curtain was lowered momentarily while the blocks were moved into a pyramid in center stage. The whirling star pattern was used around this pyramid to avoid monotony. I could have allowed the two lines of dancers to remain in one place to form a path for the new dancers who now came in and performed briefly their own personal themes. However, by having this line whirl and by having the new dancers enter from different directions, a deadness was avoided and a greater space and excitement was achieved. In this section, Variations and Conclusion, I used the Repetitional Form where the group performs the same movement. The brief solos as in Broken Form against the *basso sustenuto* of the group.

It is this method of work, which I have described for *New Dance,* that broadens the field of the modern dance, gives it a new life and a new potency. Solo dances flow out of the group and back into it again without break and the most important part is the group. Except for an occasional brilliant individual, the day of the solo dance is over. It is only through this large use of groups of men and women that the modern dance can completely do what it has always said it would do. It has not done it before mainly because a new technique and new forms had to be evolved. We were forced to work from the ground up.

Now we have reached sufficiently firm ground to be able to add those embellishments which we had been forced to discard in our search for a new technique of movement. *New Dance* and the other two works which I have not described are no longer a series of episodes strung along in a row, as too many attempts at large forms have been. They are a cohesive form in the way that symphony is and need neither music nor story as crutches to support them.

Source: Doris Humphrey papers, no date [1936].

THEATRE PIECE
Choreography by Doris Humphrey
[Choreography for *In the Theatre* by Charles Weidman]
Music by Wallingford Riegger

This dance depicts the world as it is today: a place of grim competition. Miss Humphrey has called it *Theatre Piece* to stress the fact that, even though this savage competition is dominant at the present time, it is far from being the whole of life. It distorts and kills too much of life that is good and erects symbols and numbers and figures in place of human values. Throughout the dance, Miss Humphrey plays the part of one who rebels against this way of life and prophesies a better way of living.

PROLOGUE: The roles are assigned to the various dancers so that, as in a theatre within a theatre, they may enact this partial, abortive life. In the next four sections, different phases of modern life are shown.

BEHIND WALLS: The first scene the actors show has to do with business, where brokers, stenographers and business men are seen in wild competition. One figure above the rest controls them like a dictator and directs their transactions and money-changing as though they were inhuman puppets. Here, and in the remainer of the dance, Miss Humphrey dances the part of a rebel.

IN THE OPEN (HUNTING DANCE): Here we see the methods of business carried over into daily life. The stenographers and shopgirls put on their hats and go out from their place of business at the end of the day. When they find a man, they exhibit themselves and have a great struggle to see which shall get him.

INTERLUDE: In a brief lull when the forces of competition are quiescent, Miss Humphrey in revolt against the world as it is dances a theme of harmony and peace. The movements are prophetic of "New Dance" in which the ideal world is depicted.

IN THE STADIUM: Everyone is champion here, whether defeated or not. The dance shows football and golf; the same repeated movements; the same crowds doing the same things and all reacting at the same time, as they sit eagerly awaiting a "thrill."

IN THE THEATRE: Again there is competition of one actor against another. They make fools of themselves in order to curry the favor of the crowd which seems slightly bored at their antics. At the least ripple of applause, they all bob up and down like loose-jointed puppets.

THE RACE: Having presented this competition, this grim race for livelihood, in four daily activities, Miss Humphrey brings this idea to a climax in this section. All of these various aspects are fused into the single fact that underlies them all: a race, made breakneck and pointless.

EPILOGUE (THE RETURN): Miss Humphrey's rebellion is carried to a climax. The group is suddenly brought out of its theatre-acting with a realization of something new and better. The dance ends on a hushed note of expectancy.

Source: Doris Humphrey papers, no date [1936].

LAMENT *
Choreography by Doris Humphrey
[Music by Norman Lloyd]

This is a dramatic version of the poem "Lament for Ignacio Sánchez Mejías" by Federico García Lorca. Lorca was, before his death during

---

* This describes the projected work; the actual production differed in a number of details.—S.J.C.

the Spanish revolution, Spain's leading poet and dramatist, and his Lament is considered his finest work. The poem concerns the life and death of an Andalusian bull-fighter of great prowess and beauty, and was chosen by José Limón because of its power and intensity.

The poem is in four parts, each of which depicts a different attitude toward the death of the bull-fighter, Ignacio, ranging from the impassioned utterances of the beholder, to the formal elegy of tribute. Since these two expressions of the theme are so marked, the dramatization provides two women to speak the poetry—one, a fateful and impersonal figure who records his destiny; the other an anguished observer of the well-loved hero. The formal introduction which precedes the actual poem serves to introduce the three characters, "Ignacio," "Guardian of Destiny," "Witness and Mourner" in their dramatic relationships. Because of the special significance with which all Spanish poets, and especially Lorca, view blood, and the spilling of it, the three are bound round by a red thread which symbolically entangles the Man, his Fate, and his Mourner.

The entire poem has been cut extensively in the interests of pace, clarity and dramatic impact; the actual wording is a compilation from many translations. The entire conception has been pointed toward a more inclusive meaning than is strictly indicated in the poem—the keynote is in the lines of the last part:

> "For you are dead forever
> like all the dead of the whole earth,
> like all the dead who are forgotten."

The drama of the bull-fighter is intended to signify the struggle of all men of courage who contend in the ring of Life and who meet a tragic end, to which they are bound by destiny, and to which they must go alone.

Edwin Honeg [Honig] says of Spanish poetry:
"(It is) alive with characters whose feet are aching to dance,
whose voices at every turn are breaking into inspired Song."

LAMENT

Based on the poem "Lament for Ignacio Sánchez Mejías" by
Federico Garcia Lorca
Dramatized and adapted by *Doris Humphrey* for
José Limón

Cast:

    Ignacio—Contender in the Ring
    First Woman—Guardian of Destiny
    Second Woman—Witness and Mourner

At Curtain:

Music   The three figures stand center, framed by a partly open curtain mid-stage. A narrow red scarf, symbol of their blood destiny, entwines them.

Scene I   ENTRANCE INTO THE ARENA:

Music   In action only, Ignacio demands that the Guardian release him so that he may meet his enemy in the ring.

    She unties the knot, he disengages himself and the Mourner, and circles the stage as an heroic preamble to his encounter. Exit right—the Witness and Mourner takes her place to watch and recount his struggle, seen only by her. The Guardian, near her, holds the red thread of his destiny in her hands and waits.

Scene II   THE CATCHING AND THE DEATH:

GUARDIAN   At five in the afternoon
It was exactly five in the afternoon

MOURNER   A child brought a white sheet

GUARDIAN   At five in the afternoon

MOURNER   A rush-basket of slaked lime

GUARDIAN   At five in the afternoon

MOURNER   The rest was death and death alone

GUARDIAN   At five in the afternoon

Music

MOURNER   The refrain of a song strikes up

GUARDIAN   At five in the afternoon

MOURNER   And, all heart, the bull charges

GUARDIAN   At five in the afternoon

MOURNER   Death laid its eggs in his wound
Bones and flutes sound in his ears
The room is iridescent with agony

GUARDIAN   At five in the afternoon

MOURNER   His wounds blaze like Suns

GUARDIAN   At five in the afternoon

MOURNER   Now from afar-off comes gangrene
A lily trumpet through his green veins

GUARDIAN   At five in the afternoon
At five in the afternoon

MOURNER   Ay, that terrible five in the afternoon

GUARDIAN   It was five by all the clocks
It was five in the shadow of the afternoon

Scene III   THE SPILLING OF BLOOD

    The Guardian with one hand retains the red scarf and with the other opens the curtain at right, where Ignacio's struggle with death has taken place. This revealing of the place of his defeat continues through the first half of the dialogue in Scene III.

MOURNER   I do not want to see it!
for I do not want to see the blood
of Ignacio over the arena.
Do not bid me to see it!
(*Ignacio* enters the arena during the following lines)

GUARDIAN   Up the stairs went Ignacio
With all his death upon his shoulders

Music

His eyes did not close
When he saw the horns near

Music   IGNACIO, during the following dialogue, expresses the meaning of the words through gesture and movement, moving sparsely when the words are spoken, and freely during musical interludes.

GUARDIAN   There was no prince in Seville
Who could compare to him
Nor any sword like his sword
Nor any heart so fervent

Music   two minutes

GUARDIAN   The air of Andalusian Rome
gilded his head
on which his smile was a nard
of grace and intelligence.
What a great bull-fighter in the ring!

Music   one bar

GUARDIAN   What a mountaineer in the mountains!

Music   one bar

GUARDIAN   How tender with the dew!

Music   one bar

GUARDIAN   How dazzling at the fair!

Music   one bar

GUARDIAN   How tremendous with the last
Banderillos of darkness!

Music   continues through following dialogue. The Guardian, with her red scarf, slowly encircles IGNACIO with her fateful step, also speaking. IGNACIO gradually yields to the red circle.

GUARDIAN   But now he sleeps endlessly
Now the moss and the grass
Open with sure fingers
the flower of his skull.
And now his blood comes out singing
like a long, dark, sad tongue
to form a pool of agony
close to the starry Guadalquivir.

Music   two minutes—through the struggle between them, the Guardian has bound him to her, and leads him toward the left of stage, passing before the Mourner

MOURNER   Oh nightingale of his veins!
No.
I do not want to see it!
No chalice can contain it
No swallows can drink it
No frost of light can cool it
No crystal can cover it with silver.
No.
I do not want to see it!

Scene IV   BODY PRESENT

Music   The Guardian reappears center alone, and opens the curtain at left to reveal a rude catafalque of stone on which the body of IGNACIO appears to be resting, (or a symbolic representation of this idea). Music of a funereal nature continues under the dialogue.

GUARDIAN   Stone is a forehead where dreams moan
Where is no curving watercourse
              nor frozen cypresses
Stone is a shoulder to carry time
with its trees of tears and ribbons
            and planets.

The Mourner moves to the left at the head of the catafalque—music more agitated and accented. The Guardian at extreme left stage.

MOURNER   What do they say? Here lies a stinking silence.
We have before us a laid-out body, which is fading
A bright form, once with nightingales,
And we watch it fill up with bottomless decay.

Music

I do not want them to cover his face with handkerchiefs
that he may get used to the death he carries.
Go! Ignacio; do not hear the hot bellowing of the bulls
Sleep, fly far, rest; even the sea must die!

Music

The Mourner moves quickly away to the opposite stage—her movements carrying out the desperate cry to Ignacio—Go! fly far—

Scene V   ABSENT SOUL

The Mourner and the Guardian ceremoniously move to far sides of the stage—music throughout.

MOURNER   For you are dead forever
like all the dead of the whole earth,
like all the dead who are forgotten—

(She   The bull does not know you, nor the fig tree
wanders   nor horses, nor the ants in your own house.
through   The child does not know you, nor the afternoon
the place   For you are dead forever.
of his
killing)   Nobody knows you, no. But I sing of you
I sing for a later time, of your profile and your grace
The celebrated ripeness of your skill
Your appetite for death and the taste of his mouth
And the sadness lying beneath your valiant joy.

(The Guardian and the Mourner begin to draw the curtains together, one from each end. The shadowy person of IGNACIO
as he was in Scene III, but moving more slowly, seems unendingly to exist with strength and grace in the memory. He is
unseen by the two women. The moving curtains obscure him,
and before they finally close, the Mourner speaks:

MOURNER   I sing his elegance in words that tremble
And remember a sad wind through the olive trees.

Music   The Guardian holds open the curtains for the Mourner, who
exits through them, bearing on her shoulders one end of the
red scarf which the Guardian holds. The Guardian re-ties the
knot with which she first entangled the three and follows the
Mourner.

Curtain

25 to 28 minutes

Source: Doris Humphrey papers, no date [1946].

INVENTION
[Notes for Norman Lloyd, composer]

movement

I Solo (José') (you have this)

II. 1st Duet — A - Betty - B - José *allegro*

A 3/8 | 4 | 16 | 2/4 7 | *add 8*
B 2/4 | ___ | 12 | 3/8 8 | 2/4 1 | *mms 35*

A (A) (Themes in José's solo)
B 5/8 | 2 | 7/8 2 | 2/4 4 | V
   F Broder

A Tempo

A 2/4 | 4 | (B) 1 | 3/8 2 | } like
B   P rit. | F ___ | music   P alone | inter lude

A 2/4 | ___ | 3/8 2 | 2/4 3 |
B   1 | music P alone | M7 |
   7

A 2/4 | (C) 12 | 4 | Sforz. 3/4 6 |
   M7 . legato rest | stac. | Broder FF
B

A Tempo

A 2/4 | 6 | (D) 6/8 11 | 6/8 1 |
B   P. rit. | F Con brio | ♪ ♪ ♪ ♪ ♪ |
  Piz.

Segue

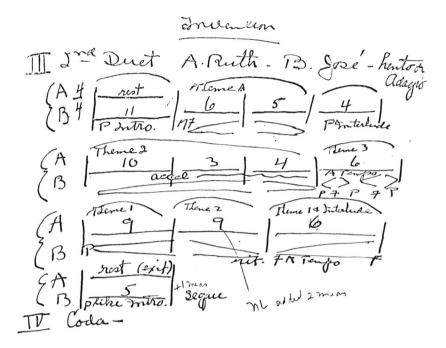

Notes: The single line in a measure means two dances are in unison. Separate lines for A. & B. means two different parts in the same measure or phrase.

Don't be bound absolutely by the phrase lengths—they can be a bar or two longer or shorter. Also in 2nd duet if you want to deviate from the 4/4, do that.

The character of 1st duet is bright, even maestoso in passages marked "broader."

The second duet I based on "breath rhythm" as differing from metric rhythm in the solo & 1st duet, so that, within almost every bar there is a rise & fall like breathing. The whole is slightly romantic and mysterious.

When you send the music, please indicate how the phrases correspond with my notes.

Source: Doris Humphrey papers, no date [1949].

INTERPRETER OR CREATOR?
A Young Dance-Teacher Outlines the Difficulties in
Becoming a Serious Artist—As They Seem to Her

Now that the dance has overflowed the narrow banks of the folk dance and the ballet, and has spread like a mighty river in all directions, no one can be sure which is the main artery, or venture to be dogmatic about the proper course. Hence, any statement concerning the subject is an opinion, and should be labeled with a large sign reading: "It seems to me." Having hung this in a conspicuous place, we can begin with a clear conscience to diagram a course down one of the new channels.

Learning to dance is primarily learning to mold the body into a fluid and transparent state, so as to express ideas or emotions in an art form. Achieving this end obviously falls into two parts of training, the comparatively sure and simple mechanical molding process, classed as technique, and the more vague and difficult intellectual and emotional development loosely known as inspiration. Both must have their full share of time and study or the resulting art will be abortive, a fact which a great many students have failed to recognize sufficiently. If the mechanical process were all, one could admit the hosts of technical experts as artist-dancers, or if spirit were all, a great many "arty" people with lots of feeling and imagination but no form could be accepted as true exponents of the dance. But the principal fact that an equal proportion of each should be the aim of the dancer is well established, and is accepted by almost all artists; although as to what constitutes form, and what spirit, there is a very wide divergence of opinion. It is a common fault, for instance, to confuse physical vitality with spiritual power. I mean by spiritual, loosely speaking, both imagination and emotion. Often a dance lacking in imagination is said to be done with spirit when it is merely done with pep springing from a vital, healthy body whose owner is young and happy. A dance lacking in form is more easily recognizable as we are always more keenly alert to weaknesses in design or technique than we are to falseness in conception. Of these two parts of training, form and spirit, I will give an outline first of the way to achieve form, the process by which the body is molded so as to form a medium for those ideas and emotions necessary to make art, should they be forthcoming.

This training should begin with a foundation of rhythm and music; muscular coordination based on a natural flow of movement; a sense of design both in time and space, time as in music, space as in architecture; a copious vocabulary—as many different designs as possible, as many ways of saying the same thing as possible; pantomime, the way to tell a concrete story without words. Next should follow a general survey of the history and characteristic movement of the dance in every country so as to give the potential dancer as wide a grasp as possible, and at the same time an appreciation and understanding of its past manifestations as a background for further work. This is a difficult part of the dance to pursue, because of the paucity of teachers who really know how the people of the world dance. Even yet I venture to say there are hundreds of instructors who think the Japanese always trot, fluttering a fan in one hand, and wiggling the first finger of the other, who never heard of the Noh, the ancient dance of Japan, and whose idea of headdress is the traditional chrysanthemum over each ear.

After this direct study of the art should come at least a cursory survey of closely related subjects, such as color, costuming, stage setting, lighting and make-up, and a few miscellaneous but important bits of knowledge: such as program building and picture posing. All this outline of training forms a technique adequate to express any idea, provided the student has that thing vaguely designated as talent.

Parallel with the technical training should flow the study of actual dances, compositions which use the technique, but have as a motive power an idea removed from the physical plane. And this is the rock on which so many artistic careers are wrecked. Dancers do not know how to practice technique for its own sake at one instant, and then vitalize those same movements with spiritual power at the next. Now is the time to train the emotions, to stimulate feeling by every possible device, for emotion vitalizes motion. Now is the time to encourage ideas, everybody's ideas, and train taste and discrimination in their selection, for imagination may be fanned to a flame by the breath of the fantasy of other minds, and a constant association with esthetic ideas. This spiritual quickening will make clear that some individuals are naturally creative and will never lose that flame once it is kindled, and others are interpretive and will respond to inspiration from without. Now having trained our dancer theoretically, let us consider just one of the difficulties confronting a student looking forward to a career as a serious artist.

There is the problem of obtaining dances, from the standpoint of the interpretive artist. It is obvious that an artist of this class should have a wide choice in compositions to be used. That this is not true is a sad fact, due to the lack of a satisfactory way of recording the dance, so that interpretation has the appalling limitation of space, a difficulty not shared by any of the other arts. That is to say, if the creator or teacher is not physically accessible to the would-be interpreter, nothing can be done. Often the interpreter finds that he has exhausted the resources of his instructor in dances that are suitable to him, and that the instructor has not the means to gather material for him from far away sources. When, in addition to this, one realizes that in the Occidental world there are probably not more than twenty cities which hold true creative artists of the first or even second calibre, it is small wonder that thousands of sincere interpreters are thrown upon their own resources of creation, or allow themselves to be dragged through the tasteless and uninspired creations of dull minds. It seems to me that the only solution of this problem is the motion picture, which, when it is adapted to our requirements, will do more to raise the art of the dance than any other one thing I know of. However, in spite of the confusion in which the dance is now involved, it is bound to stumble on, due to its tremendous new-found vitality, until it reaches the perfection attained by the other arts. In that day learning to dance will be less of a dark uncertain adventure and more of a joyous pilgrimage on a shining road.

Source: *The Dance Magazine*, January 1929.

WHAT SHALL WE DANCE ABOUT?

There is only one thing to dance about: the meaning of one's personal experience and this experience must be taken in its literal sense as action, and not as intellectual conception. Art, like religion, is based on events; physical manifestations which have been lived through and therefore represent action, emotion. It is important in the "dance" to remember to keep drawing on the well-springs of experience of this nature, as movement is the very essence of the dance.

So long as the dance moves, it lives as dance but the moment static ideas are introduced either in the form or the conception, it becomes something other than itself—drama, painting, literature—or it collapses of inanition. For this reason, static ideas are dangerous. They tend to stop the flow of movement. For instance, democracy is a static idea, a collective noun representing many actions, many desires, and as a thing in itself—a symbol—is useless to the dance. Such a crystallized conception could not be represented by one figure or even a number of them, although such attempts are made with lamentable frequency. But how some part of democracy works, or should work, or how its various actions interlace might be suggested in movement convincingly, even when the form seems far removed from the original idea. Four abstract themes, all moving equally and harmoniously together like a fugue would convey the significance of democracy far better than would one woman dressed in red, white and blue, with stars in her hair.

On the whole, symbolism is too dead for the dramatic dance. I do not mean to infer that the dance must always have a specific theme such as democracy behind it but that there must be some conception even in the most abstract composition—and static ideas must be guarded against throughout. The common fault in abstractions is to throw the emphasis on design, either of mass or line, and so achieve an effect as dead as that of democracy in a flag. The obvious conclusion is that the dance must move and not pose; and that the dancer must choose from experience that which is dynamic—and not static. It is not sufficient, however, for the artist merely to record his personal experiences, even assuming he has chosen dynamic ones, for they have meaning only as he is aware of their relationship to other people and things both past and present. He must know not only how his experience originates, how it affects others, of what it is made, what its proper place is among things; but also what part it takes in the organic progression of his race. A race is an entity evolving from form to form just as other biological entities do and experience is most truly meaningful when it is seen as a part of this whole.

The most difficult problem for the American dancer is the realization of this relationship, both because of his conglomerate racial heritage without a common folk-lore or mythology; and because his environment has divested him of his religious faith. For people in other times and countries, a common religion has been so well-established, at least during the life-span of any one artist, that he was provided with a ready-made attitude about experience. He knew what the past meant, what he could expect the future to hold, and therefore with what it was important to concern himself in the present. But the modern artist is adrift in a maelstrom of conflicting interpretations of life and must determine truths for himself by an individual analysis. Some sort of philosophy is implied in all human activity and no matter how the artist may abstract or mathematize his experience, there must be implicit some attitude toward the meaning of existence. If his conclusion is that human existence has no meaning, that too, is an attitude toward the very thing he disbelieves. In this realm there can be no rules for modern artists. The meaning of experience is an individual matter. All that may be done is to lay out general boundaries within which fertile material may be found—to elucidate form which can be quite definite—and to state some simple restrictions as to what is and what is not suitable for the dance among experiences.

American dancers are especially fortunate in having rich and vivid outer stimuli for sensual experience, and no less vital inner life. Some of our dancing reflects this. There are an encouraging number of subjective dances on concert programs now. Titles appear such as "Conflict," "Revolt," "Exuberance," "Remorse." These prove a sincere if slightly pretentious belief in subjective experience for dance material. Then there is the unself-conscious tap dance which is certainly our own and is born of our hearty adolescence. Occasionally objective works in a strictly American vein appear, such as "Skyscrapers," "Krazy Kat," or "Men and Machines"; but on the whole, the dancer turns away from his known experience to the unknown. He dances like the Orientals, the Indians, or the Germans, with the charming naiveté of an enthusiastic child. It is obvious that he does this because he must be dancing about something in a hurry and lacks either the patience or the talent to discover a form, his experience-form in the American dance being still embryonic. Consequently he turns to formalized foreign dances and thereby becomes that most pitiable thing, an artist without integrity. There are exceptions, of course. For the extraordinary dancer it is possible to use vicarious experience as thematic material, but emphatic power accurate enough to translate foreign experience into convincing movement is so rare as to be negligible in considering what to dance about. The usual outcome of these attempts is either a nondescript impression of the original, or an imitation, obviously spurious, or a satire mostly of the dancer's insight. In general, no man can dance convincingly like any other man whose experience lies outside his own, and this is because the body, mirror of every thought and feeling, cannot disassociate itself readily from its movement habits. Here the dance is unique in the aesthetic world. In those arts that deal with words, stone or steel, exotic experience is frequently made convincing through the very impersonality of the medium. Thus Spanish music might be written by an Englishman that would catch the inherent character of the people; but no Englishman could do a Spanish dance. Under very special circumstances foreign or antique frame-works for dances may be suitable for contemporary use if they do not involve body movements of the original people, and are really conveyances for the experiences of the dancer. A good illustration of this point is the ballet "The Prodigal Son" which has been done here in a way that is true for us by translation into American terms. My ballet, "Dionysiaques," although stemming from ancient days is a modern psychological drama about ourselves.

The confusion as to what to dance about would be dissipated if American artists would adhere to known experiences seen as part of a whole, and if they would distinguish between dead and alive parts of these experiences. Form, added to this knowledge would provide them with the understanding that they so urgently need to give the dance integrity.

Source: *Trend: A Quarterly of the Seven Arts*, June-July-August, 1932.

ON CHOREOGRAPHING BACH

After seeing the all-Bach program at the Studio Theatre, John Martin wrote an extended article, taking exception not only to particular dances, but to the general principle of choreographing to music intended solely for listening. On February 14, 1943, he graciously published the major part of the artist's reply. Since he made some deletions, the original letter is reproduced in full here.

January 23, 1943

Mr. John Martin,
New York Times,
New York.

Dear John:
I read your most provocative article about the Bach program, now on view at our studio, and I think that it calls for a reply, if only to clarify my point of view about which you seem to be a little vague. We are going to disagree violently in the matter of dancing to Bach, but as we are in perfect accord on fundamentals in general, I'm sure we'll still be speaking at the end of this.

Let's take your statement—"why Miss Humphrey should have felt the necessity of turning to Bach must be clear to her," quoted from your article, January 17, 1943. Indeed, yes. "Perhaps Miss Humphrey is dancing to this music because she loves it." I admit the charge that I admire the music of the master to distraction, but I deny that this is my sole reason for composing with it as a base, or that self-expression, in the narrow sense, is the strongest motivation.

It seems to me that the motivation behind all my dances, from the Shakers to the Choral Preludes (fifteen years) has been the same to the point of monotony—and can be epitomized in the Shaker faith that "ye shall be saved, when ye are shaken free of sin." In fact, this seems so obvious to me that I am surprised and also pleased to find myself uncriticized for evangelism, and a general paucity of fresh ideas. Perhaps this can be attributed to the limitless possibilities of the theme and my skill and imagination as a choreographer. Viewed as a part of the consistent program of my life's work, I think the Bach compositions fall logically and relevantly along with the New Dance, the Race of Life, which was never so much comedy to me, as a sugar-coated indictment of the cheapness of the average aspiration, marked, I thought, with a sign, "This is Sin," and With My Red Fires, a much more obvious and immoral tale.

Specifically as to Bach, I intended the Chorale Preludes to be a naive and stylized miniature, greatly simplified and understated, of the respective rewards of unity and disunity in human behavior. The Chaconne, not being my conception, does not fall into my line of progression exactly, and is at the same time more abstract and more personal than any of my dances. I think José Limón had no conscious program at all, yet the total effect is of a man, not Man, with a particular background, who at thirty-four, has a discipline of mind and body in relationship to his environment, evidenced in a high degree of strength, endurance, grace, coordination and balance; yes, so has a fine athlete all the attributes—but it is precisely here that the dancer comes in and the athlete leaves off. Remember our old friend, meta-kinesis? I see in the Chaconne implications of what one of the Greek philosophers meant when he said, "every man should dance in order to understand the State and be a good citizen." Here are courage, balance in every sense, authority without boastfulness, power tempered with intelligence, the possibilities of the whole mature man brought to a high degree of perfection—yes, says the opposition—possibly —but not to Bach's Chaconne. And I very respectfully say, Are you sure you know what you want? Do you want to see this man's contribution to the development of the human race to the music which happens to inspire him in this way (as no other music does), or do you want to listen to the music and behead the dancer? This latter attitude sounds very much like the sacrosanct opinion of the conservative musician who can't bear a breath of air to blow through the pages of "absolute" music.

Next we come to the Partita in G Major. Now that is a piece which is out of line somewhat, if you will, in the progression of the behavior of

Man, but it is in there for two reasons—recreation for me and the art lovers for whom Bach says he wrote it, and also because I am show-woman enough to know that a suite of dances like that is a necessary balance on the program. If it doesn't prove to be a recreation for all the art lovers who come to the performance, that is a matter of personal taste, and possibly faults in the performance or choreography. However, I defend the idea of composing it at all on the grounds that Bach, whose humble admirer I am, thought it was fun to do a set of these Partitas on odd Sunday afternoons, and three centuries later people, and even dancers, are entitled to have fun, too; that having fun to the same music is legitimate, as it was built on the rhythms and shapes of folk dances, by people with legs and feelings and impulses like ours; that the dance is an invention around the music, as the music was an invention around the original folk forms.

Now we come to the Passacaglia—as you didn't mention this, I can be brief about it. I'll just ask a question—having been extremely complimentary in the past about this work, do you now class it with the rest of the program? "One recalcitrant spectator would willingly forfeit all the musical excellence of the repertoire for one even moderately successful venture into truly creative movement."

One more thing—as to why I chose Bach music at this time. I think this has to do primarily with my feeling about the world war. I remember telling you this once before. My reaction is strong as anybody's must be who has sensitivity that the convulsive drama going on simply cannot be expressed, at least not by me. Any attempt would be pallid and unconvincing. My creative impulses run as rapidly as possible in the other direction. Now is the time for me to tell of the nobility that the human spirit is capable of, stress the grace that is in us, give the young dancers a chance to move harmoniously with each other, say, in my small way, there is hope as long as corners remain where unity prevails. Perhaps I am not succeeding in expressing these ideas—however, this is the intention. I picked Bach for music because I still think he has the greatest of all genius for these very qualities of variety held in unity, of grandeur of the human spirit, of grace for fallen man; not only this, but I sincerely believe the music has movement in it, based on dances of forgotten men and women who are the unknown authors of much of the music of this or any other age.

Mr. Martin concluded: "Here is not only reason but eloquence."

ADVICE TO YOUNG CHOREOGRAPHERS
*(Notes from the opening session of a class in choreography,
February 1956, Juilliard School of Music)*

Man has composed dances throughout the ages from the earliest pre-historic era to the present time, but it is only within the last thirty years that theories of dance composition have been developed and taught. Dance has done extraordinarily well for itself by virtue of the efforts of gifted individuals who up to the recent past, had no theoretical framework to work within such as music had with its counterpoint and harmony or painting with its laws of perspective and proportion. The social upheaval of the first World War was, more than anything else, responsible for the emergence of a choreographic theory, because it produced a penetrating reevaluation of everything pertaining to the dance art, the movement, the sources of movement, the subject matter, the music, the notation, the costumes and décor. Lastly, there was a great need for a plan to tie all these new approaches together which gradually produced several well-defined theories. I was one of the dancers who was fortunate enough to be in at the beginning of those stirring times, and this stimulated me to think about movement and form in new ways, resulting in a theory which is the subject of this course. I have been putting these ideas into practice for the last twenty-five years and they work for me, but in giving them to you I do not intend them to be a formula. I am merely saying, "See if you think these things are true; see if they will work for you."

Before we go into that, however, let us consider what sort of person a choreographer should be in order to insure a reasonable success. Choreography is a very special field, and calls for special characteristics, just as performing or teaching need particular qualifications.

The choreographer is observant; he is not just interested in, but fascinated with all manifestations of form and shape. He notes the shapes of his environment, wherever he may be. In the city? He sees the architectural variations, the skyline, the tangled grotesqueries of water tanks, television wires, ventilators, the "feel" of the congestion, the preponderance of rectilinear lines, and the comedy of the small defiant brownstone squashed between two mammoth chromium and glass monsters. He sees the people, *en masse*, as in a street moving in kaleidoscopic patterns, or as individuals, old, middle-aged, young, who are meeting, parting, talking, walking, working. He is never bored when alone in public places; the world's people are always giving a show. He is also a close observer of people in more intimate situations; what movements do they make under the stress of various emotions: anger, affection, enthusiasm, boredom? If you would much rather think about your own personal problems, and find your greatest interest lies in perfecting a technique; if you have recurrent visions of yourself performing before vast audiences; or if you would like to have a job dancing in television and live comfortably—you are a potential or already-arrived dancer and not essentially a choreographer. As a dancer you have an entirely different set of problems, much more subjective, though fully as complicated as those of a choreographer.

The choreographer likes to discover and invent. He never ceases to be curious about the meaning of movement, and never stops wondering at the infinite possibilities and gradations of movement. The finding of a new sequence, or even a single gesture, has all the excitement of high adventure. He is acutely aware that other people differ from him physically and emotionally and he takes delight in discovering where their potentials lie, resisting the temptation to impose all his own idiosyncrasies on them.

And finally, the choreographer had better have something to say. This, to some young people, seems very formidable indeed and they immediately search their souls for grandiose or cosmic themes which are not only unnecessary but ill-advised. Leave the massive themes to the older heads and hands; they are difficult enough even for the veterans. All you really need is a genuine enthusiasm for something rather simple inspired by a subject you understand, an incident or a feeling in your own experience, music or poetry which will bear the added weight of dancing, a dramatic idea or a figure from history—there are many things to dance about. The important ingredient is your enthusiasm for it, plus its practicability: there are some things that cannot or should not be danced about. An apathetic approach, or a vague desire to be doing something is a good recipe for failure and, moreover, you need that initial excitement about the subject to tide you over the inevitable slump that besets all choreographers.

Having had a chance in four decades to make many choreographic mistakes, and having observed other people make them too, I have compiled a short list based on these experiences, which I hope will serve as a warning to you to avoid the commonest errors befalling choreographers. These I state in the most positive terms so that they will have more impact, although I am quite aware that they could be modified or qualified. For instance, one of them is, "All dances are too long." Now obviously this can not be 100% true, but it recurs so often that it is almost an axiom and you had better keep it in mind. I recommend that you copy this list and tuck it in your mirror where you can see it every day:

> Symmetry is lifeless.
> Two-dimensional design is lifeless.
> The eye is faster than the ear.
> Movement looks slower and weaker on the stage.
> All dances are too long.
> A good ending is 40% of the dance.
> Don't be all gray or all red. Look for contrasts.
> Don't be a slave to the music.
> Don't fall in love with it. Be ready to change.
> Don't intellectualize—motivate movement.
> Don't leave the ending to the end.

In this course we will examine first all the major ingredients of movement, which I name design, dynamics, rhythm and gesture. These, I think, are the component parts of any kind of dance, not just modern dance. It is essential that you have as great an awareness as possible of the materials you work with so that you can make intelligent choices in composing a dance. Then we will inquire into the origin and structure of the phrase, and the combining of phrases into over-all forms, the use of stage space, the subject of subject matter, the use and mis-use of music, and the combining of words with movement and music. All this will be considered both in regard to the solo dance and the group dance.

And now a few words about the general position of the choreographer in the world of esthetics. You should always remember that the dance is the only art without a permanent record of itself, and I say this in spite of the fact that dance notation is making headway and that a few films have been made. In comparison to the durability of paintings, musical scores, books and sculpture, dance is highly perishable. It has a moth-like existence and dies in the spot-light. This means, among other things, that dancers do not have hundreds of scores from which to learn as musicians do, but must be in a place and a position to acquire any finished compositions from a live teacher or choreographer, from mouth to foot, so to speak. There must be thousands of young dancers with good technical equipment who, through various circumstances, have nothing to dance, or, worse than nothing, some trash thrown together in utter ignorance or desperation. The obvious answer to this is more choreographic information through notation, which is slow, or through more study of the subject at first hand, which is faster. If you, through me, can acquire some of the knowledge and skill you need in order to compose, you will be better equipped to deal with any situation in which you must depend on yourself. Suppose you were to wake up some morning to find that Fate had deposited you in a small town, any small town, or even a medium-sized city. The chances are that there would be no one who could teach you a good dance, nor any group you could join which had a knowledgeable director at its head. But you would not be at a loss completely because you would know something about choreography and could make dances of your own. They might not be masterpieces, but they could not be utterly without value. And one more thing I shall expect, wherever Fate may lead you: that you will spread the light of understanding among the people you meet, and do your bit to further the progress of the dance either as a teacher or a dancer or, best of all, as a choreographer.

Source: *The Juilliard Review*, Spring 1956.

DORIS HUMPHREY ANSWERS THE CRITICS

The José Limón company with Doris Humphrey as its director and choreographer, came to London in the late summer of 1957. In the November issue of Dance and Dancers of that year, Clive Barnes wrote an enthusiastic article on the season which criticised a few of its features. Several months after that he received a long letter from Miss Humphrey answering some of his criticisms. Owing to lack of space at the time and because the season was long since past, we did not publish the letter. On December 29 of last year, Doris ·Humphrey died (an obituary by Arthur Todd appears on page 34 of this issue), and we feel that this is the moment to publish the letter as it gives great insight into certain aspects of the American Modern Dance as well as into a very remarkable personality.

"I am moved," as they say in Quaker meetings, "to bear witness" about the José Limón Co. Season in London, taking as a springboard your review in the November issue of *Dance and Dancers*, which, although in the main thoughtful and perceptive, has, I think, some blind spots. One of these is in the area of music and rhythm, and the phrasing of movement. That you and your fellow-critics should be quite unaware of the imagination and subtlety of the Limón Co. in matters musical and rhythmic is quite understandable, as this company is probably unique in this respect, and foreign critics have no eyes to grasp it. Moreover, since this is so, it is no doubt our fault for not making a detailed explanation on the programme. There was a brief outline of the sources and aims of the Limón company on the back of the souvenir programme, which I trust you and others saw, but did you? You state in your review that "the right place for an explanation was in the programme." However, as there was no room to go into detail anyway, here is, belatedly, a brief analysis of our approach to rhythm and movement in relationship to music.

First of all, the choreographers and leading dancers in this company are all extremely musical. My own mother and father were musicians and music was familiar to me from earliest childhood. My dance training included the study of piano and Dalcroze Eurythmics. The background was useful when, as a young dancer, I was with Ruth St. Denis during the period when she composed music visualisations for her company. This gave me a keen ear and an enduring love of music as the basis of dance. Mr. Limón came early to music, too, and learned to play the piano classics with a devotion which he has never lost. Similarly the others, Pauline Koner, Lucas Hoving, Betty Jones, Ruth Currier, are all expert musicians with fastidious ears. With musical resources such as these, unique in dance companies I imagine, it was inevitable that music of unusual merit would play a dominant part in the Limón repertory. Incidentally, this is the first point overlooked by the critics. Nowhere was there a mention of the unusually high standard of the music which I affirm was unhackneyed, admirably suited to the needs of the dance and in impeccable taste. And here I must diverge to disagree with your estimate of the Priaulx Rainier score as "dry and uninventive." Although the performance of this work was below par, and therefore not at its best, even so it seemed original and provocative to me—can it be that this neglected English composer, whom I found to be quite unknown in her native land, has something to say which you have not ears to hear?

To go back to the use of music in the dances. Early in the nineteen-thirties I discarded the idea of music visualisation. It seemed quite unnecessary, and indeed false, to force the dance to follow music exactly. The two arts have such utterly different media that the dance could only be damaged by being cut to fit every phrase, every beat and every measure. Moreoer, it was a redundant practice. As the composer has said it all once, why repeat it in movement terms? So I evolved a theory of relating the dance to the music, while leaving each its individuality intact. This results in a dance and music partnership in which neither dominates nor imitates the other, in short a true collaboration. Often the movement is in counterpoint to the music, both in rhythm-phrase and tempo, and this applies not only to musically based dances but to the dramatic pieces as well. However, this is so skilfully done, I say with pardonable pride, that at worst there is no jar to the onlooker, and at best he sees and enjoys the fitting together of the two entities. I'm afraid this escapes almost everybody in Europe, where they are used to conventional rhythmic phrasing procedures. This lack of perception was particularly apparent in the appraisal of the music dances, such as Vivaldi's *Concerto Grosso* and Pergolesi's *Concertino*. Mr. Limón and Miss Koner, the respective choreographers, quite agree with me about the rhythmic dance structure above the music, and looked at in this way, not just as Baroque art, or patterns or moods, these two dances are seen to be imaginative and inventive pieces of choreography with a highly sensitive regard for the relationship of movement to music. But nowhere were these subtleties perceived or mentioned.

Other important elements went unnoticed as well, such as dynamics; every movement phrase of this repertory is consciously coloured by dynamic shifts consonant with the theme, we are at great pains to keep movement alive by constant changes in texture; originality—there are no outworn clichés in the Limón repertory; structure—these are all firm with no long padded passages, no meaningless introduction of irrelevant material; communicability—the aim is not intellectual or esoteric or pyrotechnical, but seeks to convey in quite simple terms some aspect of human experience.

One more comment, and this is specifically about the *Lament for Ignacio Sánchez Mejías*. Here again I must explain the approach, which is, in a way, similar to the theory about music. My attitude to the use of words with dance is that they must form a collaboration, each staying within its own orbit. I see words as a means of conveying facts, and the dance as the means of expressing emotion. Of course the word can be eloquent in describing feeling too, but in a fusion of the two arts, I believe the feeling should be the function of the dance and the words should convey whatever we need to know about place, time, state of being, or any fact which the dance, by its nature, cannot express. Consequently your comment that "she has made no attempt to match the poet's very precise verbal symbolism" is quite correct and quite conscious on my part. All the poet's vivid words of a descriptive nature are left to stand alone, once the emotional reactions to these things form the choreographic structure. It is not intended to be a dance *per se*, but a theatre piece, a synthesis of the dramatic arts. I must say, however, that there was one damaging circumstances in the presentation of the piece. Formerly all the lines had been spoken by the dancers themselves, but in Europe I was persuaded to substitute a speaker in the pit because of the performers' American accent. This was a disastrous mistake which I was immediately aware of. The focus was lost, and the immediacy of the drama hitherto coming entirely from the stage was dissapated [sic] and weakened.

I realise that all the foregoing will savour of the stigma that you complain of in American modern dancers, our monastic asceticism and our deadly seriousness, but is it too much to ask dance critics to consider us seriously as a temporary antidote to more Giselles, Sleeping Beauties and Graduation Balls? And yes, I agree wholeheartedly with your criticism of London critics who did not find either the time or the interest to examine the Limón Co. intelligently as to its aims, technique or place in the dance picture.

There is much more, but I am sure this is quite enough for one effusion. Thank you for being London's most sympathetic, perceptive commentator on the Limón Co. Season.

Sincerely,
DORIS HUMPHREY.

Source: *Dance and Dancers,* March 1959.

DORIS HUMPHREY SPEAKS . . .

These are excerpts drawn by Walter Sorell from a speech delivered by the late Doris Humphrey at the Dance Department of Juilliard School of Music on November 7, 1956. The Editor expresses his gratitude to Martha Hill for making the publication of this speech possible.

On the Problem of Projection

By projection I suppose we mean how do you convey the meaning or the mood of what you are doing to the best possible advantage to the people who are in front of you? How do you accomplish this? Projection has a lot of different facets, particularly for the modern dance. I don't think it is such a problem for the ballet, because the ballet has a long tradition of movement by which the body has been trained to show its best line or its most provocative movement in the proper direction so the whole impact of it is immediately apparent. But the modern dance has a different premise, that of improvisation and choreography of an original kind; so the problem of projection really has to be reexamined as a part of the technique of performing.

First of all we have to remember the picture-frame stage. Communication comes from only one direction. Whatever you are saying in movement has to be stated so that there is the greatest possible projection in this one direction. This seems very obvious, but it's something that young dancers are very likely to forget. Perhaps the most important thing one could say about projection is that there certainly will be none unless there is conviction back of what you are doing. Unless you believe in yourself, no one else will, I assure you. The tentative dancer, the one who is afraid or is very uncertain, either of his movement technically or because of the theme, cannot project. The body is extremely revealing. It tells us more than speech, more than almost any kind of communication what is really felt, what is going on in the inside; so that without the conviction, there is automatically very little projection.

That is number one. But there are technical aspects to this. You can believe in yourself thoroughly and have all the assurance in the world, but if you do your dance in the wrong place, for instance side to side against the back wall, it is not going to convey very much power. The stage is an area which is divided into different sections with dynamic differences according to where you are. If you are going to do something which you want to make very personal, then this should be brought forward, very close to the edge of the stage where we get the impact of the personal equation. It would be quite wrong and you would have great difficulty in making this carry to an audience if you were to put it way back in the corner or way back against the side. And so forth. There are many technical know-how points to remember about where to put your dance.

Then there also is the question of the line, and where the face is and what it says. I am one of those who believe that the face is the most expressive part of the body. Other parts are communicative and expressive too, but the face is the part of the body we are most used to reading. When you meet people you talk to the faces, you glean the meaning of the conversation by the responsiveness of the face. One does not watch the hands or the body very much, one watches the face. So it seems to me that unless the movement is backed up with a face, so to speak—which is a kind of metaphor—the most eloquent and familiar part of the body is lost. The face will tell us what the feeling is, whether it is one of grief, exultation, or happiness, more quickly than any other part of the body. I am afraid many young dancers do not realize this. They work impersonally in class and then they are suddenly called upon to do some kind of a dramatic movement in a particular dance; the movement may be very expressive, but the face is still the impassive one of the classroom.

Projection must take into account the architecture of the theatre, and the relationship of the audience to the performer. We are, at the moment, in a conventional kind of theatre, an orchestra floor that has a little rise, a balcony above. If you are going to project down to the first few rows, those in the balcony are going to see nothing but the top of your head. The face has to be raised to an unnatural degree, and the whole line of the body too, much higher than in the conversational level. One of the most amusing and also, I think, instructive illustrations of this is in some of the old movies. I am thinking of one of Sarah Bernhardt in *Camille*. She stands in a doorway at the back of the stage about to make an entrance into the room. She leans on the door with her head lifted high, communicating her sense of imminent tragedy not to the actors in the room with her, nor to the orchestra, but to the balcony, thereby taking in the full sweep of the theatre. This was part of the grand manner of the day and much of this seems dated, but the high projection is still valid.

One more thing about projection, namely about the line. Because of the one-sided stage we have, this picture-frame, box-like stage, not just any body-lines you can think of will do; to be effective they should be only those which will carry to the front. For example, if you stand in profile with the arms extended to the side, you have lost most of the design. The line of the arms is invisible, and the whole movement becomes a wasted effort. I don't mean that you should always dance facing front and stare at the balcony. By no means. This would be quite wrong. Sometimes a dramatic situation demands a communication between people. This may often mean that you don't look up and out at all. But almost any movement can be altered slightly so as to project it with the greatest possible impact in the line even in scenes like this.

On Subject Matter

There are hundreds of things to dance about beginning with your own experiences. There are also hundreds of things that you shouldn't dance about. There are both do's and don'ts: The don'ts would include too intellectual concepts that do not lend themselves to movement, scientific subjects. I got a letter from a dancer the other day about the peaceful uses of the atom bomb. How can you dance about the atom bomb? The subject would have to be put into some specific situation. It would have to be concerned with some reaction of people to the bomb and this would put the emphasis on feeling, and if the idea of "bomb" could be retained at all it would be minor. You can't dance about scientific subjects. There are also plots from literary sources which are too vast for the dance. It is all very well for the movies to attempt Tolstoy's *War and Peace*, but I wouldn't like to see a group of dancers try this. There are limitations.

In general, it is a good idea to dance about something you understand. Don't feel that in order to be different or to be original you must fasten on something very remote from what you know about. If we are going to promote the American dance, then we had better try to work indigenously, that is, foster what we have and try to understand that better, rather than go far away for thematic material.

On Denishawn, and on How It Started in the Dance World

I was brought up in Chicago, and then when I was eighteen my family moved to a suburb. That was Oak Park where I was born and where I returned right after high school. I began teaching; it was necessary to earn a living. I had had some ballet training by then, some ballroom dancing and whatever passed for aesthetic dancing, and clogging and gymnastic dancing. It is probably a little hard to realize that not too long ago there was no such thing as modern dance. I studied ballet with an ex-Viennese ballet mistress who was in Chicago. Her name was Josephine Hatlanck [sic], and she taught with a stick and high button shoes. So I had what there was, and by eighteen I was fairly accomplished and began teaching children and ballroom classes.

But this was doubtless the most unhappy time in my life. I thought I was going to be buried alive in Oak Park, Illinois, because there did not seem to be any way to be released from the drudgery of teaching in a small town and, of course, like all young dancers I wanted very much to dance.

The opportunity came with Denishawn, and the reason it came is another point I went to emphasize. I had a wonderful teacher, and a wonderful teacher is something that you should cherish when you find one. This teacher not only had vision, but was interested in the whole field of dance. She used to go abroad and bring back whatever seemed to be of value as she was going on from year to year with her classes. She also had an individual interest in her students, and I was one of those she advised and encouraged and it was she who brought the Denishawn school to my attention. It was on the West Coast at that time, so I went out to Los Angeles where the school was and never came back to Oak Park. It was one of those very fortunate things; it was the right time and the right place for me.

I had by this time a very flourishing school of my own in Oak Park, but fate made it very easy for me to get away. At Denishawn was another teacher who was looking for a school, a place to settle. She wasn't from Oak Park, but she was interested in getting something to do that was secure, and she didn't mind small towns, in fact she liked them. So I handed her my school; she went back to Oak Park and I went on with Denishawn. They were fascinating years, and this was the first time that I had ever been able to step my foot on a professional stage which had been the goal and the objctive for such a long time.

Then, of course, there were the magnetic and stimulating personalities of the two leaders, Ruth St. Denis and Ted Shawn. I think everybody who has ever been with Ruth St. Denis has come away with a little of her vitality and her spark. She was and is a magnificent person. I think that we didn't learn from her too much about dancing, because none of us who were with her has really gone on as she did. She was at her greatest in Oriental dancing and also in religious dance, and I don't know of anyone who has carried this out. But what we did gain from her was vision. Here was a woman who saw the dance whole, complete. She was not interested in a little segment but in all of it and was a major influence in inspiring the future leaders of the American modern dance.

It was like a university of the dance at Denishawn; we did absolutely everything. Any kind of dance that they could lay their hands on we had some part of, which included American Indian, Spanish dances with roses and a black wig, and Hopi dances with squash blossoms and the legs all done up in white wrappings, and American folk dancing, Japanese, Siamese, Burmese, the world's dances. After a while it began to seem a little scattered. I felt as if I were dancing as everyone but myself. I knew something about how the Japanese moved, how the Chinese or Spanish moved, but I didn't know how I moved or what the American heritage should be. As dancers they had a different point of view, they felt that all dance was universal, the common property of all dancers. But it came to me and, I think, to a good many others who were with them, that it was imperative to find out what we were as Americans and as contemporary dancers. This led to a break, of course, and to a completely new start.

The life of the dancer at that time was so different from the way it is now. I had the incredible luck of going to the Denishawn School, immediately going into their company and touring year after year after year, and then teaching in between; so that there was no question of a living; everything was ready and provided. Nowadays this is almost nonexistent. There are very few modern companies which offer continual performance and plenty of teaching in between. Now we have a new problem quite different from that as to how young dancers are going to perform, how they are going to earn a living.

This succession of performances of the Denishawn Company went on for something like ten years, but there was one break. After I had danced with them for a number of seasons there was a shift in their policy and what they were doing came to an end, and they didn't have a new plan ready. So all of a sudden I was faced with nothing, no Denishawn, no company, no school any more. It was in Little Rock, Arkansas, that I gave the last performance with the Denishawn Company. Then what? Well, I had $100 saved in my pocket, and I went back to Oak Park where I still had some pupils who were pretty good. I got together four girls and some dances and costumes and I rented some scenery and got an agent. I bought five tickets for them and myself to open in Detroit in vaudeville on $100.—.

This was way back, then you could do it. And of course vaudeville was a familiar outlet for me because I had played with the Denishawn Company in vaudeville for years on the Keith circuit, the Orpheum circuit, the Pantages circuit, two a day, three a day, four a day, even five a day. This was by no means unusual. Vaudeville was a wonderful experience. Too bad you don't stand a chance to try it. You learn first of all discipline. Now for a concert to begin five or ten minutes late is standard procedure, and if you are not quite ready between dances, they'll hold the curtain for you. There was nothing like this in vaudeville. You learned to be exact, you had to be there. The curtain went up, and if you were not there they played the music anyway, and nobody cared except the manager who came tearing back from the front and said where was so and so. There was no such thing as holding the curtain.

The opportunities we had were unique, and they are not duplicated now. Denishawn was a large company, it had something like fifteen dancers or so and the two stars and toured year after year. They also went to the Orient two years where I went with them. They were very generous; they gave me and other people solo work. They composed dances for me, also they allowed me to compose dances of my own and present them on their programs. I don't know of any company which will allow its members all these different things and keep them working the year round and also give them teaching opportunities. We have to adjust to new times, and this is an important question about which I have some opinions.

Some Practical Advice for the Young Dancer

Everybody wants to dance, just as I did. I know you do. I know that all the young dancers in all the studios want to dance. How are you going to do this now? There are a few companies, but you'll have to wait till these people retire before you can get in. By that time you will be creaking in your bones. So there must be other ways. First of all, I think it is very unlikely that you can do anything alone. There are a few I know who have made a name for themselves and are able to function alone; that is, they have a studio and settle themselves in it, work all alone. This is the most difficult way to do it and the least likely to make a success unless you are a genius, and genius is scarce. This is apt to strike the young dancer as being very desirable, because the ego is very strong, our sense of independence. You think, "I'll do something by myself; I've got ideas." The surge of youth and vitality and everything leads you to make this error sometimes, but I don't believe it will work very well.

I think that the only way we can hope to find some success for young dancers in the concert field is in collaboration of some kind. Either you should collaborate with each other in small groups or affiliate yourself with an institution or a company which has some opportunities to offer. It hurts me to see some young dancers who are so eager to perform that they will accept some of the sporadic things that are offered. Maybe an individual dancer decides to give a concert once a year and gets a group of people together who probably have not worked with her before, who do not understand her approach, and they all work like dogs and then give it, and that's the end of it. This is not what I mean by collaboration. I mean a collaboration with a plan of continuity.

There are opportunities for small ensembles, small groups, two or three, at the most four, in this country where individual initiative would count for something. It won't count for much if you go off and bury yourself in a studio. It's a big country, and there are lots of colleges and institutions of various kinds where there are dates to be had for anywhere from $100 to $300 or $400 each. Now this would only take care of a few people, but these opportunities are there.

You must plan realistically. The way not to do it, it seems to me, is to aim with a hammer. You are going to strike New York City with what you have. You are going to do a whole program with your choreography, and you're going to put it on the Y stage for one performance, and the result will be first of all that you will lose money because everybody always goes in for too much rehearsing, too much costuming, too much music, too many dancers. Also, you are likely to win the disapproval of people and critics; because there are very few young dancers who can sustain a whole program with just their pieces and their ideas. Young dancers don't have enough resources to hold the attention.

Now there is, of course, a difference between the audience in New York and in the rest of the country. This is a very sophisticated audience, probably much more so than in Europe. They see absolutely everything. What would not be acceptable here is acceptable there very often. It can be simpler, less sophisticated. But if you are going to go on with any such ideas, this had better be with a plan. This business of just one shot somewhere isn't going to work. You will be discouraged, you will lose money. You're going to find that people drift away from each other because there is no plan, there is no future for it, there's nothing to build on.

Also, in the pursuit of a general career which might include some performances here as well as elsewhere, it is very helpful to ally yourself with some center in the sense of a studio, institution, people. Juilliard is a very good example of a valuable center where you have services—to put it very coldly—of various kinds. There is the Placement Bureau; there is a personal interest in your welfare and what you are going to do, what your plans are, and it is a center where opportunities come, and questions are asked about who is available for jobs and performing.

One of the saddest things, I think, is to be a drifter in this field. If you go from studio to studio looking for something you have never quite found, and you never stay in any place long enough to make a mark, then you have no one really to help you, no one to advise you, or to be concerned about what becomes of you. You are always a new student, and you don't stay long enough to form any attachments. I am a great believer in alliances, in planning, in cooperation. My advice is: don't try to do it alone, don't try to do whole programs by yourself. Get other people to collaborate. They will supply new ideas, more audiences and so forth.

This is all about dancing on the concert stage. But there are other ways of functioning. There is the teaching field. There is the show-business, there are the ballet companies and there is television. These are all of varying degrees of value. One of the most important and rewarding of these is teaching for which there are many opportunities all over the country. But I have had very little success in persuading young dancers to leave New York and go out into the middle of Nebraska, for example. They say, "Oh, me go to Nebraska? I want to stay here, something might happen in New York!" But there are good positions out there and it is not nearly such a desert as you might think. The rest of this country has a lot of intelligent people in it, and one of the great advantages is that you are going to be one who knows the most wherever you go. There all the opportunities, whatever they were, would gravitate toward you, in the studio, the theatre, or in the university. You can't all dance here, it's impossible. Somebody has to go away.

On Isolation and Egocentricity

When I was young my personal experience tended to isolate me and the people I was with a good bit from other dancers because, as I said, we went on very long tours—one-night stands all over the country. When you are travelling like this, you don't see anybody else, you hardly hear about any other dance that is going on. Therefore, under such circumstances, it is very difficult to even keep track of what others are doing, let alone be concerned with it. That was then, with no magazines in existence, but there isn't so much reason now, even when you travel a great deal.

Now all are very well conversant with what goes on in the field, and there should be a greater sympathy and a greater interest and action than there is. We must not tend to discount any kind of modern dance in which we are not personally concerned—"Mine is the only kind!" This viewpoint is very narrow and destructive. We had better have more concern for the whole field, or we won't have any.

Do not listen to isolationist kinds of talk or rejecting or ignoring other dancers or movements; resist such influence for the good of the whole. Do not forget: You are the ones who are going to be responsible for carrying the work on.

Source: *Dance Observer*, March 1962.

Chronology

BY CHRISTENA L. SCHLUNDT

For assistance in preparing this chronology, and for the use of materials in its archives, I am grateful to the Dance Collection, Library & Museum of the Performing Arts, New York Public Library; and especially to its director, Miss Genevieve Oswald.

—C.L.S.

A. Companies and Performers in Premieres of Concert Works by Doris Humphrey

Denishawn groups (Dn)

Three separate (though slightly overlapping) Denishawn groups performed premieres of works by Doris Humphrey. They were billed as: Ruth St. Denis Concert Dancers, 1920; Ruth St. Denis, Ted Shawn and Denishawn Dancers, 1923, 1924, 1926; Doris Humphrey with Charles Weidman and Students of the Denishawn School, 1928. Dancers involved were:

DH ('20, '23, '24, '26, '28)	Katharine Laidlaw ('20)
CW ('23, '26, '28)	Dorothy Lathrop ('28)
Cleo Atheneos ('28)	Pauline Lawrence ('26)
Ruth Austen ('20)	Katherine Manning ('28)
Elizabeth Bodé ('20)	Sylvia Manning ('28)
Dorothea Bowen ('20)	Ara Martin ('26)
Louise Brooks ('23)	Betty May ('20)
Grace Burroughs ('26)	Claire Niles ('20)
Grace Carson ('20)	Virginia Millar ('28)
Ernestine Day ('26)	Jean Nathan ('28)
Ann Douglas ('23, '26)	Della Nuckols ('20)
Evelyn Fields ('28)	Frances O'Meara ('28)
Olga Fry ('28)	Celia Rauch ('28)
Nina Garrett ('26)	Theresa Sadowska ('23)
Leja Gorska ('28)	Lenore Scheffer ('23)
Geordie Graham ('23, '26)	Jane Sherman ('26)
Martha Hardy ('23)	Frances Shinn ('28)
Katherine Hawley ('20)	Gertrude Shurr ('28)
Lenore Hellakson ('20)	George Steares ('26)
Mary Howry ('26)	Helen Strumlauf ('28)
Edith James ('26)	Pearl Wheeler ('26)
Eleanor King ('28)	Rose Yasgour ('28)

Humphrey-Weidman groups (HW)

The Humphrey-Weidman company was billed, over the years, under at least ten different titles; e.g., DH, CW and The Concert Group (or some variant on that pattern), 1928–1932; DH, CW and Company, 1929–1942; The Humphrey-Weidman [Repertory] Company, 1942–1944; it was also one of the component groups associated with The Dance Repertory Theatre, 1929–1931. It was, however, substantially a single ongoing company with a strong continuum of membership. The following lists only company members who performed in DH premieres; student dancers and workshop participants, as at Bennington and Connecticut College, numbered several score and are not mentioned by name.

DH ('28–'44)
CW ('28–'44)
Louise Allen ('36)
Ruth Allred ('30–'32)
William Archibald ('38, '39)
Cleo Atheneos ('28–'34)
Helen Bach ('34, '35)
Morris Bakst ('35)
William Bales ('35–'38)
Patricia Balz ('41, '42)
Mirthe Bellanca ('38)
Joseph Belsky ('36)
Marcus Blechman ('33, '34)
George Bockman ('34–'38)
Kenneth Bostock ('34–'36)
Jerry Brooks ('35)
Lillian Burgess ('36)
William Canton ('36)
Noel Charise ('35)
Lee Cherman ('35)
Jack Cole ('34)
Debby Coleman ('33, '34)
Jack Coleman ('33)
Rose Crystal ('29–'33)
Maxine Cushing ('36)
Molly Davenport ('40–'44)
Jerry Davidson ('35, '36)
Eva Desca ('38–'40)
Helen Douglas ('43, '44)
Justine Douglas ('28–'30)
Evelyn Fields ('28–'32)
Ezra Friedman ('35)
Gloria Garcia ('40–'44)

Margaret Gardner ('28, '29)
Gertrude Gerrish ('29)
Beatrice Gerson ('35)
Joseph Gifford ('44)
Maurice Gilbert ('35)
John Glenn ('33, '34)
Doris Goodwin ('44)
Philip Gordon ('36, '37)
Leja Gorska ('28–'30)
Geordie Graham ('28)
Harriette Anne Gray ('37–'40)
Peter [Charles] Hamilton
 ('40–'42, '44)
Ernestine Henoch ('31–'34)
Gene Hirsch ('32)
Letitia Ide ('30–'37)
Harry Joyce ('34)
Elizabeth Kendall ('42)
Frances [Kinsky] Kinney ('38, '43)
Ada Korvin ('31–'36)
Miriam Krakovsky ('35, '36)
Virginia Landreth ('28–'31)
Charles Laskey ('31)
Dorothy Lathrop ('28–'34)
Paul Leon ('36)
Florence Lessing ('43)
Joan Levy ('35–'38)
José Limón ('31–'40, '42, '43)
Katherine Litz ('34–'42)
Joey Luckie ('40)
Marie Maginnis ('40–'42)
Ethel Mann ('42–'44)
Katherine Manning ('28–'38)

Sylvia Manning ('28–'32)
Gene Martel ('33, '34)
William Matons ('33–'36, '40)
Claudia Moore ('41)
Jean Nathan ('28)
Edith Orcutt ('35–'38)
Joseph Precker ('44)
Miriam Raphael ('37)
Celia Rauch ('28–'32)
Frances Reed ('33, '34)
Hyla Rubin ('33, '34)
Gail Savery ('33, '34)
Nona Schurman ('40–'42)
Marion Scott ('44)
Beatrice Seckler ('35–'42)

Sybil Shearer ('35–'38)
Jane Sherman ('28)
Lee Sherman ('38–'42)
Gertrude Shurr ('29)
Lillian Spevak ('32)
Helen Strumlauf ('31–'33)
Mildred Tanzer ('35)
Barbara Thomas ('44)
Lily Verne ('36)
Helen Waggoner ('42–'44)
Allen Waine ('41)
Frank Westbrook ('44)
Paula Yasgour ('34)
Rose Yasgour ('28–'33)
Gabriel Zuckerman ('33, '34)

José Limón and Dance Company (JL)
Members of this company who danced in Humphrey premieres, 1946–1957, were:

José Limón ('46–'57)
John Barker ('56)
William Burdick ('54)
Ruth Currier ('49, '51–'57)
Charles Czarny ('53)
Crandall Diehl ('53)
Richard Fitz-Gerald ('55, '56)
Ray Harrison ('53)
Michael Hollander ('56, '57)
Lucas Hoving ('51–'57)
Lola Huth ('57)
Letitia Ide ('46–'48)

Betty Jones ('48, '49, '51–'57)
Pauline Koner* ('48, '52–'54, '56, '57)
Ellen Love ('46)
Harlan McCallum ('56)
Melisa Nicolaides ('47)
Lavina Nielsen ('52–'57)
Miriam Pandor ('47, '48)
Beatrice Seckler ('46)
Alvin Schulman ('56)
Lucy Venable ('57)
Chester Wolenski ('56)

*(Guest Artist)

Juilliard Dance Theatre (JDT)
Members of this group who danced in Humphrey premieres, 1955–1959, were:

Diane Adler ('56)
John Barker ('56)
Jemima Ben-Gal ('55, '57)
Sallie Bramlette ('59)
Janet Byer ('55–'57)
Bruce Carlisle ('55, '57)

Patricia Christopher ('55, '57)
Jeff Duncan ('55)
Richard Fitz-Gerald ('55)
Anna Friedland ('55, '56)
Martha Gallagher ('56)
Maureen Gillick ('56, '57)

Margot Holdstein ('56, '57)
Lola Huth ('55)
Deborah Jowitt ('59)
Cristyne Lawson ('55)
Rhoda Levine ('55)
Janet Mansfield ('59)
Harlan McCallum ('56, '57)
Martin Morginsky ('56, '57)
Melisa Nicolaides ('56, '57)
James Payton ('59)

Florence Peters ('56, '57, '59)
Durevol Quitzow ('56, '57)
Poligena Rogers ('55–'57)
Baird Searles ('59)
Jack Spencer ('55)
Joyce Trisler ('55–'57)
Martha Wittman ('57, '59)
Chester Wolenski ('56, '57)
David Wynne ('56, '57, '59)

B. Concert Works Choreographed by Doris Humphrey

Title	Accompaniment	Costumes	Type	Group	Dancers	Place & date
Valse Caprice (Scarf Dance)	Chaminade		Solo	Dn	DH	Egan Little Th., Los Angeles, Jan. 7, '20
Bourrée	Bach		Solo	Dn	DH	Potter Th., Santa Barbara, Apr. 5, '20
Soaring [1]	Schumann		Quintette	Dn	DH, group of 4	Spreckels Th., San Diego, Sept. 20, '20
Sonata Pathetique [1]	Beethoven		Group	Dn	DH, group of 10	Same
Sonata Tragica (Tragica)	MacDowell		Group	Dn	DH, CW, group of 6	Apollo Th., Atlantic City, Oct. 15, '23
Scherzo Waltz (Hoop Dance)	Ilgenfritz		Solo	Dn	DH	Acad. of Music, Newburgh, N.Y., Oct. 6, '24
A Burmese Yein Pwe [1]	Vaughan	Pearl Wheeler	Group	Dn	DH, CW, group of 12	Victoria Th., Singapore, July 15, '26
At the Spring	Liszt		Solo	Dn	DH	Shuraka-Kan Th., Kobe, Oct. 23, '26
Whims	Schumann		Group	Dn	DH, CW, group of 5	Philharmonic Aud., Los Angeles, Dec. 6, '26
Air for the G String	Bach		Quintette	Dn	Group of 5	Little Th., Brooklyn, Mar. 24, '28

1. Ruth St. Denis, co-creator.

Title	Accompaniment	Costumes	Type	Group	Dancers	Place & date
Gigue (Gigue from The First Partita)	Bach		Solo	Dn	DH	Same
Concerto in A Minor, Allegro Moderato	Grieg		Group w. solo	Dn	DH, group of 17	Same
Waltz (Valse)	Debussy		Solo	Dn	DH	Same
Papillon	Rosenthal		Solo	Dn	DH	Same
Color Harmony	Vaughan	DH	Group	Dn	CW, group of 13	Same
Pavane of the Sleeping Beauty	Ravel		Solo	Dn	DH	Same
The Fairy Garden	Ravel		Solo	Dn	DH	Same
Bagatelle	Beethoven		Duet	Dn	S. Manning, E. Fields	Same
Pathetic Study (Etude, Opus 8, No. 12, Patetico)	Scriabin		Duet	Dn	DH, CW	Same
The Banshee	Cowell		Solo	Dn	DH	John Golden Th., New York, Apr. 15, '28
Rigaudon	MacDowell		Solo	DH (solo concert)	DH	St. Stephen's Coll., Annandale, N.Y., May 14, '28

Title	Accompaniment	Costumes	Type	Group	Dancers	Place & date
Sarabande	Rameau-Godowsky	DH	Solo	HW	DH	Civic Repertory Th., New York, Oct. 28, '28
Water Study	None	Pauline Lawrence	Group	HW	Group of 16	Same
Air on a Ground Bass	Purcell		Duet	HW	DH, CW	Guild Th., New York, Mar. 31, '29
Gigue	Bach		Trio	HW	D. Lathrop, G. Gerrish, S. Manning	Same
Concerto in A Minor, Allegro Marcato	Grieg		Group w. solo	HW	DH, group of 15	Same
Speed			Solo	HW	DH	Same
Life of the Bee	Pauline Lawrence		Group w. solos	HW	DH, group of 16	Same
The Call	Rudhyar		Solo	HW	DH	Agora, Lake Placid, N.Y., Aug. 2, '29
Quasi-Waltz	Scriabin		Solo	HW	DH	Same
Courante (from Antique Suite)	Green		Solo	HW	DH	Same
Mazurka to Imaginary Music	None		Solo	HW	DH	Same

Title	Accompaniment	Costumes	Type	Group	Dancers	Place & date
A Salutation to the Depths² (To the Depths)	Rudhyar		Duet	HW	DH, CW	Maxine Elliott's Th., New York, Jan. 6, '30
Breath of Fire	Rudhyar		Solo	HW	DH	Same
Drama of Motion Processional Transition and Interlude Conclusion	None		Solo w. group	HW	DH, group of 12	Same
La Valse (Choreographic Waltz)	Ravel		Duet	HW	DH, CW	Same
Descent (Into a Dangerous Place)*	Weiss		Solo	HW	DH	Same, Jan. 9, '30
March (Parade) (Passing Parade)	Tcherepnine arr. Pond		Group	HW	Group of 13	Opera House, Boston, Mar. 7, '30
Salutation	None		Duet	HW	DH, CW	Prentiss Aud., Cleveland, May 1, '30
Etude No. 1	Scriabin		Solo	HW	DH	Same
La Valse	Ravel	DH	Group w. duet	HW	DH, CW, group of 14	Robin Hood Dell, Philadelphia, Aug. 19, '30

2. Charles Weidman, co-creator.

* A preliminary version titled *Gargoyle* (*Descent into a Dangerous Place*) was performed Nov. 15, '29, at a woman's club.

Title	Accompaniment	Costumes	Type	Group	Dancers	Place & date
The Shakers (Dance of the Chosen)	Lawrence		Group	HW	Group of 17	Craig Th., New York, Feb. 1, '31 [3]
Dances of Women (Dances for Women) (Rituals for Women)	Rudhyar		Solo w. group	HW	DH, group of 15	Same
Burlesca	Bossi		Duet	HW	DH, CW	Same, Feb. 4, '31
Lake at Evening	Griffes		Solo	HW	DH	Same
Night Winds	Griffes		Solo	HW	DH	Same
Tambourin	Rameau	Lawrence	Solo	HW	DH	Robin Hood Dell, Philadelphia, Aug. 18, '31
Three Mazurkas (Three Dances) Elegance Transition Country Dance	Tansman		Duet	HW	DH, CW	Washington Irving H.S., New York, Oct. 31, '31
Variations on a Theme of Handel	Brahms		Solo	HW	DH	Same
Two Ecstatic Themes Circular Descent Pointed Ascent	Medtner Malipiero		Solo	HW	DH	Same

3. First professional performance; recital premiere, Hunter College, New York, Nov. 12, '30.

Title	Accompaniment	Costumes	Type	Group	Dancers	Place & date
The Pleasures of Counterpoint	Achron	Lawrence	Group	HW	Group of 17[4]	Guild Th., New York, Mar. 13, '32
Dionysiaques	Schmitt	Lawrence	Solo w. group	HW	DH, group of 17	Same
Suite in E Prelude[5] Sarabande Gigue	Roussel		Duet w. group	HW	DH, CW, group of 21	Lewisohn Stadium, New York, Aug. 8, '33
Rudepoema (Sacred Dance) Dance to the Gods Love Dance Play Dance	Villa-Lobos	Lawrence	Duet	HW	DH, CW	Guild Th., New York, Apr. 15, '34
Pleasures of Counterpoint No. 2	Pollins	Lawrence	Solo	HW	DH	Same
Pleasures of Counterpoint No. 3	Horst	Lawrence	Solo w. group	HW	Ide, group of 23	Same
Exhibition Piece	Slonimsky	Lawrence	Trio	HW	DH, CW, Limón	Same
Theme and Variations	Brahms	Lawrence	Solo	HW	DH	Severance Hall, Cleveland, Apr. 14, '34

4. Performed twice on the same program, as opening and closing numbers; DH danced in the reprise.
5. Choreography by Charles Weidman.

Title	Accompaniment	Costumes	Type	Group	Dancers	Place & date
Credo	Chavez	Lawrence	Solo	HW	DH	Dance Th., Baltimore, Nov. 18, '34
Duo-Drama Unison and Divergence Phantasm Integration	Harris	Lawrence	Duet	HW	DH, CW	Guild Th., New York, Jan. 6, '35
New Dance Prelude First Theme Second Theme Third Theme Processional Celebration	Riegger	Lawrence	Group w. solos, duets, trios, etc.	HW	DH, CW, group of 17 HW members and 24 workshop members	Bennington College Th., Bennington, Vt., Aug. 3, '35
New Dance Variations and Conclusions	Riegger	Lawrence	Group w. solos	HW	DH, CW, groups of 6 and 13	Guild Th., New York, Oct. 27, '35
Theatre Piece Prologue Behind Walls In the Open Interlude In the Stadium In the Theatre The Race Epilogue	Riegger	Lawrence	Group w. solos	HW	DH, CW, group of 17	Same, Jan. 19, '36

Title	Accompaniment	Costumes	Type	Group	Dancers	Place & date
With My Red Fires Part I: Ritual Hymn Search and Betrothal Departure Part II: Drama Summons Coercion and Escape Alarm Pursuit Judgment	Riegger	Lawrence	Group w. solos, duets, trios	HW	DH, CW, group of 16 HW members and 29 workshop members	Armory, Bennington, Vt., Aug. 13, '36
To the Dance [2] (Preludes to the Dance)	Leonard, arr. Lloyd	Lawrence	Group w. duet	HW	DH, CW, group of 13	Alumni Hall, Bloomington, Ind., Feb. 23, '37
American Holiday Death of the Hero Dance of the Living	Mamorsky	Lawrence	Group w. solo	HW	DH, group of 12	Guild Th., New York, Jan. 9, '38
Race of Life	Fine	Lawrence	Group	HW	DH, CW, group of 6	Same, Jan. 23, '38
Passacaglia in C Minor (Passacaglia and Fugue)	Bach	Lawrence [6]	Group	HW	DH, CW, group of 12 HW members and 11 apprentices	Armory, Bennington, Vt., Aug. 5, '38
Square Dances Country Dance Tango Schottische Waltz	Nowak	Lawrence	Group	HW	DH, CW, group of 6	Washington Irving H.S., New York, Nov. 25, '39

6. Décor by Arch Lauterer.

Title	Accompaniment	Costumes	Type	Group	Dancers	Place & date
Variations[7]	Lloyd	Lawrence	Group w. solos	HW	DH, CW, group of 6	Vassar College, Poughkeepsie, N.Y., Jan. 20, '40
Song of the West The Green Land Desert Gods	Nowak Harris	Lawrence	Solo Group	HW	DH L. Sherman, Seckler, group of 7	Madison College, Harrisonburg, Va., Nov. 8, '40
Dance "ings" Leap-ing Runn-ing Fall-ing Turn-ing	Nowak	Lawrence	Solos	HW	L. Sherman, Maginnis, Schurman, Litz	HW Studio, New York, Apr. 18, '41
Decade (A Biography of Modern Dance from 1930 to 1940) [A montage in 3 parts, 27 numbers, inc. 7 choreographed by CW]	Bach, Copland, others; arr. Nowak; script, Alex Kahn	Lawrence[6]	Group w. solos, duets, trios	HW	DH, CW, group of 9 HW members and 7 apprentices	Bennington College Th., Bennington, Vt., Aug. 9, '41
Decade [Reprise, w. 4 new numbers, 1 by CW]	Same	Lawrence[6]		HW	DH, CW, L. Sherman, group	HW Studio, New York, Dec. 26, '41

7. Co-created with performing dancers.

Title	Accompaniment	Costumes	Type	Group	Dancers	Place & date
Song of the West Rivers	Harris	Lawrence	Group w. solo	HW	DH, group of 8	Same, Jan. 17, '42
Four Chorale Preludes Introduction In Thee Is Joy Man's Fall from Grace Love and Mercy Shall Restore Thee Awake, the Voice Is Calling	Bach	Lawrence	Group	HW	DH, group of 5	Same, Dec. 27, '42
Partita in G Major Préambule Allemande Courante Sarabande Tempo di Menuetto Passepied Gigue	Bach	Lawrence	Group w. solo	HW	DH, group of 6	Same
El Salon Mexico	Copland	Lawrence	Group	HW	Limón, group of 7	Same, Mar. 11, '43
Inquest	Lloyd; narration, Norman Rose	Lawrence	Group	HW	DH, CW, group of 12	Same, Mar. 5, '44

Title	Accompaniment	Costumes	Type	Group	Dancers	Place & date
Canonade	Nordoff	Lawrence	Group	HW	Group of 4	Same
The Story of Mankind	Nowak	Lawrence [8]	Duet	JL	Limón, Seckler	College Th., Bennington, Vt., July 11, '46
Lament for Ignacio Sánchez Mejías Prologue The Catching and the Death The Spilling of the Blood Body Present, Absent Soul	Lloyd; text, Lorca	Lawrence [9]	Trio	JL	Limón, Ide, Love	Same
Day on Earth Man's Work and First Love The Family Loss, and the Refuge of Work	Copland	Lawrence	Quartette	JL	Limón, Ide, Pandor, Nicolaides	Beaver Country Day School, Brookline, Mass., May 10, '47
Corybantic	Bartók	Lawrence	Group	JL	Limón, Koner, Ide, Pandor, Jones	Palmer Aud., New London, Aug. 20, '48

8. Décor by Jean Rosenthal.
9. Décor by M. Czaja.

Title	Accompaniment	Costumes	Type	Group	Dancers	Place & date
Invention	Lloyd	Lawrence	Trio	JL	Limón, Jones, Currier	Same, Aug. 13, '49
Quartet No. 1 (Night Spell)	Rainier	Lawrence	Quartette w. solo	JL	Limón, Hoving, Jones, Currier	Same, Aug. 16, '51
Fantasy, Fugue in C Major, Fugue in C Minor	Mozart	Lawrence	Quartette, duet, group	JL	Limón, group of 5	Same, Aug. 24, '52
Deep Rhythm (Ritmo Jondo) Of Men Of Women Of Meeting and Parting	Surinach	Lawrence[9]	Group	JL	Limón, group of 7	Alvin Th., New York, Apr. 15, '53
Ruins and Visions "Oh, which are the actors" "The Storm Rises"	Britten	Lawrence[10]	Group	JL	Limón, group of 7	Palmer Aud., New London, Aug. 20, '53
Felipe el Loco The Arrival The Lesson The Madness	Gomez Montoya Segovia		Group	JL	Limón, group of 6	Same, Aug. 20, '54
The Rock and the Spring	Martin	Bailey[10]	Group w. solo	JDT	Nicolaides, group of 13	Juilliard Concert Hall, New York, Apr. 18, '55

10. Décor by Paul Trautvetter.

Title	Accompaniment	Costumes	Type	Group	Dancers	Place & date
Airs and Graces	Locatelli	Lawrence [10]	Group	JL	Limón, group of 5	Palmer Aud., New London, Aug. 18, '55
Theatre Piece No. 2 / In the Beginning / Ritual / Satires from the Theatre / Poem of Praise	Luening	Sherman [11]	Group w. solos	JL	Limón, group of 11	Juilliard Concert Hall, New York, Apr. 20, '56
Dawn in New York	Johnson	Sherman [11]	Group w. solos	JDT	Trisler, Barker, group of 14	Same, Apr. 27, '56
Descent into the Dream	Petrassi	Roberts [12]	Group w. solos	JDT	Gillick, Peters, Wynne, Nicolaides, group of 12	Same, Jan. 11, '57
Dance Overture	Creston		Group	JL	Limón, group of 12	Palmer Aud., New London, Aug. 15, '57
Brandenburg Concerto No. 4 in G Minor [13] / Allegro / Andante / Presto	Bach	DH [14]	Group	JDT	Group of 10	Juilliard Concert Hall, New York, May 12, '59

11. Décor also by William Sherman.
12. Décor also by William Roberts.
13. Ruth Currier, co-creator.
14. Décor also by DH.

C. Choreography by Doris Humphrey for the Musical Stage

Die Glückliche Hand. Production, League of Composers, Philadelphia Orchestra Association; direction, Reuben Mamoulian; music, Schönberg; design and costumes, Robert Edmond Jones; opening, Metropolitan Opera, Philadelphia, April 11, 1930; dancers, DH, CW, 4 others.

Lysistrata (incidental dances and concluding bacchanale).[1] Production, Philadelphia Theatre Association; direction and design, Norman Bel Geddes; music, Leo Ornstein; costumes, Helene Pons; opening, Walnut Street Theatre, Philadelphia, April 28, 1930; dancers, Helen Savery, Betty Schlaffer, Ilse Gronau, Letitia Ide, Ernestine Henoch, José Limón, others.

Les Romanesques (two dance interludes, "Dance at Evening" and "Les Fêtes de L'Hymen et Terpsichore"). Production, Gerald Cornell; music, Griffes, Rameau; costumes, Raymond Sovey; performance, The Glen, Newport, R.I., July 18, 1930; dancers, DH, CW, group of 10 HW members.

"String Quartet," in a concert of organ and chamber music, with stage action. Direction and design, Irene Lewisohn; music, Bloch; costumes, Polaire Weissman; performance, Library of Congress, Washington, D.C., April 23, 1931; dancers, DH, CW, Anna Sokolow, Sophie Maslow, others.

Carmen (incidental dances).[2] Production, Laurence Productions, Inc.; music, Bizet; opening, Cleveland Stadium, June 29, 1932; dancers, CW, Robert Gorham, José Limón, group of 42.

Aida (incidental dances).[2] Production, Laurence Productions, Inc.; music, Verdi; opening, Cleveland Stadium, July 2, 1932; dancers, CW, Robert Gorham, José Limón, group of 42.

Run, Little Chillun! Production, Robert Rockmore; direction, Frank Merlin; music, Hall Johnson; design, Cleon Throckmorton; costumes, Helene Pons; opening, Lyric Theatre, New York, March 1, 1933; dancers, Tangola's Dancers (a group of 28 members including Esther Hall, Irene Ellington, and others).

The School for Husbands (ballet interlude, "The Dream of Sganarelle").[1] Production, Theatre Guild; direction, Lawrence Langner; music, Brunette, Dandrieu, Lully, Rameau; design and costumes, Lee Simonson; opening, Empire Theatre, New York, October 16, 1933; dancers, DH, CW, 12 HW members, supporting actors.

The Christmas Oratorio. Production, Delos Chappell; direction, Macklin Marrow; music, Bach; design, Donald Oenslager; costumes, Millie Davenport; opening, 44th Street Theatre, New York, December 24, 1934; dancers, Lillian Gish in mime role, CW, 18 HW members.

1. Charles Weidman, co-creator.
2. Choreography by DH and CW, assisted by Eleanor Frampton.

Iphigenia in Aulis (nine dances).[1] Production, Philadelphia Orchestra Association; direction, Herbert Graf; music, Gluck; design, Norman Bel Geddes; opening, Academy of Music, Philadelphia, February 23, 1935; dancers, DH, CW, others.

Sing Out, Sweet Land (four dances).[1] Production, Theatre Guild; direction, Lawrence Langner, Theresa Helburn; staging, Leon Leonidoff; music, Elie Siegmeister; design, Albert Johnson; costumes, Lucinda Ballard; opening, Colonial Theatre, New York, November 13, 1944; dancers, Peter Hamilton, Irene Hawthorn, group of 20.

Poor Eddy (eight dances: "Premature Burial," "The Pit and the Pendulum," "The Literary Women," "Ligeia," "The Lost Beloved," "The Tell-Tale Heart," "The Masque of the Red Death," "Delirium"). Production, The College Theatre Association of the School of Dramatic Arts, Columbia University; book, Elizabeth Dooley; music, Albert Rivett; opening, Brander Matthews Theatre, Columbia University, March 11, 1953; dancers, CW, Letitia Ide, group of 9.

The Child and the Apparitions (three dances: "Shepherds and Shepherdesses," "Dragonfly," "Frogs"). Production: Juilliard School of Music; direction, Frederic Waldman, Frederic Cohen; music, Maurice Ravel; opening, Juilliard Concert Hall, March 22, 1957; dancers, members of Juilliard Dance Theatre.

RECORDS OF THE WORKS OF DORIS HUMPHREY

NOTATED SCORES
in Labanotation by the Dance Notation Bureau, Inc.

Brandenburg Concerto No. 4; Day on Earth; Life of the Bee; New Dance; Partita; Passacaglia; Ritmo Jondo; Soaring; Song of the West ("Desert Gods"); *Water Study; With My Red Fires*

FILMS

Air for the G String (Westinghouse)
Brandenburg Concerto No. 4 (Ohio State University; also University of Oregon)
Lament for Ignacio Sánchez Mejías (Walter Strate)
New Dance (Connecticut College American Dance Festival)
The Shakers (Thomas Bouchard)
With My Red Fires (Connecticut College American Dance Festival)

Notes, Part II

Chapter 1. *Interim: Conflict*

Unless otherwise noted, all the passages cited in this chapter are taken from letters by Doris Humphrey to her parents.

p. 70. "if I stay at home . . . ." June 26, 1926.
p. 70. "I feel dissatisfied . . . ." January 28, 1927.
p. 70. "I'm going to try . . . ." March 2, 1927.
p. 71. "promise us an increase . . . ." March 20, 1927.
p. 71. "It would be the biggest . . . ." April 11, 1927.
p. 72. "He will stay out . . . ." May 27, 1927.
p. 73. "The Shawns . . . ." May 27, 1927.
p. 73. "Martha could stay . . . ." June 7, 1927.
p. 73. "the whole thing . . . ." June 7, 1927.
p. 74. "Following my theory . . . ." June 22, 1927.
p. 74. "He is most interested . . . ." n.d.
p. 75. "and went through the usual . . . ." n.d.
p. 75. "I feel more free . . . ." August 2, 1927.
p. 75. "which is that of moving . . . ." August 8, 1927.
p. 75. "None of these . . . ." September 9, 1927.
p. 76. "I like groups . . . ." December 11, 1927.
p. 77. "We haven't heard . . . ." December 11, 1927.
p. 77. "The recital used me up . . . ." January 3, 1928.
p. 77. "among dance masterpieces . . . ." Mary F. Watkins,
    Dance Magazine, January, 1929.
p. 78. "Of course it takes time . . . ." DH to TS, n.d.
p. 78. " 'The Banshee' . . . ." February 13, 1928.
p. 78. "a spooky spirit . . . ." Nickolas Muray, *Dance Magazine*, June, 1928.
p. 78. "I had an awful time . . . ." March 16, 1928.
p. 79. "It was so much better . . . ." March 29, 1928.
p. 80. "From the response . . . ." April 18, 1928.
p. 81. "our ideas . . . ." May 30, 1928.

Chapter 2. *The Start of the Struggle*

Unless otherwise noted, all the letters cited were written by Doris
Humphrey to her parents.

p. 84. "Quite a man . . . ." August 7, 1928.
p. 85. "I'm sure they won't use it . . . ." July 15, 1928.
p. 86. "the authentic feeling . . . ." Mary F. Watkins, *Dance Magazine,*
    January, 1929.
p. 86. "in the literal sense . . . ." John Martin, *New York Times,*
    April 8, 1929.
p. 86. "Yes—I have them . . . ." September 24, 1928.
p. 87. "You see I'm in debt . . . ." December 19, 1928.
p. 87. "But every time . . . ." May 8, 1929.
p. 88. "The other is my first . . . ." July 16, 1929.
p. 88. "Rehearsals are . . . ." Form letter dated October 31, 1929.
    Courtesy Ernestine Stodelle.
p. 89. "You see . . . ." November 24, 1929.
p. 90. "It has seemed . . . ." October 29, 1929.
p. 91. "quite the most extraordinary . . . ." John Martin, *New York Times,*
    January 7, 1930.
p. 91. "After all . . . ." n.d.
p. 91. "considered prose . . . ." MTP, *Boston Transcript,* March 8, 1930.
p. 93. "Another time . . . ." March 26, 1930.
p. 94. "All except Hymen . . . ." June 13, 1930.
p. 94. "You can't change . . . ." June 23, 1930.
p. 94. "I'm interested . . . ." September 14, 1930.
p. 95. "The whole place . . . ." October 8, 1930.
p. 96. "I am continually discovering . . . ." January 17, 1931.

Chapter 3. *And Afterwards a Woman*

p. 99. "I found out . . . ." DH to HBHs, July 4, 1931.
p. 100. "I feel better . . . ." DH to HBHs, July 25, 1931.
p. 100. "I think of you . . . ." CFW to DH, June 13, 1945.
p. 101. "looked preoccupied . . . ." CFW to DH, July 8, 1932.
p. 102. "Every day . . . ." DH to CFW, July 21, 1931.
p. 102. "It's hard . . . ." CFW to DH, August 11, 1931.
p. 103. "This absence . . . ." DH to CFW, n.d.
p. 104. "I am sorry . . . ." CFW to DH, October 23, 1931.
p. 104. "marriage would give us . . . ." CFW to DH, November 7, 1931.
p. 105. "Cleveland is afraid . . . ." DH to HBHs, November 8, 1931.
p. 106. "Getting them composed . . . ." DH to HBHs, February 15, 1932.
p. 106. "steel and velvet . . . ." John Martin, *New York Times,*
    January 18, 1932.
p. 106. "Once you told me . . . ." CFW to DH, January 2, 1932.

p. 106. "The decision . . . ." CFW to DH, February 13, 1932.
p. 106. "We could get married . . . ." CFW to DH, n.d.
p. 106. "Here Miss Humphrey . . . ." John Martin, *New York Times,*
    March 14, 1932.
p. 107. "I enclose criticism . . . ." DH to HBHs, March 15, 1932.
p. 107. "Every moment now . . . ." DH to CFW, n.d.
p. 108. "I'm troubled . . . ." CFW to DH, February 16, 1932.
p. 108. "I have no theories . . . ." DH to CFW, n.d.
p. 109. "my sense of male . . . ." CFW to DH, March 12, 1932.
p. 109. "Up to a certain point . . . ." CFW to DH, n.d.
p. 110. "I have changed . . . ." DH to HBHs, May 23, 1932.

Chapter 4. *Hopes and Fears*

p. 112. "I have an apology . . . ." CFW to HBHs, June 23, 1932.
p. 112. "It seems scarcely . . . ." CFW to DH, June 11, 1932.
p. 113. "It is not that I mind . . . ." CFW to DH, n.d.
p. 114. "This parting . . . ." CFW to DH, June 26, 1932.
p. 115. "in ideas . . . ." DH to HBHs, July 25, 1932.
p. 115. "I really think . . . ." DH to HBHs, August 29, 1932.
p. 116. "I thought that we . . . ." CFW to DH, September 3, 1932.
p. 116. "A stunning historical passage . . . ." Gilbert W. Gabriel,
    New York *American,* October 6, 1932.
p. 116. "gives the dance . . . ." Brooks Atkinson, *New York Times,*
    October 6, 1932.
p. 116. "I know how you feel . . . ." DH to HBHs, November 13, 1932.
p. 118. "It is a theatre art . . . ." Papers, n.d.
p. 119. "I'm between . . . ." DH to HBHs, January 23, 1933.
p. 120. "You always . . . ." JWH to DH, April 3, 1933.
p. 120. "is a plague . . . ." DH to HBHs, June 11, 1933.
p. 121. "It looks . . . ." DH to HBHs, July 2, 1933.

Chapter 5. *Family Life*

p. 122. "It's very annoying . . . ." DH to HBHs, August 1, 1933.
p. 122. "I won't be the solo dancer . . . ." DH to HBHs, August 20, 1933.
p. 124. "most kind . . . ." Cornelia Otis Skinner to DH, n.d.
p. 125. "As the evening . . . ." RSD to DH and CW, n.d.
p. 125. "My ambition . . . ." DH to HBHs, December 13, 1933.
p. 126. "I wonder . . . ." CFW to DH, February 14, 1934.
p. 126. "You can pinch hit . . . ." DH to JWH, May 13, 1934.
p. 127. "I've just got up . . . ." DH to CFW, n.d.
p. 128. "There is a permanent . . . ." DH to CFW, August 21, 1934.
p. 128. "What a waste . . . ." CFW to DH, n.d.
p. 129. "Really he must . . . ." DH to HBHs, August 21, 1934.
p. 130. "We've been busying . . . ." DH to HBHs, November 12, 1934.

Chapter 6. *Pioneering*

p. 132. "Well, we're off . . . ." DH to CFW, January 4, 1935.

p. 133. "Your heartening letter . . . ." DH to CFW, January 21, 1935.

p. 134. "Charles is having . . . ." DH to JWH, February 3, 1935.

p. 135. "If only . . . ." CFW to DH, February 14, 1935.

p. 135. "But do you suppose . . . ." CFW to JWH, February 26, 1935.

p. 136. "I wondered . . . ." CFW to DH, April 15, 1935.

p. 136. "Poor little Pussy . . . ." CFW to DH, July 3, 1935.

p. 136. "It makes me very happy . . . ." DH to CFW, June 29, 1935.

p. 137. "the world as it should be . . . ." see Appendix.

p. 137. "never appeals . . . ." DH to CFW, July 20, 1935.

p. 137. "one of the most exciting . . . ." *New York Times*, August 11, 1935.

p. 137. "Certainly . . . ." John Martin, *New York Times*, October 28, 1935.

p. 137. "the first pure example . . . ." Margaret Lloyd,
Christian Science Monitor, October 8, 1937.

p. 137. "this piece will go down . . . ." Joseph Arnold Kaye,
American Dancer, March, 1936.

p. 138. "Beyond the rent saving . . . ." DH to JWH, September 5, 1935.

p. 138. "Last year . . . ." DH to JWH, September 5, 1935.

p. 138. "Dear God . . . ." CFW to JWH, October 25, 1935.

p. 139. "Well here's the 'Times' . . . ." DH to JWH, January 22, 1936.

p. 140. "The drive was long . . . ." DH to CFW, July 12, 1936.

p. 142. "Our business . . . ." DH to JWH, October 16, 1936.

p. 142. "I think the progressive . . . ." DH to JWH, November 16, 1936.

p. 143. "If you don't have time . . . ." JWH to DH, January 8, 1937.

p. 143. "not only the greatest . . . ." Margaret Lloyd,
Christian Science Monitor, October 8, 1937.

p. 144. "Leo has gone . . . ." DH to JWH, February 14, 1937.

p. 144. "Your task . . . ." CFW to DH, February 23, 1937.

p. 145. "The net result . . . ." DH to JWH, November 15, 1937.

p. 147. "It implies . . . ." CFW to DH, January 21, 1938.

p. 147. "My girl left . . . ." CFW to DH, February 2, 1938.

p. 147. "How you balk . . . ." CFW to DH, February 23, 1938.

p. 148. "I was a little disturbed . . . ." JWH to DH, April 28, 1938.

p. 149. "The first thing . . . ." DH to CFW, July 4, 1938.

p. 149. "For a man . . . ." CFW to DH, July 10, 1938.

p. 149. "The constant living . . . ." CFW to DH, July 27, 1938.

p. 150. "It is indeed . . . ." John Martin, *New York Times*,
November 28, 1938.

p. 150. "the real triumph . . . ." Isabel Morse Jones, *Los Angeles Times*,
April 22, 1939.

p. 150. "Someday I'll get violent . . . ." DH to JWH, September 2, 1938.

p. 150. "My whole aim . . . ." JWH to DH, October 5, 1938.

p. 151. "Pauline wants . . . ." DH to JWH, December 1, 1938.

p. 152. "Of course I hate . . . ." DH to CFW, February 19, 1939.

p. 152. "At almost every gathering . . . ." DH to JWH, n.d.

p. 153. "We should meet . . . ." CFW to DH, April 6, 1939.

p. 153. "I never should . . . ." DH to JWH, June 29, 1939.

p. 153. "Looking at it . . . ." DH to CFW, July 11, 1939.

p. 154. "José and Katy . . . ." DH to CFW, August 1, 1939.

p. 155. "Martha was the first . . . ." DH to CFW, n.d.

p. 155. "It's rather a mess . . . ." DH to CFW, n.d.

Chapter 7. *Threats*

p. 157. "Even if the school . . . ." DH to JWH, January 6, 1940.

p. 158. "Nobody would describe . . . ." CFW to DH, January 11, 1940.

p. 158. "Pumba was so impressed . . . ." DH to CFW, n.d.

p. 158. "My impression . . . ." DH to CFW, n.d.

p. 159. "I realize . . . ." CFW to DH, February 27, 1940.

p. 159. "As for my having . . . ." DH to CFW, March 6, 1940.

p. 160. "I don't know . . . ." DH to JWH, April 14, 1940.

p. 161. "Let me know . . . ." PL to DH, July 15, 1940.

p. 161. ["It] considerably strengthened . . . ." DH to CFW, August 13, 1940.

p. 162. "I want to tell you . . . ." JL to DH, n.d.

p. 163. "The psychological atmosphere . . . ." DH to CFW,
      September 24, 1940.

p. 163. "I, at first . . . ." DH to CFW, n.d.

p. 163. "I am feeling . . . ." DH to CFW, n.d.

p. 164. "Queer . . . ." HMR to DH, November 28, 1940.

p. 165. "brilliantly effective . . . ." G[rant] C[ode], *Dance Observer*,
      January, 1941.

p. 165. "[I am] trying to build . . . ." DH to CFW, February 12, 1941.

p. 165. "Cecil Smith . . . ." DH to CFW, March 12, 1941.

p. 166. "a most distinguished . . . ." John Martin, *New York Times*,
      January 18, 1942.

p. 166. "you were only . . . ." DH to JWH, April 21, 1941.

p. 166. "Also we have come . . . ." DH to JWH, April 21, 1941.

p. 167. "The tone of your letter . . . ." CFW to DH, May 2, 1941.

p. 168. "It hangs over me . . . ." DH to JWH, April 17, 1941.

p. 168. "I hope the problem . . . ." CFW to DH, June 9, 1941.

p. 169. "What a pity . . . ." JWH to DH, September 16, 1941.

p. 169. "It's hard to define . . . ." CFW to DH, n.d.

p. 170. "Actually the desperate . . . ." CFW to DH, September 3, 1941.

p. 171. "I, personally . . . ." DH to CFW, November 18, 1941.

p. 171. "It is horrible . . . ." CFW to DH, December 8, 1941.

p. 172. "I'm afraid . . . ." CFW to DH, March 23, 1942.

p. 173. "He must'nt go . . . ." PLL to DH, January 19, 1942.

p. 174. "[We] get along . . . ." PLL to DH, February 22, 1942.

p. 174. "If you need me . . . ." PLL to DH, March 9, 1942.

p. 175. "The problem of the boys . . . ." CFW to DH, May 7, 1942.

p. 175. "I have wondered . . . ." HMR to DH, September 9, 1942.

p. 176. "Whether or not . . . ." George W. Crane to DH, October 16, 1942.

p. 177. "Humphrey calls me . . . ." DH to JWH, December 7, 1942.

p. 178. "sweet formality . . . ." G.W.B., *Dance Observer*, February, 1943.

p. 178. "not suitable . . . ." John Martin, *New York Times*, January 17, 1943.

p. 179. "I've seen her . . . ." HMR to DH, January 14, 1943.

p. 179. "but I've been flat . . . ." DH to JWH, January 30, 1943.

p. 179. "For the moment . . . ." JL to DH, April 28, 1943.

p. 180. "and the mama . . . ." DH to JWH, May 14, 1943.

p. 180. "my only regret . . . ." JWH to DH, October 22, 1943.

p. 180. "I've heard you say . . . ." HMR to DH, September 12, 1943.

p. 180. "It's a little . . . ." JWH to DH, October 6, 1943.

p. 182. "The piece has pointed out . . . ." Edwin Denby,
New York *Herald Tribune*, March 12, 1944.

p. 182. "I think . . . ." DH to HMR, March 25, 1944.

Chapter 8. *In the Face of Misfortune*

p. 184. "He should be starting . . . ." PLL to DH, November 17, 1944.

p. 184. "When the songs . . . ." *Cue*, January 6, 1945.

p. 187. "Maggie kyed . . . ." DH to HMR, August 13, 1946.

p. 187. "Miss Humphrey lifts . . . ." Margaret Lloyd,
Christian Science Monitor, July 20, 1946.

p. 188. "Of course I like it . . . ." DH to HMR, August 13, 1946.

p. 189. "Pumba chews . . . ." DH to HMR, December 4, 1946.

p. 191. "I am thankful . . . ." Margaret Lloyd to DH, October 19, 1946.

p. 191. "The enthusiasm . . . ." CFW to DH, January 23, 1947.

p. 191. "Through his own efforts . . . ." Walter Terry,
New York *Herald Tribune,* January 12, 1947.

p. 191. "Pumba telephoned . . . ." DH to HMR, February 12, 1947.

p. 192. "I am coming . . . ." DH to HMR, n.d.

p. 192. "I am pleased . . . ." DH to HMR, May 14, 1947.

p. 193. "one of her greatest . . . ." John Martin, *New York Times,*
January 4, 1948.

p. 193. "On my birthday . . . ." DH to HMR, October 30, 1947.

p. 194. "I came out . . . ." Agnes de Mille to DH, December 31, 1947.

Chapter 9. *Helping*

p. 197. "They have learned . . . ." DH, notes for radio interview, WNYC,
September 4, 1948.

p. 198. "remains as confused . . . ." N. K., *Dance Observer,*
August-September, 1949.

p. 199. "long, sweeping lines . . . ." Doris Hering, *Dance Magazine,*
       October, 1949.
p. 199. "The season at the City Center . . . ." DH to HMR,
       December 27, 1949.
p. 200. "no major figure . . . ." DH to HMR, April 4, 1950.
p. 200. "I can't get as much done . . . ." DH to HMR, January 17, 1951.
p. 201. "My Quartet . . . ." DH to HMR, August 16, 1951.
p. 201. "Moving . . . ." DH to CHW, October 11, 1951.
p. 203. "In that six weeks . . . ." DH to HMR, September 1, 1952.
p. 203. "You know . . . ." JL to DH, September 3, 1952.
p. 204. "I could not help . . . ." Frederik Prausnitz to DH,
       December 16, 1952.
p. 205. "the need for avoiding . . . ." "Doris Humphrey's Ruins and
       Visions," *Dance Observer,* December, 1953.
p. 205. "The medicine men . . . ." DH to HMR, November 28, 1953.
p. 206. "Naturally . . . ." DH to HMR, March 25, 1954.
p. 207. "What they'll make of it . . . ." DH to HMR, November 9, 1954.
p. 209. "I came yesterday . . . ." DH to HMR, July 9, 1955.
p. 210. "To have everything tightened . . . ." DH to HMR, n.d.
p. 211. "Endless detail . . . ." DH to HMR, March 14, 1956.
p. 212. "Works of large affirmation . . . ." George Beiswanger,
       Dance Observer, May, 1957.
p. 212. "although everything . . . ." DH to HMR, n.d.
p. 212. "This has missed . . . ." DH to HMR, June 9, 1956.
p. 213. "I was pleased . . . ." DH to HMR, January 14, 1957.
p. 213. "intellectualized . . . ." Doris Hering, *Dance Magazine,*
       March, 1957.
p. 213. "My 'Dance Overture' . . . ." DH to HMR, August 23, 1957.
p. 214. "We have an unreasoning . . . ." DH to HMR, July 29, 1957.

Chapter 10. *A Good Fighter*

p. 215. "Such a jumble . . . ." DH to HMR, October 16, 1957.
p. 220. "The rhythm . . . ." DH to HMR, n.d.
p. 220. "so I have instead . . . ." DH to HMR, December 18, 1958.

Index

NOTE: Full lists of DH premieres, with companies and dancers, will be found in the chronology, pp. 270–288. This index includes only those mentioned in text and appendix.